Pyrenees & Gascony including Andorra

The Pyrenees and Gascony made to measure

The Pyrenees and Gascony à la carte

The Pyrenees and Gascony in detail

A weekend in Toulouse

The heart of Gascony's capital is the Place du Capitole (p. 170), the symbolic centre of the 'pink city'. From this central square, walk to the Saint-Sernin basilica, a masterpiece of Romanesque art, with its perfect proportions (p. 170). As you wander through the old town, don't miss the huge Jacobin convent and its gothic fan-vaulting (p. 172). The Musée des Augustins boasts a wonderful collection of paintings and sculpture from the Middle Ages to the 19th C. (p. 172). If you are fascinated by science and technology, there is nothing more contemporary than the Aérospatiale (p. 171), the home of the French aircraft industry. Then there is the Cité de l'Espace (p. 173), which is devoted entirely to space exploration, an area where Toulouse has made an important contribution. The last excursion of a weekend which will prove all too short is a trip on the Canal du Midi (p. 160), hiring a small motor boar for an hour or a day, drifting along the waters of the River Garonne. Finally, if you have a little time left, visit the violet perfume factory (p. 178); the violet is a local emblem which is currently enjoying a welcome revival.

A weekend in the Principality of Andorra

Start your tour with Andorra's capital, Andorra-la-Vella, which perches on top of a hump-back hill (p. 225). Wander through its narrow streets lined with old houses, step into the church of Sant Esteve (p. 225), once the headquarters of the Conseil Général des Vallées, and visit the Casa de la Vall, where the council now meets (p. 225). Andorra-la-Vella is surrounded by 'silent valleys', each of which has its own individual attraction. In the north, the Casa d'Areny de Plandolit, at Ordino, has retained the atmosphere of an Andorran master blacksmith (p. 225), and the nearby rivers are ideal for whitewater sports (the Valira del Nord is the most popular fast-moving river; see p. 228). Climb to the centre of Caldea, in the east, where sulphurous water rushes out of the ground at 155 °F (68 °C) at an altitude of 3,330 ft (1,000 m) or spend time at Engolaster Lake (p. 228). Finally, visit Port d'Envalira, in the north-west, the highest peak in the Pyrenees to have a road running through it (see p. 227). In winter, the principality's ski-runs attract the finest skiers and, throughout the year, the duty-free shops (p. 229) provide yet another good reason to visit Andorra!

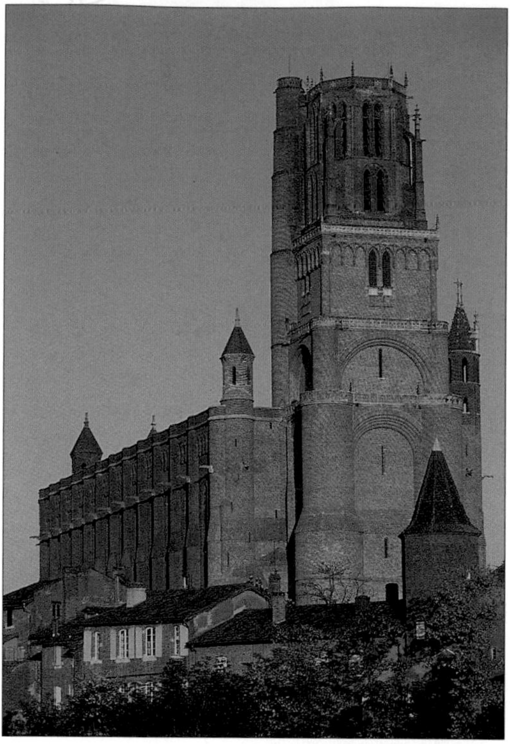

A weekend in Albi

To soak up the atmosphere, wander through the old red sandstone town of Albi, following the heritage paths (p. 136). Don't miss the cathedral of Sainte-Cécile, a vast brick edifice in which a magnificent *son et lumière* show is held during the summer. For a little relaxation after such splendours, why not take a trip down the river Tarn in an old barge (p. 137). Water sports enthusiasts may prefer to paddle a canoe down the river, as an alternative way to explore all its meandering banks (p. 138). On the way back, stop off for a delicious treat at one of the town's chocolate shops (p. 137) or, if you prefer, taste the foie gras of the Maison Lascroux, one of Albi's most famous establishments (p.138).
The next day, make time for a cultural tour around the Musée Toulouse-Lautrec, which contains more than 1,000 works of art by this local genius (p. 137). An excursion outside the walls of the town will take you to Saint-Juéry to see the Saut-du-Tarn Museum (p. 138), dedicated to the history of the river. Visit a glassblower's workshop (p. 139), take a carriage ride through the Forest of Sérénac (p. 139) or laze about at the Aiguelèze leisure centre on the banks of the river Tarn (p. 138).

MESSING ABOUT ON THE RIVER

A trip down the Tarn on a barge is a great way to see the beautiful countryside without exerting yourself. Sit back, soak up the sun and watch the scenery roll by. If you are feeling energetic, however, you could try a spot of kayaking. See pages 101 and 138 for more details.

A weekend in Comminges

Comminges is an area south of Lannemezan, the gateway to Spain. Even a whirlwind trip will take you into another world. You will be walking in the footsteps of the Romans when visiting the ancient city at the foot of Saint-Bertrand-de-Comminges (p. 204), the ruins of the Montmaurin villa (p. 202) or the Gallo-Roman palace of Valentine (p. 202). Eat in Roman style at Lugdunum (p. 205) at Valcabrère, then visit the lovely church of Saint-Just, a medieval masterpiece which stands in isolation in the midst of fields. Go back even further in time at Aurignac, at the Musée de la Préhistoire (p. 202), to find the earliest Frenchmen. At Louron you will discover that the churches were painted by shepherds in the 16th C. (p. 198). On the way, stock up on the local sweets *flocons pyrénéens* (Pyrenean snowflakes) at Saint-Lary (p. 198) or go hang-gliding at Vieille-Aure (p. 199). You are now very close to the Néouvieille nature reserve, high in the mountains, which has a variety of mountain flora and fauna. Enjoy the restorative powers of the pure waters of the Bagnères-de-Luchon spa. The natural steam baths of this famous health resort offer guaranteed relaxation (p. 200). Taste the local delicacies, including *pétéram*, a tripe dish, and *pistache*, which contains preserved duck (p. 201). To find peace and tranquillity wander through the hundreds of species of trees at the magnificent Joueou arboretum (p. 201).

A week in Haute-Garonne

There are two ways to get to the Lauragais district (p. 146) from Toulouse: by sailing down the Canal du Midi (p. 160) in a small barge called a *penichette* or by riding or driving along the course of this major engineering feat, classified as a World Heritage Site (don't miss the Négra lock). You can stop on the way to eat *cassoulet* (pork and bean casserole) at Villefranche-de-Lauragais (p. 161). When you reach Revel, visit the marquetry workshops (p. 149) and look for the medieval covered market. The pretty village of Saint-Félix-de-Lauragais (p. 149) still makes the pastel paints for which the region was once justly famous. Take a trip to Rieux-Volvestre (p. 169), south of the Garonne, and enjoy a delightful stroll through this beautifully preserved papal town. End the excursion at Saint-Bertrand-de-Comminges mountain (p. 204), a miniature St. Michael's Mount in the Pyrenees, with its beautiful cathedral and monastery. The Roman villa at Montmaurin (p. 202) is well worth seeing, in addition to the ancient tile workshops of Martres-Tolosane (p. 203). For a breath of fresh mountain air, ascend more than 3,330 ft (1,000 m) to the Joueou arboretum (p. 201), before relaxing in the natural steam baths of Bagnères-de-Luchon (p. 200).

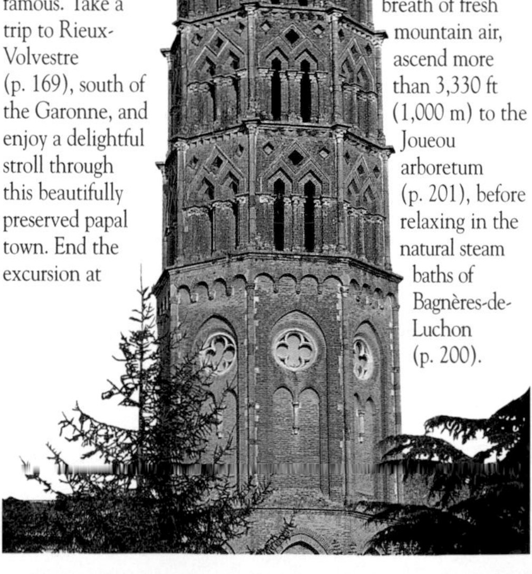

A week around Albi

Between Albi and Toulouse, the landscapes are varied, with brick-built villages, rounded hills and gentle slopes. Albi, with its red-brick tiled buildings, is a lovely place to linger. Attractions include the cathedral of Sainte-Cécile (p. 136), the Musée Toulouse-Lautrec (p. 137), the banks of the Tarn and the ancient, narrow streets of the old town. It is a paradise for food-lovers. Indulge yourself with delicious ice cream and hand-made chocolates (p. 137), not forgetting the foie gras for which the region is famous (p. 138). Follow the river Tarn from Albi to the magnificent forest of Grésigne (p. 150), the largest oak forest in southern France. You can explore it on foot or by bicycle, as there are plenty of forest paths. The narrow valley of the Vère contains pretty hilltop villages, such as Castelnau-de-Montmiral (p. 150), Penne-du-Tarn (p. 151) and Puycelsi (p. 150). Take advantage of your stay by visiting an angora goat farm and stock up on mohair wool or knitwear. (p. 151). The Aveyron Gorge, at the northern end of the valley, can be seen from the corniche on the road from Saint-Antonin-Nobleval (p. 151). Further south, Cordes-sur-Ciel, with its head in the clouds, has winding, ancient streets and a group of sandstone houses with carvings of imaginary animals (p. 140).

In the lower town, Le Jardin des Paradis is a lovely public garden with a water-lily pond (p. 141). Taste spit-roasted pork at the Bellevue farm (p. 141), before leaving for the Gaillac region, where wine-tasting is a must for those who enjoy touring the vineyards. (p. 143), You can also linger beneath the *pountets* of Isle-sur-Tarn (see p. 144) or pick up a second-hand book at Rabastens (p. 145). The highlight of this excursion is the church of Notre-Dame-du-Bourg, at Rabastens, which is decorated with scenes from the Crusades.

A week in the Val de Garonne

The Val de Garonne, north of Toulouse, is reminiscent of Tuscany. A grape variety called Négrette is grown on the hills of Frontonnais, and is the main ingredient in the Côtes-du-Frontonnais wine.

Taste the wine at the Château de Bellevue-la-Forêt (p. 154). This is where the French children's writer, the Comtesse de Ségur, once lived with her daughters. She spent her summer holidays at Verfeil in a huge 18th C. château (p. 155). Other châteaux worth a visit are Larra and Merville (p. 154), built in the days of Louis XV. Montauban (p. 164), to the north, is a fine city of pink brick. It boasts beautiful mansions, lovely gardens, old arcaded frontages and the Musée Ingres, dedicated to the work of this 19th C. painter. The Domaine de Montels offers wine-tastings (p. 167) and the cheese factory at Ramier (p. 167) is open to visitors. Make your way across the plain of the Garonne, the great orchard of the Midi-Pyrénées, where picturesque Castelsarrasin (p. 152) is renowned for its flowers and fruit-trees. The nearby 'water-slope' of Montech is a unique

engineering feat (p. 153). There is a wood nearby which is popular for walks and horseriding (p. 153). To complete the excursion, drive from Valence-d'Agen to Moissac, through a narrow plain dotted with poplars and fruit-trees. Stop off at Auvillar, one of the prettiest villages in the region, and visit its museum which contains a collection of pottery. This is the land of black wine, artists, medieval fortified villages and weirs on the river. Discover the pottery made at (p. 158), the Donzac cellar (p. 158), and the villages of Castelsagrat and Monjoi (p. 159). Explore the banks of the Tarn and the Garonne from a boat (p. 159), or at Moissac you can wander among the sculptures of a Romanesque monastery (p. 162) and visit the workshops in the Rue Mourrat. Alternatively, you can simply laze about on the shores of the lake of Saint-Nicolas-de-la-Grave (p. 163).

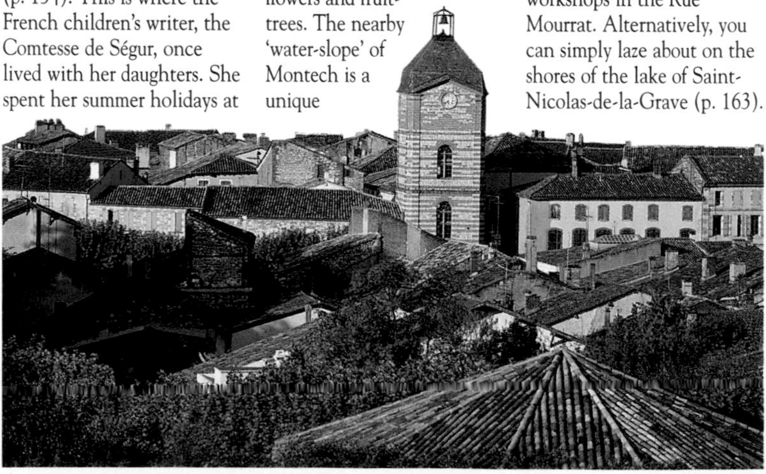

Two weeks in Ariège

Start at Saint Lizier, the capital of Couserans, by exploring the cathedral with its marble pillars (p. 218). Nearby, you can pan for gold (p. 219) and visit a cheese-makers, where

the black-rinded Pyrenean cheese is made (p. 207). At Moulis, French scientists have set up a laboratory in a cave to investigate subterranean life forms (p. 206), and you can also visit the famous Mas-d'Azil, whose caverns contained many prehistoric artefacts (p. 210). Nearby, you can see the Mérens, a local breed of horse, and drink asses' milk at the Castelnau-Durban donkey farm (p. 211). Traditional wooden clogs can be purchased at Audressein (pp. 206-207). Stop at the hill-top town of Foix, to the east, the capital of the département. It has a fine château which has retained traces of its Albigensian heritage (p. 208). The nearby escarpments are popular for hang-gliding. Then go down to Tarascon-sur-Ariège (p. 220) to

delve into prehistory. Discover the Parc Pyrenéen d'Art Préhistorique and its dolmens, and explore the extraordinary caves of Niaux, Bedeilhac and Lombrives (pp. 221 and 222). In this region, sharpening stones and raw wool are still produced (p. 223). To the east, Roquefixade and Monségur, in the Pays d'Olmes (p. 214), were important centres for the Cathars. There are ruined castles and lovely landscapes. At nearby Lesparrou (p. 215), buy a horn comb, a symbol of local craftsmanship, before making for Camon (p. 213), a fortified village dominated by an abbey. End your tour at the medieval town of Mirepoix (p. 212), the final stage in this taste of the Ariège.

Two weeks in Gascony

Eauze, the capital of Armagnac, was prosperous in Roman times, to judge from the Roman treasure trove (p. 116) found there. Taste the famous Armagnac (p. 116) brandy before moving on to the Lac d'Uby, near Barbotan, before visiting Condom and its elegant mansions (p. 122). The biggest flower market in the region is held in the pretty fortified village of Fourcès (pp. 124-125). The countryside is dominated by châteaux, of which the most notable are Cassaigne (p. 124) and Laressingle (p. 123), and abbeys such as Flaran and La Romieu (p. 125). Lectoure (p. 126), to the east, is known for producing melons; it also holds an annual photography festival. This is a good moment for a lengthy wander through the streets of the old city, then you can enjoy the gentle valleys of the Lomagne, famous for their garlic, wines and foie gras.

Star-gazers will enjoy an evening contemplating the heavenly bodies at the Ferme des Étoiles. The Save Valley to the south has farms and markets which are dedicated garlic (p. 128). At L'Isle-Jourdain, discover wooden *béjouets*, beautifully carved pieces of Gascon folk art (p. 134). Auch, former seat of the counts of Armagnac, is the next stop. This is the home of d'Artagnan, Alexandre Dumas' hero, whose statue stands on the monumental flight of steps of the Colline d'Auch. Stroll through the maze of streets called *Les Pousterles* in the old town (p. 118), then visit the twisted spire of the church at Barran (p. 120). At nearby Lavardens (p. 121) there is an annual scarecrow competition! To complete your trip, stop at the pretty fortified village of Mirande and continue to the Val d'Adour (p. 112). Taste the wines at Madiran and Plaisance-du-Gers, and listen to jazz at the Marciac festival (p. 115).

Two weeks in the Pyrenees

In Tarbes (p. 196), the local capital, famous for its French beans, visit the cathedral before going on to Lourdes (p. 190). A pilgrimage to this shrine will get your week off to an auspicious start and the funicular of the Pic du Jer will help you climb even higher! The Lavedan river to the south (p. 186) has many waterfalls and flowing waters, and is a paradise for anglers and kayakers. Cauterets is a popular ski resort in winter – and also specialises in humbugs, known as *berlingots* (p. 189). The truly adventurous can take a bungee jump from the Napoleon Bridge at Luz-Saint-Sauveur (p. 188). Opt for a moment of relaxation at the Thermes de Luz spa (p. 188), before moving on to the Cirque de Gavarnie (p. 184), a geological formation. Take a look at the nearby cirques, at Troumousse, Estaubé and Barroude. On the way back to Bagnères-de-Bigorre (p. 180), stop at the Médous caves (p. 180) and spend a moment on the Pic-du-Midi, at an altitude of 9,550 ft (2,865 m). Visit the amazing painted churches of the Valley of Louron (p. 198), via the Col d'Aspin (one of the mountain passes on the Tour de France route; p. 195). You may be watched by the bears which inhabit the Pyrenees, but you are most unlikely to see them. South of Saint-Lary, you'll find the Néouvielle (p. 199) nature reserve, the gateway to the Pyrenees Natural Park (p. 192). Don't miss the Pont d'Espagne and the deep blue waters of the Lac de Gaube.

The Pyrenees and Gascony à la carte

In the countryside 16

Food shopping 26

Wines and spirits 38

Regional dishes and sweet treats 44

Markets 50

Arts and crafts 62

History of the region 68

In the countryside

From deep forests to rocky peaks, Midi-Pyrénées offers wonderful landscapes for nature-lovers.

Trees and forests

1. Forêt de Sérénac **p. 139.**
2. Forêt de Grésigne **p. 150.**
3. Forêt de Sivens **p. 142.**
4. Forêt de Montech **p. 153.**
5. Cardeilhac: Arboretum **p. 203.**
6. Joueou: Arboretum **p. 201.**
7. Forêt de Berdoues **p. 133.**

Local wildlife

8. Cambounet-sur-le-Sor: bird sanctuary **p. 148.**
9. Rieux: Aquarium of the Garonne and Pyrenees **p. 168.**
10. Saint-Lizier: L'Œil aux Aguets, nature ramble **p. 218.**
11. Nature Sanctuary of Néouvielle **p. 199.**
12. Nogaro: learning about woodpigeons **p. 115.**
13. Bax: Cétonia Centre insectarium **p. 169.**
14. Plaisance-du-Touch: African safari **p. 177.**
15. Le Houga: deer and wild boar **p. 117.**

Rivers and lakes

16. Boucle d'Ambialet **p. 136.**
17. Underground river of Labouiche **p. 208.**
18. Léran: Montbels lake **p. 212.**
19. Gaube lake **p. 192.**

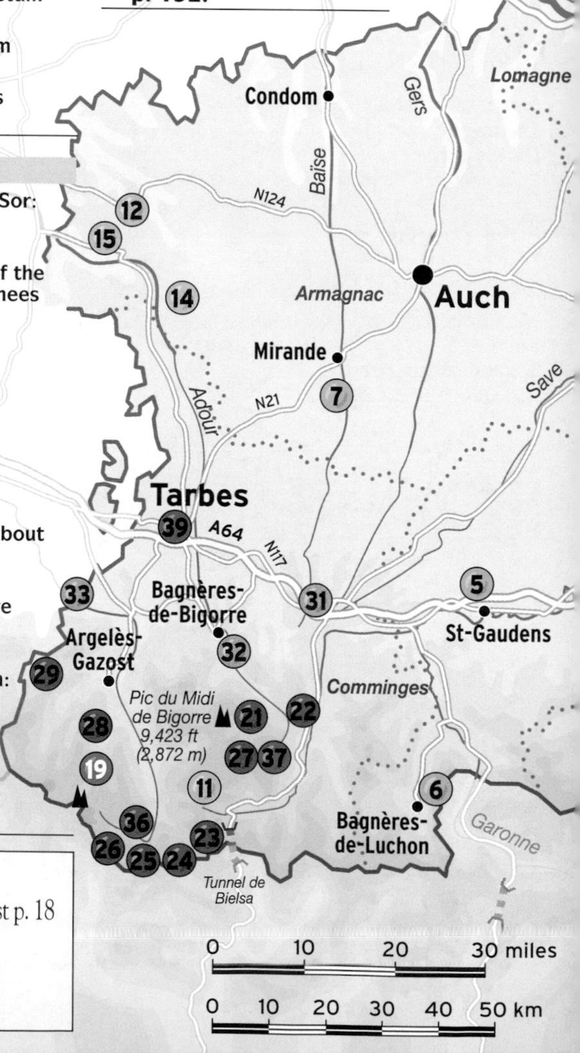

See also:

A walk deep in the forest p. 18
Water and stone p. 20
Flowers and animals everywhere p. 22

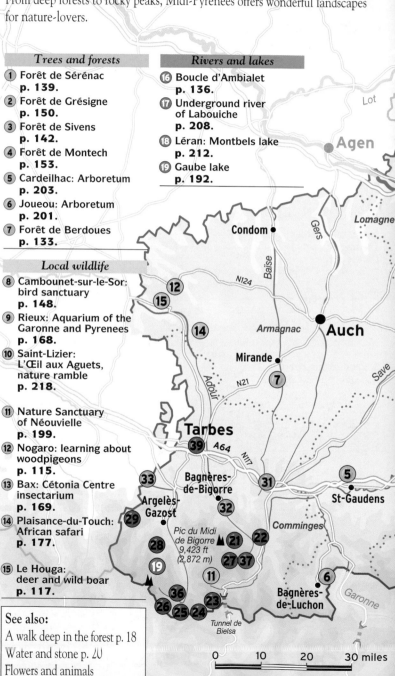

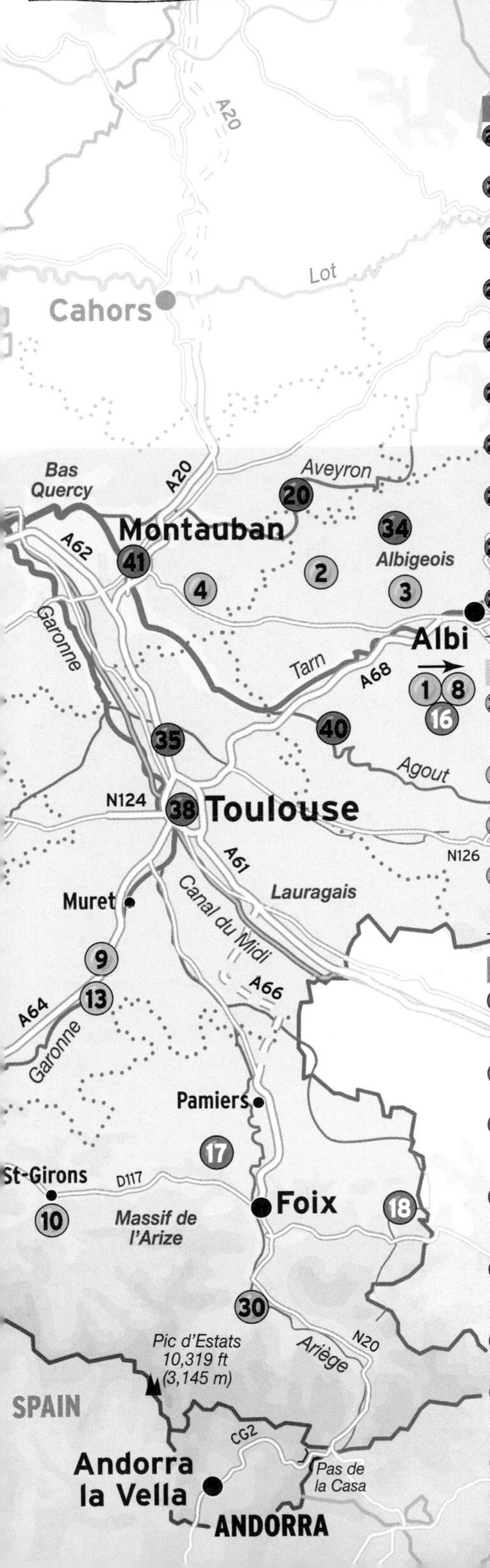

Gorges and mountains

20 Gorges de l'Aveyron **p. 167.**
21 Pic du Midi **p. 180.**
22 Col d'Aspin **p. 195.**
23 Cirque de Barroude **p. 184.**
24 Cirque de Troumousse **p. 184.**
25 Cirque d'Estaubé **p. 184.**
26 Cirque de Gavarnie **p. 184.**
27 Col du Tourmalet **p. 194.**
28 Crêtes du Lys **p. 192.**
29 Col du Soulor **p. 194.**

Caves and chasms

30 Ussat-les-Bains: Lombrives caves **p. 221.**
31 Esparros caves **p. 182.**
32 Asté: Médoux caves **p. 180.**
33 Saint-Pé-de-Bigorre: Bétharram caves **p. 186.**

Parks and gardens

34 Cordes-sur-Ciel: Le jardin des Paradis **p. 140.**
35 Merville park **p. 154.**
36 Pyrenees National Park **p. 192.**
37 Barèges: botanical gardens of the Tourmalet **p. 189.**
38 Toulouse: botanical gardens **p. 170.**
39 Tarbes: Massey gardens **p. 197.**
40 Giroussens: Martels gardens **p. 146.**
41 Montauban: rose-garden of the Espace François-Mitterand **p. 166.**

A walk deep in the forest

A walk in the countryside is a healthy, pleasurable activity. Marked trails attract families and mushroom-pickers, while horse- and bicycle riders can use the bridle and cycle paths. In summer, guides are on hand who can tell you all about the pine-martens, inch-worm caterpillars and the mountain spruce.

More than 2½ million acres of forest

More than one quarter of the Midi-Pyrenees is covered in forest (up to 39% in the Ariège, the most densely wooded département). The trees in the more than 2½ million acres are mainly deciduous, with timber forests accounting for more than half the wooded area.

The owners

The woodlands are divided between three types of owner. 80% of the forests are private, and the rest is shared between local authorities and the state. Public forests are mainly in three Pyrenean départements: Ariège, Haute-Garonne and Hautes-Pyrénées. Royal and church-owned forests confiscated at the time of the French Revolution belong to the state and there have been a few more acquisitions since the early 19th C., so that 111 forests are now state-owned, covering an area of 322,500 acres (129,000 ha).

Leisure for all

In the past, the forest was a frightening place, where few dared venture. Today, it is a favourite with hikers, both local and tourists, and for exploring nature, discovering the flora and fauna and the landscape. There are picnic areas, footpaths, cycle paths, bridle-ways and tracks for skiers. The state-owned forests are particularly well served with facilities for visitors. You can run, hike, walk and enjoy the fresh air, take a picnic, watch the birds and animals or simply sit and daydream.

USES FOR WOOD

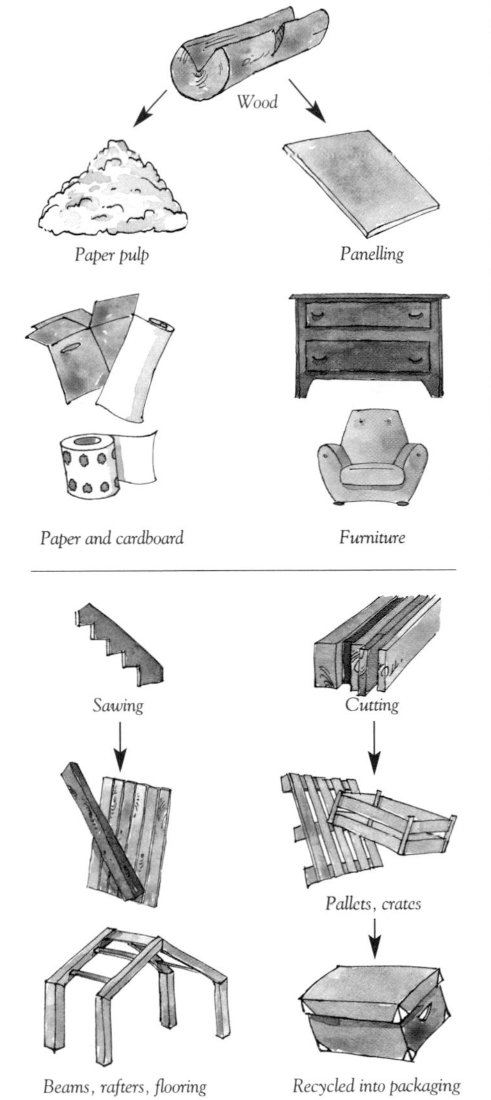

A guided tour of the larger forests

The Office National des Forêts (☎ 05 62 73 55 00) arranges guided tours of the state-owned forests in July and August (lasting about 2 to 4 hours). The foresters will explain the fauna, flora and natural ecological balance. You will learn about timber-growing, conservation and forest management. Themed guided tours are also organised, for instance to hear the stags roaring during the rut (Sept.-Oct.) or to learn to recognise different animal tracks.

A great natural treasure

Trees play a regulating role in controlling water courses. Woodland purifies the air and takes the harshness out of the climate. It stabilises land and helps to reduce the pollution created by carbon dioxide by storing part of the carbon in the wood fibres. French forests are particularly rich in wildlife. The population of larger animals is increasing. In the space of only 20 years, the number of stags has doubled and the number of roe-deer has tripled!

The importance of tree-felling?

The trees grow bigger every year and their volume of wood increases. Felling provides the space they need for growing. This insures the renewal of the forest and makes it possible to harvest wood of various types. Large trunks have a variety of uses. The best quality logs are cut and sliced for fascias and veneers, the rest are sawed into appropriate lengths of planking to use for buildings, furniture, and as packaging materials. Smaller trees, cut to clear shrubbery or undergrowth, begin a new life as paper pulp, wood panels, or are simply used as fuel. Even the sawdust has a variety of uses and is never wasted. Today, a lot of wood is

recycled, either by re-using it or by reducing it to pulp

THE RAMBLERS' CHARTER

Ramblers know that fire is the enemy of the forest. They pick flowers sparingly, because flowers that are pulled up do not grow again. They ask for permission to gather dead wood. They don't leave their litter behind in the forest. They observe closure signs on forest paths and keep to sign-posted routes. This is home for the animals and the rambler should leave them in peace.

Water and stone

In this land of earth and rock, water is everywhere. It flows between the rocks in the mountains, lingers in the green valleys, is channelled into large reservoirs for purists who only drink rainwater and pours from the sky on stormy days. All these rain-soaked landscapes make the Midi-Pyrénées a region of the most diverse views, which are exciting to discover.

The land of geological faults

The Midi-Pyrénées consists of many 'little landscapes' which were created thousands of years ago by movements in the tectonic plates. In the north, faults isolated asymetrical blocks of stone which created a mountain landscape from the Montagne Noire (4,000 ft (1,200 m)) of the Monts de Lacaune (4,200 ft (1,260 m)). The same land movements also caused subsidence, creating deep river-beds, whose picturesque gorges added to the isolation of these areas.

Ruled by the mountains

In the south, above the plain through which the river Garonne runs, all the landscapes were forged and sculpted by sediment brought down from the peaks of the Pyrenees. For a long time, the landscape and the altitude prevented communication between the main mountain valleys. However, a century ago, the establishment of roads and railway lines ended this splendid isolation (Andorra, for example, was particularly isolated).

Storm clouds

Atlantic and Mediterranean weather systems frequently clash in the skies above the Midi-Pyrenees, sometimes violently. There are frequent forecasts of summer storms, the rainfall in spring and autumn is heavy and blizzards are frequent in the Pyrenees during winter. The central plains seem to have been spared some of this turbulence. Toulouse, for example, benefits less than Tarbes from the temperate climate – yet it has a lower average rainfall for the whole year!

A WRITER TAKES THE WATERS

Prosper Mérimée, the writer, wrote to the Countess de Montijo while taking the waters at Bagnères in 1862: 'I have been here for two days and I am taking baths and drink very nasty hot water. The doctor has diagnosed two fatal illnesses, one in my heart, the other in my stomach. He tells me that this nasty water will cure me. Meanwhile, it prevents me sleeping. Add to this the fact that I bathe in the same water as Mlle Anna Deslion, which ought to arouse her, although I have noticed no change in her'.

A long, but not lazy, river

The Garonne is 404 miles (647 km) long and links the Pyrenees to the Atlantic. Its peaceful banks are colonised by birds and it moves in wide meanders through the plain making it appear tranquil. Yet, the waters gushing down from the Pyenees into the river can cause it to swell with coursing water. Before the coming of the railways, the Garonne was a hive of commercial activity. Today, there are no more *sapines*, large heavy rowing-boats weighing 160 tons (160 tonnes) which moved downriver in Spring. Nor does the Garonne carry the rafts which used to come out of Saint-Béat. Their owners used to sell wood on arrival, and bring marble from the Pyrenees as far downstream as Toulouse, before returning to the mountains.

The hot springs: a long history

The hot springs of Luchon, Capvern, Bagnères, Cadéac and Cauterets were well-known and heavily patronised from the 1st C. AD. Fifteen hundred years later, Montaigne praised the hot waters of Bagnères in his famous *Essays*. Mme de Maintenon, second wife of Louis XIV, stayed at Barèges long before the first stone of its hot baths was laid in 1823 by the Duchess of Angoulême, eldest daughter of Louis XVI. But it was the writer Lamartine who enthused about the spas of the Pyrenees in the 19th C. He was soon followed by all the literary figures of his day, as well as high society, from Chateaubriand to Baudelaire, via George Sand and Alphonse Daudet, as well as non-literary figures such as Napoléon III, Bismarck and even … Mata Hari, the spy!

Good for the health

Spas and health resorts make an essential contribution to today's local economy. The resorts generate more than 1,000 direct jobs and 10,000 indirect jobs, especially in the countryside and mountain regions. The 17 spas are visited by more than 100,000 people a year.

Flowers and animals every-where...

Visitors should respect the flora and fauna of this area by not disturbing the animals or picking wild flowers. In the Midi-Pyrénées, unusual wildlife and rare plants are mainly to be found in the mountains, where they are heavily protected by conservation measures. If you love flowers and animals, a detour through the mountains is essential.

The izard or Pyrenean chamois

FAUNA

The brown bear

The bear is the most regal member of the local wildlife. This giant omnivore stands over 6ft (2 m) tall on its hind legs. Few people have encountered a bear, because only ten or so are left in the forests of the Vallée d'Aure. However, a few years ago, three brown bears were imported from eastern Europe and released into the wild at Melle (Hautes-Pyrénées). Cubs have been born, so it is to be hoped that this will be the start of a new community.

The wood-grouse

The wood-grouse is seen mainly in the Néouvielle range between June and October. This denizen of the woods prefers the mountain pine of the Pyrenees. It is a large bird, with a wing span of 4ft (1.20 m) and it can live for nine years. In March, the male fluffs up his feathers, extends his tail and bobs about on the spot in order to impress the females and to eliminate rivals. He's a bit of a show-off!

CE SITE EST UNE RESERVE
ORNITHOLOGIQUE
POUR OBSERVER LES OISEAUX
RESTEZ SILENCIEUX

The izard

The izard or Pyrenean chamois can be seen at up to 8,300 ft (2,500 m). It leaps from rock to rock with astonishing agility. The izard males live alone, but the females live in herds with their young. The izard can be seen in summer in the mountain pastures where it feeds on the lush grass and in winter in the forests, where it hunts for lichens and mosses. It is about 4 ft (1 m) long and 2ft (70 cm) tall at the ithers, weighing up to 88 lb (40 kg).

The Pyrenean ibex

The ibex is a champion sprinter over the rocky slopes of the high mountains at an altitude of 2,500 to 8,500 ft (800 to 2,600 m). This sturdy animal is instantly recognisable by its two enormous, powerful horns, which are 3ft (1 m) long and curve back slightly. They are used mainly for fierce fighting during the rutting period (in December) when the males fight over the females. The ibex is one of the two species of mountain-goat that are native to France.

The crimson-ringed butterfly

This magnificent butterfly flies over the flowery lower and middle slopes of the mountains between June and August. It is easy to recognise because the back wings have distinctive red rings outlined in black, while the front wings are covered in black patches. Look for it carefully. The caterpillar is spotted with red and the chrysalis is completely wrapped in white silk.

The purple heron

This species of heron is dwindling in numbers throughout France, but it can still be found in the Garonne valley. It emerges at twilight and is solitary, living close to shallow water where it feeds on insects, amphibians and fish. Its elegant body with its grey plumage is graced with a long neck and narrow, pale yellow beak. The head is reddish with a little black skull-cap. Its large rounded wings measure 5 ft (1.50 m) across.

FLORA

The Pyrenean thistle

This large, striking plant, which can grow to 16 ins (40 cm) in height, is easy to spot. It is a metallic bluish colour from stem to leaf, including the thorns. The older the plant, the more noticeable the colour. Despite its attractive colour, visitors should resist the temptation to pick the Pyrenean thistle, allowing it to re-seed itself and flourish throughout the mountain range.

The Pyrenean lousewort

This unfortunately named flower grows everywhere at between 4,600 and 9,000 ft (1,400 and 2,700 m), in pastures, beside streams and pathways. It is native to the Pyrenees, and stands 4 to 8 ins (10 to 25 cm) tall. It produces huge, dark-pink flowers between June and September. Its sharply defined leaves grow in a rosette. There are about 250 species of lousewort, some of which are parasitic.

Mountain stonecrop

Only mountain-climbers will see this tiny 1 to 2 in (3 to 5 cm) flower growing on rock faces, as well as granite and sandstone boulders at between 6,500 and 10,000 ft (2,000 and 3,000 m). Its tiny, plump leaves form large reddish patches. Between June and September it produces two or three pink flowers on each stem.

The fine-flowered detawia

If you don't find this flower it is because you are only looking at your feet. In the Pyrenees, this native plant attaches itself to every rocky outcrop of limestone between 1,400 and 7,000 ft (300 and 2,100 m). The thick base of the stem and long, thin strips of shiny leaves are distinctive. In midsummer (July-August), the plant produces umbels bearing clusters of pretty white flowers.

Dragon-mouth

Horminum pyrenaicum is rare in the wild and causes great excitement when spotted, (its name comes from the Greek *hormao*, which means 'I excite'). The dragon-mouth is said to have health-giving properties and was once used medicinally. However, it should now not be picked. It grows about 8 in (20 cm) high and between June and August it produces a mass of deep-purple, almost black, blossoms. It has a distinctive lemony fragrance and grows between 4,000 and 8,000 ft (1,000 and 2,400 m).

Pyrenean valerian

Valerian grows in shady, damp places, such as near springs, at an altitude of between 3,281 and 7,875 ft (1,000 and 2,400 m). This large plant grows in clumps and can grow as tall as 5 ft (1.5 m). When studied closely, it can be seen that the leaves at the top are very small, where as the lower leaves are very large and heart-shaped. Between June and August, the plant produces pinkish-white to purple flowers.

The mountain pine

This hardy conifer grows to a height of 66 ft (20 m), and is resistant to extremely harsh weather conditions. It will survive the heaviest snowfall and most intense cold, as well as a prolonged drought. It is found at great heights, in the Vallée d'Aure, for instance, or places where the winter is particularly cold, such as the Cirque de Gavarnie. It is known in French as the hook-pine, because the cones appear to have a hook at the base. It is also known as the Spanish pine.

The Pyrenean aquilegia

The Pyrenean aquilegia adores both the sun and damp conditions. The flowers are a brilliant blue (sometimes tending to reddish-purple), appearing at the top of a stem about 12 in (30 cm) tall. The stamens are golden yellow. It is found at altitudes of between 5,000 and 8,000 ft (1,500 and 2,400 m) on rocky, limestone outcrops. Be warned: it should not be touched on any account, as it is extremely poisonous, even though it was once used to treat wounds.

The Pyrenean iris

This is the iris from which all cultivated forms were developed. You can admire this original wild iris, especially at the foot of the Cirque de Gavarnie where it grows in profusion. However, there is a complete ban on picking it! Its dark-blue, almost violet, flowers with their contrasting yellow centres are a beautiful sight. The flowers are 5 to 6 in (12 to 13 cm) in diameter and appear from mid-June to early August.

The amethyst hyacinth

Hyacinthus amethystinus, this pretty member of the lily family, grows on sunny, limestone soils.

As its name implies, the flowers are bluish-violet. The thin stem carries 12 little bells with 6 short lobes in rather floppy clusters. The amethyst hyacinth grows from a bulb and flowers in May and June at the Cirque de Gavarnie.

Food shopping

The region is well known for its gourmet food, including duck breast, preserved meats and foie gras. Here are some of the best local producers.

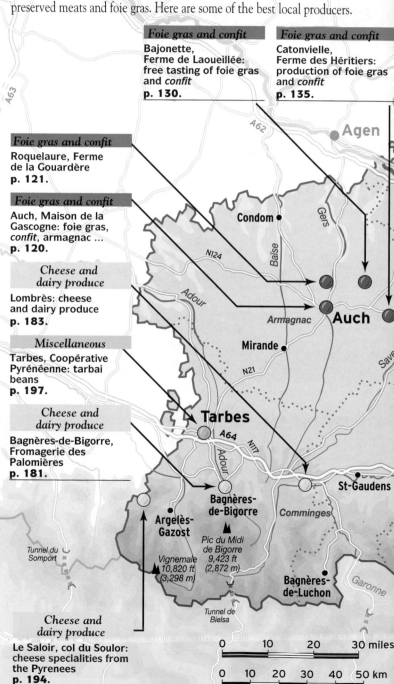

Foie gras and confit

Bajonette, Ferme de Laoueillée: free tasting of foie gras and *confit*
p. 130.

Foie gras and confit

Catonvielle, Ferme des Héritiers: production of foie gras and *confit*
p. 135.

Foie gras and confit

Roquelaure, Ferme de la Gouardère
p. 121.

Foie gras and confit

Auch, Maison de la Gascogne: foie gras, *confit*, armagnac ...
p. 120.

Cheese and dairy produce

Lombrès: cheese and dairy produce
p. 183.

Miscellaneous

Tarbes, Coopérative Pyrénéenne: tarbai beans
p. 197.

Cheese and dairy produce

Bagnères-de-Bigorre, Fromagerie des Palomières
p. 181.

Cheese and dairy produce

Le Saloir, col du Soulor: cheese specialities from the Pyrenees
p. 194.

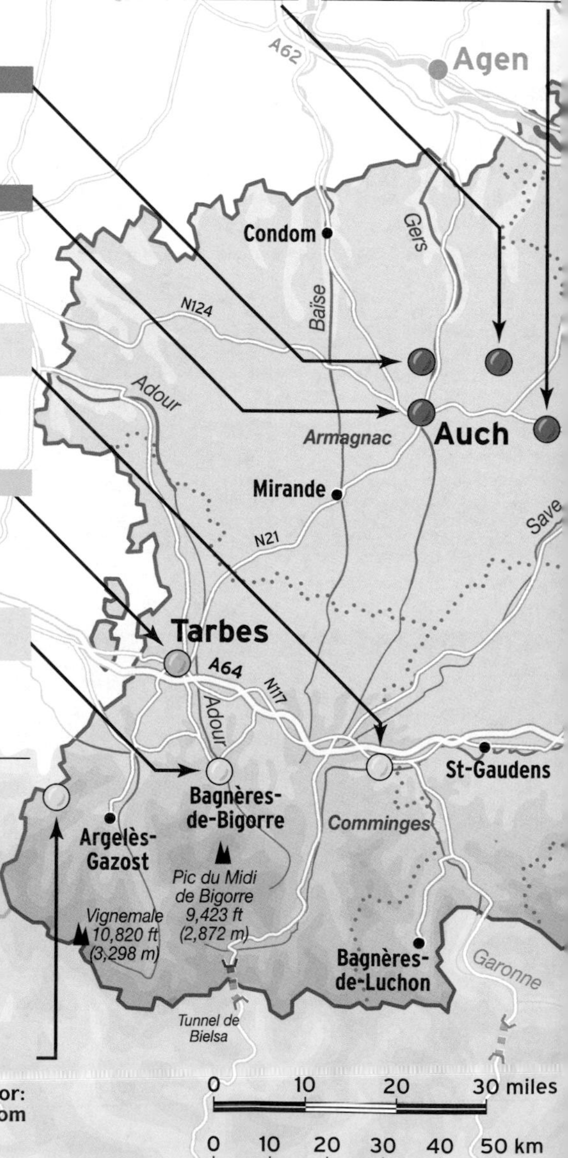

See also:
Cheeses p. 28
A thousand and one ways to cook pork p. 30
Meat and poultry specialities p. 32
Traditional duck and goose p. 34
Foie gras p. 36

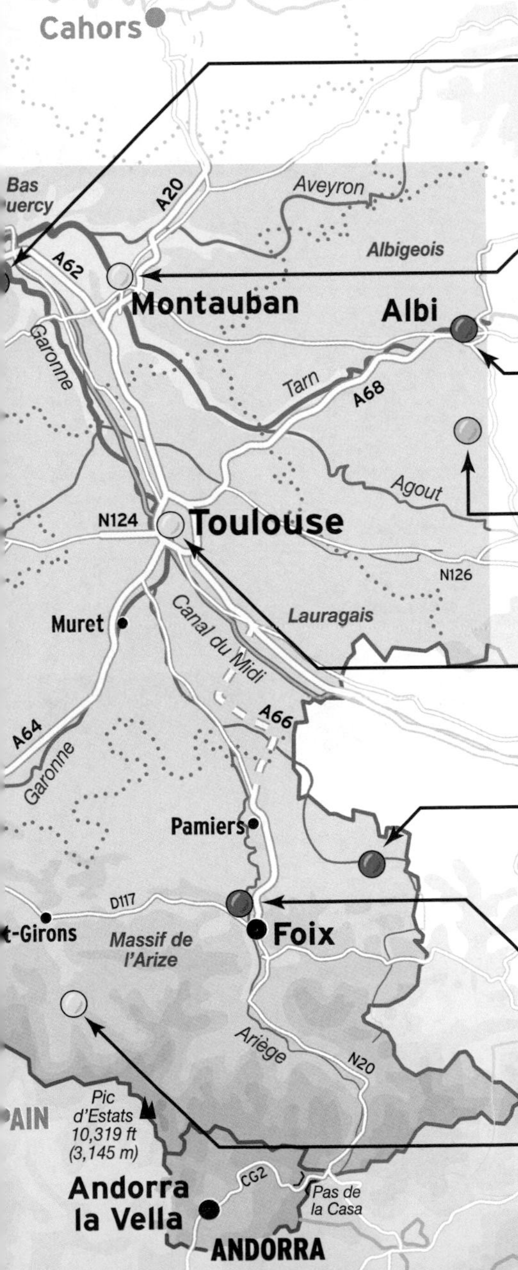

Foie gras and confit

Angeville, Ferme des Jouberts: duck foie gras, *confit*, stuffed duck breast ...
p. 153.

Cheese and dairy produce

Montauban, Ferme du Ramier: local tomme cheese
p. 167.

Foie gras and confit

Albi, Maison Lascroux: foie gras, *confit* of goose or duck, tinned food ...
p. 138.

Miscellaneous

Lombers, the pigeons of the Mont-Royal: pâtés, *confit*, stuffed pigeon
p. 148.

Cheese and dairy produce

Toulouse,Pascal dairy: fresh cheeses
p. 174.

Foie gras and confit

Mirepoix, Domaine de Sié: duck foie gras, *confit*, duck breast ...
p. 212.

Foie gras and confit

Vernajoul, Ferme du Plantié: foie gras and traditional duck *confit*
p. 208.

Cheese and dairy produce

Seix, Fromagerie Coumes: Rogallais cheese
p. 207.

Cheeses
cow, goat or ewe's milk?

Whether they are made from cow's, goat's or ewe's milk or a mixture, the cheeses of Midi-Pyrénées are all equally delicious. The most famous cheese, known simply as *Fromage des Pyrénées*, is made in the Ariège, Hautes-Pyrénées and Haute-Garonne. It is a mature, hard cheese, and is typical of the cheeses of the region. Enjoy it with a fruity red wine.

CHEESE-MAKING

1. *Souring the milk*
2. *Cutting the curd*
3. *Mashing the curd*
4. *Moulding and pressing*
5. *Salting the curd*
6. *Ageing*

Barousse

Barousse used to be made from ewe's milk, but now cow's milk is used instead. This farmhouse cheese is the pride of the region west of Saint-Bertrand-de-Comminges. The pressed curd is made from unpasteurised milk, and is semi-hard, perforated with tiny holes. The flavour varies depending on the diet of the cows, but it is always sharp and strong. The cheese is matured for six weeks and turned every day for the first two weeks.

Bamalou

Bamalou comes from Castillon-en-Couserans, near Foix (Ariège), and has the strongest aroma of all the cow's milk cheeses of the Pyrenees.It is smooth, rich, and well protected by a solid brown rind, splashed with red spots. The cheeses are made in two sizes: 1 lb 12 oz (800 g) for the small and 12 lb 16 oz (6 kg) for the large one. Complement it with a red wine that is high in tannin (Vin de Cahors, for example).

Rogallais

This cow's milk cheese is made in small batches in the village of Seix, near Couserans in the Ariège. Eyes (or holes) perforate the curd, and aerate it as the cheese matures. The curd is semi-hard, slightly elastic and is pressed but not heated. It has a distinctive smell of damp cellars. The rind is well matured and is brown or pinkish-brown. It should be served with a Graves (Médoc) red wine.

Tomme de chèvre de Loubières

This goat's milk cheese looks like an old piece of stone. It is very large,measuring 8 in (21 cm) in diameter, and is made near Foix (Ariège). It is allowed to mature for a considerable time, the dry rind protecting a yellowish-grey, crumbly cheese whose strong flavour has a hint of dampness, the result of its two-months' maturing in a cellar. The cheese is also called Cabrioulet.

Tourmalet

This 100% pure ewe's milk cheese is also made in small quantities and is named after the Pyrenean mountain pass which is also a well-known stage in the Tour de France. It is smaller than the other mountain cheeses, measuring only 4 in (10 cm) in diameter, and is only 2¾ in (7 cm) thick. It has a strong flavour which compares well with the other, larger, cheeses of the region.

Galet de Bigorre

This little white farmhouse cheese consists of 7 oz (200 g) of pure unpasteurised goat's milk, and combines several flavours which succeed each other in the mouth. First there is a fresh, slightly acidic flavour which gradually matures and expands into a creamy mildness. It should be eaten very fresh, if possible with ripe apricots.

Bethmale

This is the most famous cow's milk cheese of the Pyrenees. This cheese can weigh as much as 12 lb 16 oz (6 kg). It bears the name of the village near Foix where it was first made. It is said to have been favoured by Louis VI 'the Fat', who loved its semi-hard texture (it is pressed but not heated) and its damp flavour. It is always turned and brushed while maturing, so that it can absorb the smell of the cellar more effectively.

A BRIEF HISTORY OF CHEESE-MAKING

The history of cheese-making goes back a long way. Prehistoric man began domesticating animals and drank the milk they produced. Efforts were made to preserve the milk, and it is quite probable that vessels were made to contain and keep it when sour. The first pressed curds appeared in Greek and Roman times, but soft cheese did not emerge until the Middle Ages. As for the shape and size of different cheeses, these are no accident. In the mountains, where cold weather lasts for longer and travel is difficult due to heavy snowfalls, the cheese is made into larger wheels than elsewhere in France, as this protects the cheese from drying out and over-ageing. In the low-lying parts of the region, where the weather is warmer and drier, the cheese is mainly made from goat's milk, since it is easier and cheaper to feed goats than cows.

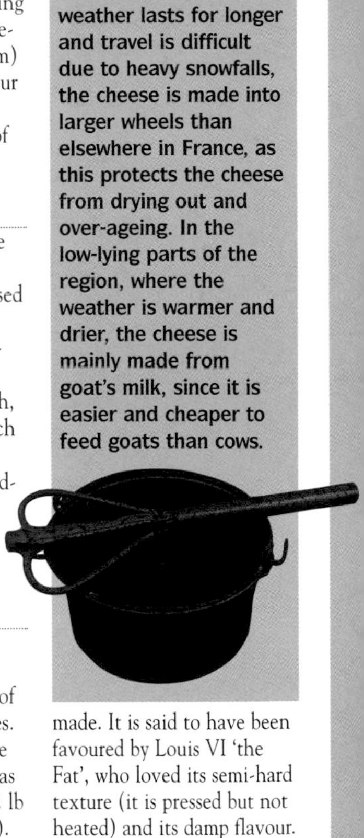

A thousand and one ways to cook pork

In Midi-Pyrénées, charcuterie and pork dishes have long been the basis for home cooking. There is an old French adage, according to which '*Sans maison, sans jardin et sans porc, mieux vaut être mort,*' (without a home, a garden and pork, it's better to be dead). Nowadays, this tradition has become a local craft and every part of the region has a great tradition of making pork products. Here is a quick, but certainly not exhaustive, survey of a real feast.

Saucisse de Toulouse

This sausage, famous throughout France, is the only regional sausage whose quality is guaranteed by a red label. It consists of coarsely chopped fresh lean pork, from which all gristle has been carefully removed, and is only allowed to contain 10% fat, salt, spices and a pinch of sugar. The large sausage, purchased ready-sliced from the butcher, will only keep for a week and must always be stored in the refrigerator, at 37.4°F (3°C).

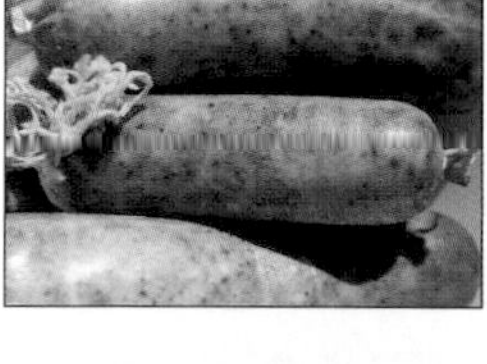

La saucisse de foie de porc

This unusual pork liver sausage is long, thin and brown and is dried for a fortnight before it is ready to eat. When at its best, it has a wonderful flavour of foie gras. Its home town is Varilhès, near Toulouse.

Boudin noir

In this region, black pudding is encased in a bladder and looks like a large, aromatic

LA MIQUE AU SANG
This is another type of pig's blood sausage. In Bigorre, it is made by mixing cornmeal with fresh pig's blood. Mique blanche (white pudding) is a preparation of cornmeal and minced aged bacon, which is flavoured with parsley and garlic and poached gently in stock. Both these varieties of pudding are shaped into large balls which are wrapped in two cabbage leaves.

soft ball which is sliced by hand. It can be eaten cold as it is, or cut into large pieces and fried with goose fat.

Menscate

This local delicacy is largely reserved for Christmas and New Year and other winter celebrations. It is also encased in a bladder and contains a rich mixture of pig's head, bread and eggs. It is exclusive to the region.

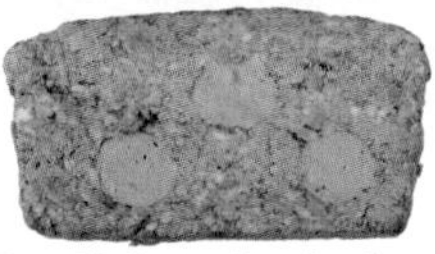

Traditional pâtés and cured ham

Revel, in the Haute-Garonne, is one of the places where large pâtés are made containing duck breast, and smooth goose or duck *rillettes* (potted meat). The well cured ham owes its flavour to the quality of Gascony pork, and the fact that the hams are dried for a whole year.

Ventrèche and camette

The speciality of Bigorre is ***ventrèche***, a piece of well-aged salt bacon, taken by shepherds as part of their summer provisions when they drive their flocks to the mountain pastures. Bigorre also produces ***camette*** or shoulder of pork, a winter delicacy resulting from the Pèle-Porc celebrations (the day on which the pig is slaughtered). It is customary to eat ***truse*** on that day. *Truse* is a small cake of cornmeal, kneaded with goose fat and lightly fried.

Meat and poultry specialities

One big farmyard, Midi-Pyrénées has such an important tradition of animal husbandry that the population of geese, duck, guinea-fowl and capons outnumbers the human population! The poultry vies in popularity with local beef, veal and lamb. This has led to a lot of good-natured rivalry in the region, as to which district makes the best *cassoulet*!

The poultry of Gers

The ***poulet gris*** (grey chicken) of Gers is well known throughout France. The free-range birds are killed when 105 days old. This is late by poultry rearing standards but this tardy execution produces tender, lean, meat. The free-range **guinea-fowl** is also famous for its lean meat. It is reared for 94 days on a diet of 70% **grain** in a fairly restricted area. This prevents the bird from putting on too much weight.

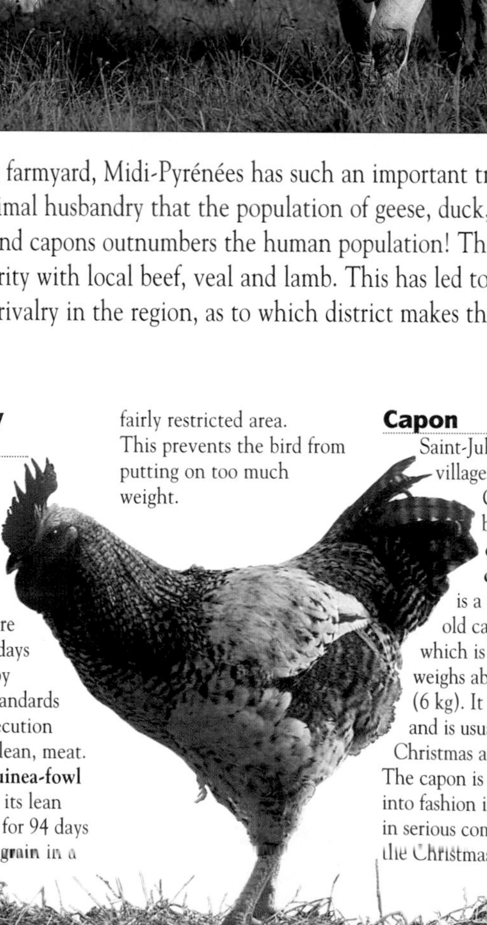

Capon

Saint-Julia is a little village in Haute-Garonne, where breeders specialise in the **fat capon**. A capon is a nine-month-old castrated cock which is fattened until it weighs about 12 lb 16 oz (6 kg). It is very tender and is usually served at Christmas and New Year. The capon is coming back into fashion in France and is in serious competition with the Christmas turkey.

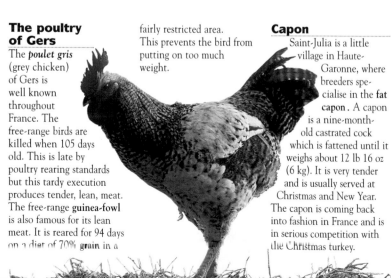

Hunters' game in the Ariège

Although many centuries have passed since bear meat was eaten, you can nevertheless find many other types of game in the markets or restaurants during the hunting season. There is partridge, hare and wild boar, prepared in a variety of ways, marinated, roasted or jugged.

Gascony beef

The sturdy mountain cattle of the region are renowned for their tender red meat. The cows and bulls are reared to be hardy, and graze in summer on the slopes of the Pyrenees. In this harsh climate, they are satisfied with meagre mountain pastures in summer and a single ration of hay per day in winter. This spartan lifestyle has not prevented Gascon beef from attaining such high quality that in 1997 it earned the famous red label. The best Pyrenean beef originates from Villeneuve-du-Paréage, in the Ariège.

White veal and black pork

The Comminges **white veal** market was once held at Saint-Gaudens, in the Haute-Garonne. The tradition of rearing these milk-fed calves exclusively with their mothers in small sheds has been maintained here (and in the Lauragais). **Black Gascon pigs** are also reared in the Hautes-Pyrenees. This robust breed produces hams of the highest quality.

Pyrenean farmyard lamb

Pyrenean lamb is reared in the Hautes-Pyrénées, Haute-Garonne, the Ariège and Gers, and comes from a very hardy Tarascon breed. The lambs are fed on ewe's milk and grain. The meat has a delicate pink colour. The lamb here is so good that you will see it sold in packaging bearing a prestigious red label, which signifies the quality of the meat. The best Pyrenean lamb is labelled Saint-Gaudens (Haute-Garonne).

Traditional duck and goose

The goose is now the traditional symbol of Gascon gastronomy, but for a long time it was also a staple of ordinary country-dwellers. From feathers for goose feather beds to drumsticks and thighs for *confit*, every part of the bird was used in some way or other. While duck breast and foie gras are special delicacies, the French connoisseur equally appreciates *demoiselles* (grilled breast meat on the bone), gizzard, heart kebabs and stuffed neck.

Preserving using goose fat

The goose was certainly the first animal to be domesticated. Geese were raised in flocks on common land and the meat was guaranteed to be a nourishing, calorie-rich food from early winter to late spring. Because of the high fat content it is possible to preserve the meat without having to dry or salt it. Thighs, drumsticks and other joints are simmered over low heat and stored in earthenware pots under a thick coating of goose fat. This is known as *confit*.

Serving *confit*

The jar or pot of *confit* simply needs to be placed in a

COOKING WITH GOOSEFAT

The cuisine of the South West is based on goose fat. Goose fat will only burn at 482°F (250°C), as opposed to 266°F (130°C) for butter and 392°F (200°C) for lard. This means that goose fat is the best fat for frying. Here is a cooking tip: save the goose grease from a canned foie gras or *confit* and use it for frying eggs or sautéing potatoes.

simmering saucepan of water and heated gently on the stove. Then the pieces of meat are removed and browned in a frying pan. Allow one goose thigh or duck breast for two people. Potted duck or goose can be stored for about four years from the date on which it was made, and actually improves with age.

Duck versus goose

Barbary duck or mallard are now more frequently reared than geese. They are easy to breed and the portions of meat and liver are smaller, and thus easier to market. Nevertheless, the goose remains the symbol of gastronomy in Gers. At the time of writing, there are moves afoot to allocate an AOC (*appellation d'origine contrôlée*) for a typical Gers breed of goose.

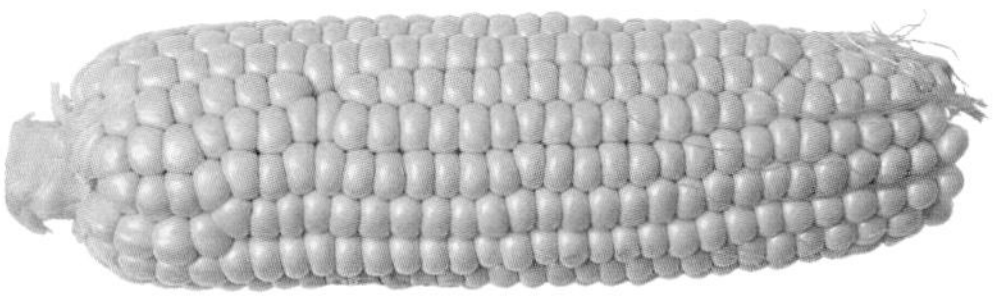

Figs or maize?

The tradition of force-feeding harks back to Roman and Egyptian times, when geese were force-fed with figs. Figs were also fed to the geese in the Midi-Pyrénées before the arrival of maize in the 16th C. Local breeds of goose, such as the grey geese of Masseube, Gimont and Toulouse, are fed on white maize, a variety which is specific to the region. Force-feeding ducks with figs has come back into fashion, however. The fruit gives the meat a special finesse and smoothness, improves the flavour by making it milder, and imparts a pinker colour to the flesh. This new delicacy is sold under the name of *figuigers*.

The pride of the South West

Of course, foie gras is not the exclusive preserve of the South West. It is produced in Alsace, as well as Hungary and Israel, yet true gourmets swear by the duck and goose livers produced in Gers, Haute-Garonne and Hautes-Pyrénées. Gers is the largest producer of fattened goose livers, with 250,000 force-fed geese and more than 50,000 goslings a year. It is the second-largest producer of duck foie gras.

Breast meat (*magret*)

This is a boneless piece of meat taken from a goose or duck which has been used to produce a foie gras. The flesh is a bright red, even though it is as low in calories as chicken breast. *Magret* lends itself to many recipes, but it is at its best when grilled with its skin on, over a wood fire, until the flesh is rare or pink. Smoked *magret* is often used in salads.

Foie gras
liver at its best

Subtle and delicate goose foie gras is an exceptional food item which has always been considered a delicacy in France. Yet the gaggles of geese are letting themselves be overtaken by flights of ducks. Currently, duck liver is even more popular than goose. Duck liver is stronger in flavour, but also has a certain panache.

Fattening a duck for foie gras

Force-feeding (whereby a funnel is placed in the open beak and food pushed down) is claimed to be a reinforcement of the natural tendency of ducks and geese to overeat during winter, though some might consider this treatment to be cruel. Force-feeding geese and ducks is considered perfectly reasonable and normal by the local people. You may feel revolted by this practice, and we are certainly not advocating it, but it is a tolerated and inescapable part of the culture of the South West.

Raw, pasteurised or canned?

The minimum weight at which raw foie gras may be sold is $10\frac{1}{2}$ oz (300 g) for duck and 14 oz (400 g) for goose. **Raw foie gras** is usually vacuum-packed. The liver is usually firm and supple to the touch and is a beige, ivory or ochre colour. **Fresh foie gras** has, in fact, been lightly cooked. **Foie gras mi-cuit** (partially cooked foie gras) or **semi-conserve** (partially preserved) has been pasteurised.

DIRECT SELLING FROM THE FARM

If you want to buy direct from the farmer, you need to look out for roadside signs bearing the words '*Conserveurs à la ferme*'. This guarantees that the geese and ducks used are bred locally. It also ensures the high quality of the preserves processed on the premises, which will have been inspected by the veterinary service. The Gers producers who benefit from this labelling are happy to welcome visitors and gourmet shoppers, and to show them how the foie gras is produced, explain the production processes involved and to enable their customers to benefit from the advantages of buying direct from the farm.

None of these three methods of processing permits the foie gras to be stored for long and it must be refrigerated at between 32°F and 39.2°F (0°C and 4°C). **Canned foie gras** has been subjected to heat treatment. It can be stored for several years in a cool, dry place.

How to choose the best liver

In winter, most of the towns in the Gers district hold foie gras markets, where you can buy raw foie gras and cook it yourself. The best duck livers weigh 14 oz (400 g) and the best goose livers 2 lb (900 g). Be aware that the heaviest livers are not necessarily the most suitable for preserving because they will ooze out too much fat. It is best to take your time and buy direct from the producer. And, if possible, buy the foie gras from October onwards. The geese that are culled early always have excellent livers.

Making your own foie gras

Foie gras is simple to prepare. All you need is a whole, raw foie gras, salt, white pepper and 10 fl oz (300 ml) of wine or spirit. Soak the liver in lightly salted water for several hours. Separate the lobes, discard the membrane, the central vein and the blood vessels. Wipe the liver and season it with salt, pepper and alcohol, then

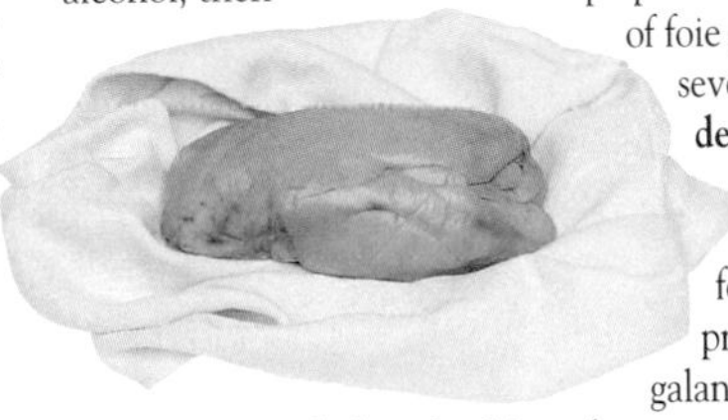

store it in a cool place for 24 hours. Arrange the liver in a terrine, cover it with a lid and place the whole dish in a roasting tin filled with water. Cook in the oven at 400°F (200°C), gas mark 6 for 1 hour. Leave to cool, then serve with some fresh, wholemeal bread.

Regulated appellations

To avoid any confusion, here is a quick overview of the official foie gras appellations. A **foie gras entier** consists of one or two pieces of liver lobe seasoned with salt and pepper. It is the Rolls Royce of the foie gras world. **Foie gras** is a preparation consisting of lobes of foie gras taken from several birds. The **bloc de foie gras** is a block of liver pâté made from reconstituted foie gras. The other preparations (pâtés, galantines, duck and goose liver mousses) must contain at least 50% foie gras in order to be allowed to use the name.

Wines and spirits

Both little-known and famous vins de pays, aperitifs and liqueurs can all be found in this region. This could be a good opportunity to start your own wine cellar or restock your selection of spirits.

① *Albias*
Domaine de Montels
p. 167.

② *Cadalen*
Alain Rotier, wine grower
p. 144.

③ *La Ville-Dieu-du-Temple*
Cooperative cellar
p. 153.

④ *Saint-Mont*
The Plaimont cooperative cellar
p. 112.

⑤ *Donzac*
Cave de Donzac: sales of 'black wine'
p. 158.

⑥ *Condom*
Musée de l'Armagnac, Maison Papelorey (Armagnac) and Maison Ryst-Dupeyron
p. 122.

⑦ *Fronton*
Côtes du Frontonnais at the Château de Bellevue-la-Forêt (Fronton)
p. 155.

⑧ *Viella*
Domaine de Berthoumieu
p. 113.

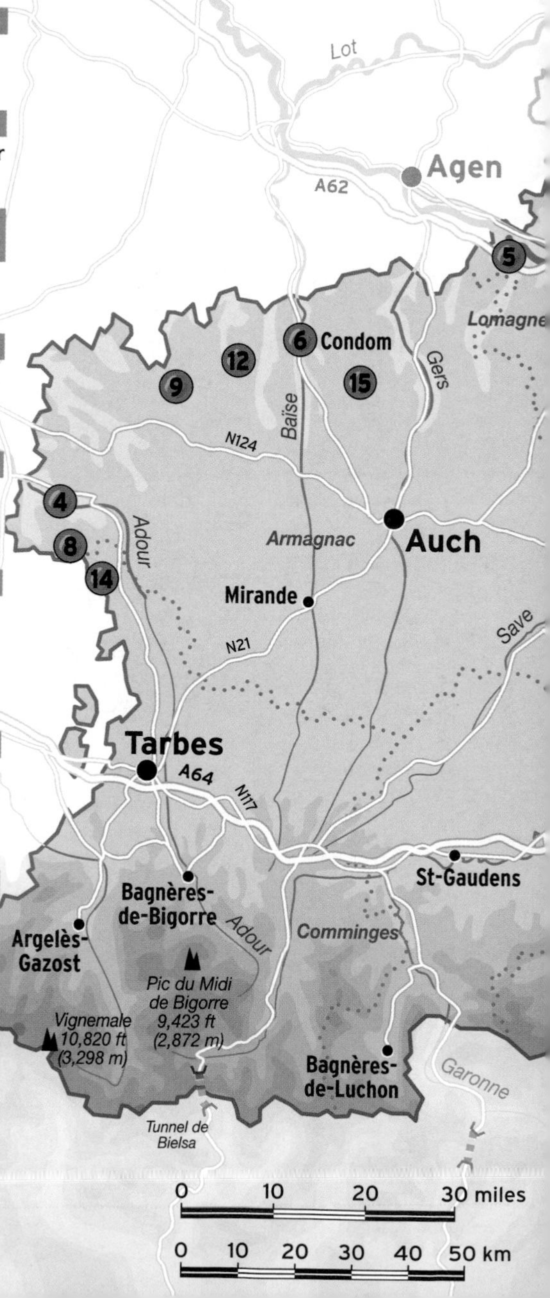

See also:
Wines of the South West: the pleasure of discovery p. 40
Armagnac: the king of brandies p. 42

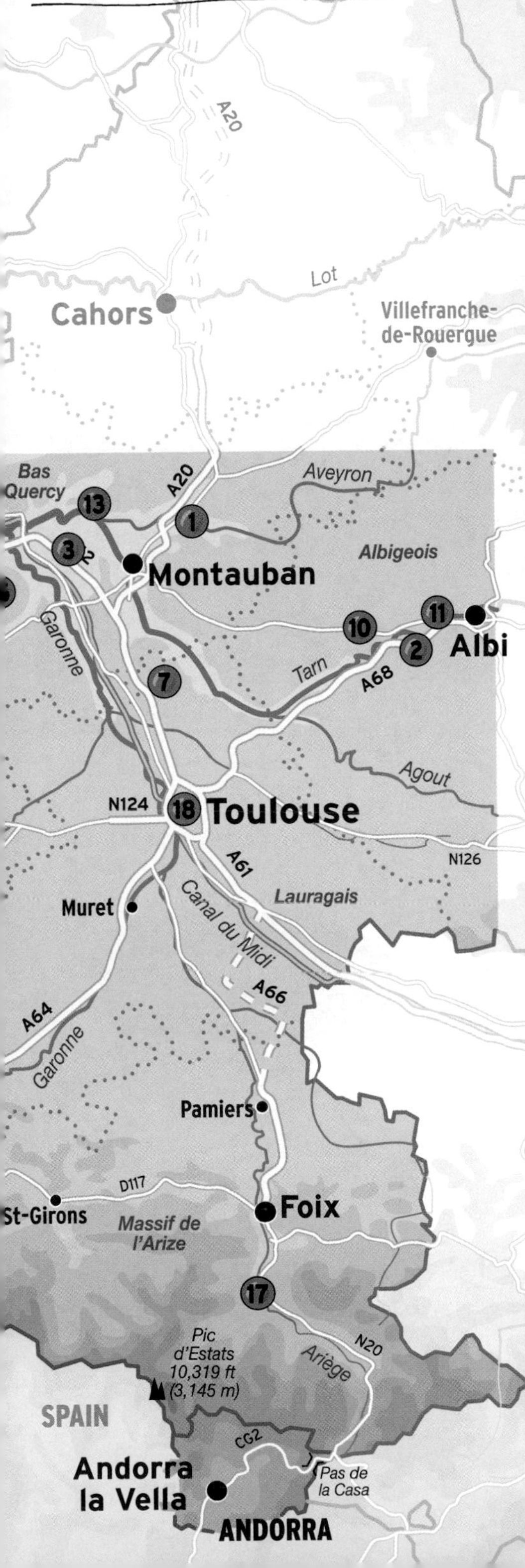

9 *Éauze*

Floc de Gascogne: aperitif makers
p. 116.
Domaine de Lagajan: production of Armagnac and a small museum
p. 117.

10 *Gaillac*

Route des Vins de la Fédération des caves particulières
p. 143.

11 *Labastide-de-Lévis*

Guided tours, tastings and sales at the cooperative cellar
p. 144.

12 *Gondrin*

Domaine des Cassagnoles: country wines, Armagnac and Floc de Gascogne
p. 125.

13 *Labastide-du-Temple*

Domaine du Gazania
p. 152.

14 *Madiran*

Madiran wines at the Châteaux de Perron and Montus and at the Domaine de Bouscassé
p. 113.

15 *Saint-Puy*

Château de Monluc: Pousse-rapière (Floc de Gascogne and sparkling wine)
p. 125.

16 *Saint-Sardos*

Saint-Sardos cellar: vin de pays
p. 131.

17 *Tarascon-sur-Ariège*

Maison Séguélas: production of *hypocras* (a local aperitif)
p. 221.

18 *Toulouse*

Maison Busquet: violet liqueurs
p. 177.

Wines of the South West
the pleasure of discovery

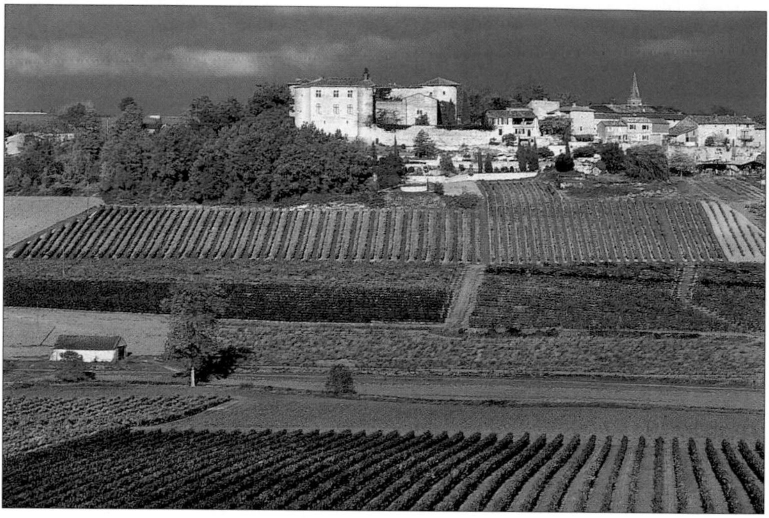

The vineyards of the Midi-Pyrénées consist of a patchwork extended from the valley of the Lot to Gascony, from south of the Massif Central to the slopes of the Tarn and from the terraces overlooking the Garonne to the gates of Toulouse. They consist of 22 *Appellations d'Origine Contrôlée* (AOC) of which five have the most excellent reputation – Gaillac, Cahors, Fronton, Madiran and Marcillac.

Gaillac

This is one of the oldest vineyards in France. Grapes have been grown in the western part of the département of Tarn since the 6th C. A variety of wines are produced: Gaillac Blanc Sec (a fruity white wine), the famous Gaillac Blanc Perlé (elegant and subtle), Gaillac Moelleux (mellow), Gaillac Rosé (light), Gaillac Rouge (dark and robust) and Rouge Primeur (a young red wine). The whites, rosés and primeurs should be drunk young but the reds are *vins de garde* which should be left to age. The Blanc Perlé is an ideal accompaniment to charcuterie, Moelleux goes well with Roquefort cheese and foie gras, and the reds are perfect with roasts and other cheeses.

CRU DU PARADIS

The wines of Frontonnais

These are made from a grape variety called Négrette, grown exclusively for centuries in the region between Toulouse and Montauban. The rosés of Frontonnais are famous for their flexibility and fullness and are general drunk young. The reds, on the other hand, improve with age (vintage reds mature well in a wine cellar for four to seven years). Their alcohol content is quite high and they are robust and full-bodied with a distinctive flavour of blackcurrant and prunes. Drink the rosés with fish and charcuterie, and the reds with grilled meat and cheeses from the Pyrenees (choose vintage wines to drink with *cassoulet*, *confits* and game).

Madiran and Pacherenc du Vic-Bilh

Madiran has had an AOC since 1948. This wine from the northern part of the Hautes-Pyrenees is the best known of the region. It is recognisable by its strong aroma, due to Tannat, the grape variety from which it is made. The wine was improved by the Benedictines in the 11th C. It is rich in tannin and full-bodied even when young. The neighbouring Pacherenc is a white wine as light as a flower. It is dry and mellow, and its fragrance combines perfectly with that of Madiran, which can be left to age for 20 years and goes particularly well with red meat and cheese. Pacherenc is often drunk nine months after harvesting, with fish and shellfish.

Little-known wines worth trying

The South West also offers a range of agreeable little wines which deserve to be discovered. The Côte-de-Saint-Mont, from Auch, benefits from ageing. Lavilledieu-du-Temple is a Vin Délimité de Qualité Supérieure (VDQS) from Montauban, an aromatic fruity rosé best drunk young. Another aperitif, Hypocras Ariègeois, is a subtle blend of wine, ginger, rose petals and cardamom, which has just been saved from obscurity.

FLOC DE GASCOGNE

This regional aperitif deserves greater recognition. Floc was once consumed only at home by the Gers winemakers, hence the label. It is a simple combination of grape juice and Armagnac. The process was soon copied to produce other liqueurs, notably Pineau des Charentes and Ratafia de Bourgogne. Floc finally received its local AOC in 1990. Drink it with strawberries, raspberries, peaches, or pour it into the scooped-out hollow of a Lectoure melon. It is delicious poured over foie gras or one of the strong-flavoured cheeses of the region.

Armagnac
the king of brandies

Armagnac is the symbol of Gascony and d'Artagnan. This prestigious brandy, heir to an ancient tradition, characterises the richness of the soil and reflects a certain style of good living. The secret lies in its long period of maturing in oak barrels which gives it its lovely golden colour and subtle aroma, all due to the skill of the *maître de chai*.

Distillation by craftsmen

Armagnac is produced in small quantities from white wines by skilled craftsmen. The wine is distilled in winter in a distillery or on the producer's premises, often using a mobile still. A still for making Armagnac is made of hammered or laminated copper which operates continuously. When it emerges from the still, the colourless spirit (*la blanche*) has between 52% and 72% alcohol.

Ageing in oak casks

The spirit is transferred to new oak casks (the best are made of white oak from the forests of Gascony) which are stored in *chais* (wine cellars). The skill lies in choosing exactly the right moment (generally after

A STILL FOR DISTILLING ARMAGNAC

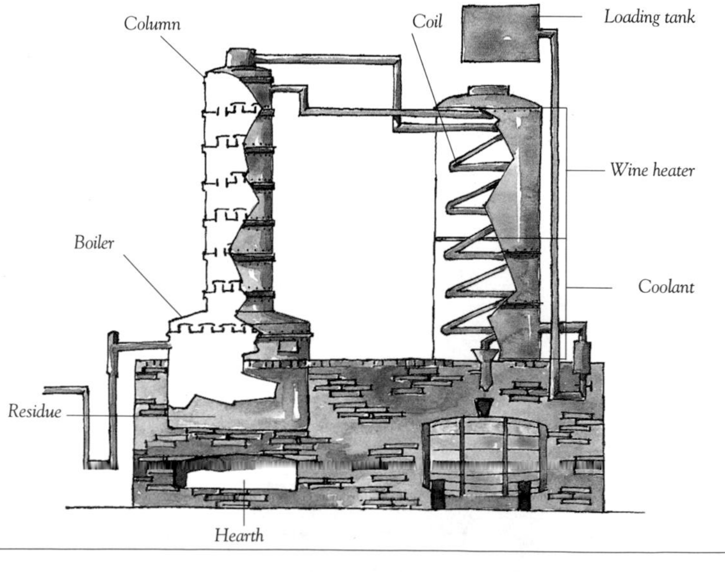

eight to ten years) for transferring the Armagnac into older casks. This second maturing gives the Armagnac its lovely amber colour. The degree of alcohol reduces through natural evaporation. The amount which evaporates is known in French as *la part des anges* (the angels' share). When the *maître de chai* considers that the Armagnac has aged sufficiently, he 'cuts' it, that is to say he blends it with several other brandies of different origins and ages.

Understanding the label

Armagnac is characterised by its long ageing in oak casks. Three-star Armagnac contains brandies of which the youngest must be at least two years old. VO, VSOP or Réserve on the label indicate a blend in which the youngest brandy is at least five years old. Bottles labelled XO, Extra or Napoleon contain Armagnacs which are at least six years old. Hors d'Âge (ageless) has an age, in fact, despite its name. It is a blend in which the youngest brandy is at least ten years old. The vintage year (*Millésime)* on the label represents the year in which the grapes were harvested. Once purchased, your bottle of Armagnac does not need to age. Brandy, like all distilled liquids, does not mature in the bottle. To store it correctly, keep the bottle upright, so that the alcohol does not damage the cork.

The Armagnac regions

The AOC area covers 37,067 acres (15,000 ha) of vines and three production regions, of which Bas-Armagnac is considered the best. Its sandy soil produces delicate, fruity brandies. Ténarèze produces more robust brandies which require prolonged ageing. Upper Armagnac makes excellent wines but they are not usually distilled.

The privilege of age

For 700 years, Gascony has been distilling a brandy which used to be famous for its antiseptic properties. This usage developed in the 17th C. when the merchants added it to Bordeaux wines to preserve them. The brandy used in this process was stored in oak casks, and so, by pure chance, the virtues of ageing were discovered! In 1878, all the vines of the Armagnac region were destroyed by phylloxera, the plant louse infestation which ruined so many French vineyards. Only one quarter of the area was replanted after the devastation.

SERVING BRANDY

A great Armagnac deserves to be presented in the proper manner. Serve it in quite a large snifter, with a large bulb and narrow rim, to concentrate the aroma. Armagnac should be allowed to rest and breathe and its nose is all important. Pour it in small quantities to fully appreciate it. Never add a vintage Armagnac to a warm cup of coffee and avoid smoking when tasting it. For a sublime treat, leave the last little drop in the bottom of the glass for a few hours, then come back and inhale the magnificent bouquet. Armagnacs from Bas-Armagnac, will retain this aroma for up to 24 hours.

Regional dishes and sweet treats

Food-lovers will find a range of delights to suit every taste in the Pyrenees-Gascogny region, from local sweetmeats to food festivals.

① *Miscellaneous*

Moissac, the Uvarium: sampling of grape juice **p. 163.**

② *Cakes and confectionery*

Montauban, *Pâtisserie Marty:* the montoriol **p. 165.**

③ *Cakes and confectionery*

Montauban, *Confiserie Pécou:* boulets **p. 165.**

④ *Chocolates*

Albi: Michel Belin **p. 137.**

⑤ *Ice cream*

Albi: Michel Thomas Défos **p. 137.**

⑥ *Restaurants*

Toulouse, *Jardins de l'Opéra*: haute cuisine **p. 170.**

⑦ *Restaurants*

Villefranche-de-Lauragais, *Hôtel de France*: cassoulet, **p. 161.**

⑧ *Restaurants*

Valcabrère, *Le Lugdunum*: Roman cuisine **p. 205.**

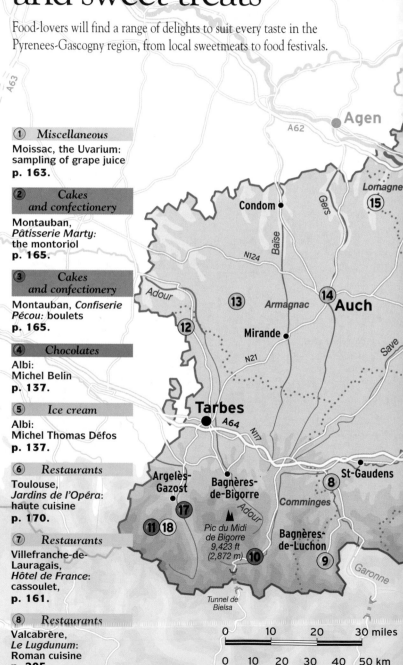

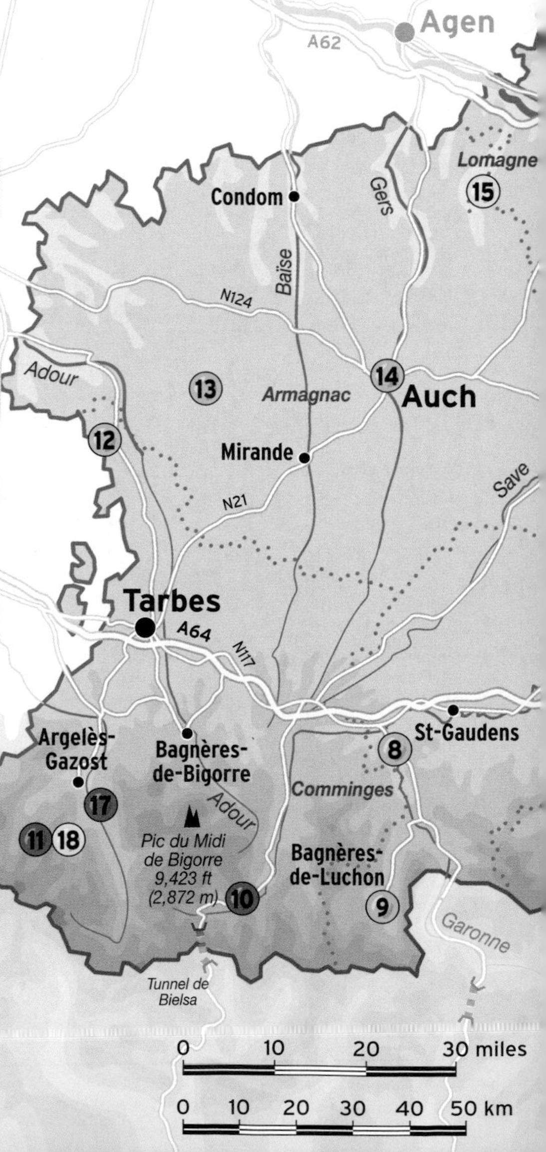

See also:
Favourite dishes from the land of gourmets p. 46
Assortment of treats for a sweet tooth p. 48

Cahors

⑨ *Restaurants*

Bagnères-de-Luchon, *Hôtel d'Étigny*: pétéram and pistachio p. 201.

⑩ *Chocolates*

Saint-Lary-Soulan: chocolates and *Flocons pyrénéens* p. 198.

⑪ *Cakes and confectionery*

Cauterets, *La Reine Margot*: humbugs p. 189.

⑫ *Restaurants*

Madiran, *Le Prieuré*: country dishes p. 113.

⑬ *Restaurants*

Plaisance-du-Gers, *Hôtel Ripa-Alta*: French cuisine p. 114.

⑭ *Restaurants*

Auch, *Hôtel de France*: country dishes p. 120.

⑮ *Honey*

Gramont: museum and honey tastings p. 131.

⑯ *Honey*

La Borde, Trebas, Apis Vinaegria: honey and vinegar p. 139.

⑰ *Cakes and confectionery*

Beaucens, *Biscuiterie des Pyrénées*: *croustades* p. 187.

⑱ *Honey*

Cauterets, *Pavillon des Abeilles*: honey and gingerbread p. 189.

⑲ *Honey*

Esplas-de-Sérou, Liliane Martin: mountain honey p. 211.

⑳ *Cakes and confectionery*

Saint-Girons, Martine Crespo: *croustades* filled with prunes, apples and pears p. 219.

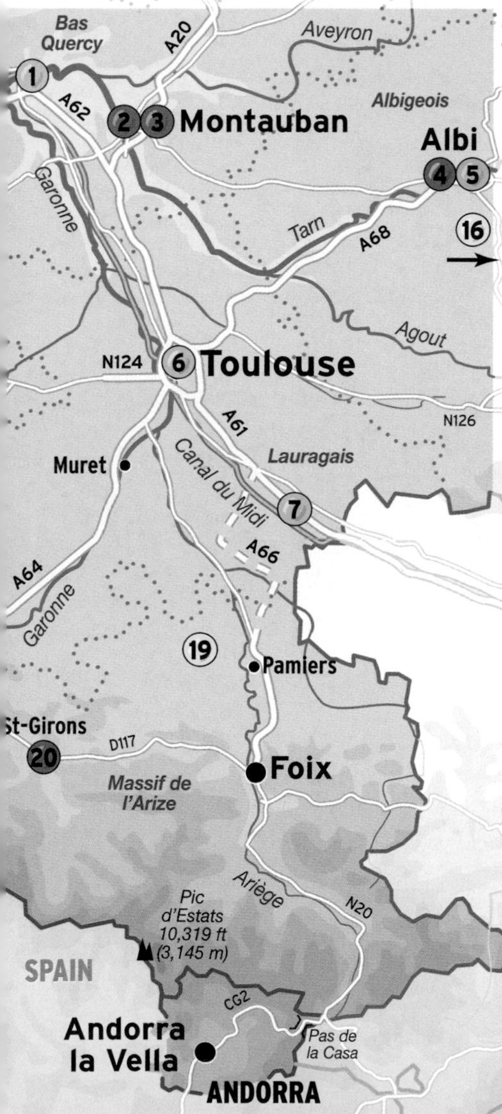

Favourite dishes

from the land of gourmets

Midi-Pyrénées is a food-lovers' paradise. Its rich and varied gastronomy, created mainly on around the local produce, has justly earned it a great reputation. Here are a few delicious regional dishes which will make your mouth water!

The cream of Midi-Pyrénées

Although the region boasts several local cuisines, certain foods are of prime importance wherever you go. **Goose** is still unquestionably the staple meat of Gascony and Toulouse. **Pork and pork products** are eaten mainly in the south, but **beans** are a popular dish everywhere, since they combine so well with preserved pork, pork dishes and goose, especially the recently revived Tarbes bean (see p. 54).

A reviving bowl of *garbure*

Garbure is a rich, thick, creamy soup that is typical of the region. In a steaming pot, numerous fresh vegetables (turnips, potatoes, carrots and onions) are combined with Tarbes beans, salt pork, and potted meat (*confit*). To this is added a mixture of chopped garlic and parsley. This is the basic

recipe, but there are many variations throughout the entire region. For example, in Hautes-Pyrénées, the famous **camayou ham**, or at least a knuckle bone, is added. The dish is always served in the same way. The master of the house first cuts slices of wholemeal bread which he places in the bowls and the soup is poured, piping hot, over the bread.

Civet of pork

This ancient dish is made to celebrate the pig festival at Trie sur Baïse. Take 2¼ lb (1 kg) of cubed belly of pork and fry it in fat with diced carrots, onions and shallots.

Sprinkle with flour then add Armagnac and set alight. Add 1¾ pt (1 l) of strong red wine with thyme, bay leaf, salt, peppercorns and 2 cloves. Cover and simmer until the meat is very tender.

HOME COOKING DOWN ON THE FARM

Home cooking in the Midi-Pyrénées is based on a wide variety of traditional foods, which can be discovered in a number of different ways. For instance, you can stop at a farm for a snack prepared by the farmer from his own produce. These are hearty farmhouse snacks, and the food will be wholesome and plentiful.
When mealtimes come around, head for the *ferme-auberge* (farmhouse-inn). The farmer greets the guests himself and the menu will include his own home-grown produce (poultry, eggs, cheese, fruit, vegetables, etc). Names and addresses of participating farms are available on request by calling ☎ 05 61 13 55 55.

With a little patience, you will have cooked up a real country feast.

Millas

This is one of the oldest dishes in Midi-Pyrénées. Although sweetcorn has replaced millet, the name of this dish has not changed. Each village has its own recipe. Millas consists of cornmeal sprinkled into a mixture of water, butter and milk and cooked in a deep copper pot. It is served cut into thin slices which are fried. They are sugared if eaten as a dessert, salted to accompany meat dishes. Millas can be found in all the local markets during winter.

The *cassoulet* controversy

This debate has lasted for centuries and does not look like being resolved in the near future! The bone of contention is: which is the true *cassoulet*? Is it the *cassoulet* of Castelnaudary, of Carcassonne or of Toulouse? Above the hubbub, a clear answer emerges – all three of them. Prosper Montagné, author of the *Festin Occitan*, wrote: '*Cassoulet* is the god of cuisine: the *cassoulet* of Castelnaudary is God the Father, that of Carcassonne is God the Son, and that of Toulouse is the Holy Ghost.' However, all *cassoulet*-lovers can agree on

several points. A true *cassoulet* contains 30% meat and 70% beans, pork rinds, gravy and herbs. Similarly, a *cassoulet* worthy of the name should simmer for a long time on the stove top, acquire a crust by baking in a low oven, and before it is served, the crust that forms over the top must be broken at least seven times. The fussiest people add that the stew should be so thick that a spoon should be able to stand upright in the *cassole*, the traditional terracotta dish which gave the recipe its name!

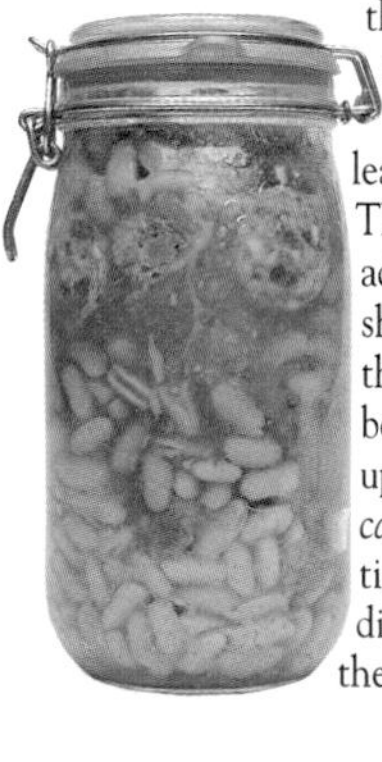

An assortment of treats for a sweet tooth

There are enough speciality pastries and cakes in this region to satisfy even the sweetest tooth! Pâtisserie, confectionery, ice-cream and chocolates are all on offer and the makers vie with each other to produce temptations that are as pretty to look at as they are delicious to eat! However, these delights have not displaced such traditional specialities as Gascony's apple *croustade* or the spit-baked cake of Bigorre.

Croustade Gasconne

This incredible pastry cake is also known as Pastis Gersois. The Croustade Gasconne is a sublime mixture of melting and crispy textures. The crispiness is provided by a pastry made from a dough which is pulled out into ribbons that are so thin and transparent that they are called *voiles de mariée* (bridal veils). The melting texture is provided by slices of apple previously soaked in Armagnac. These are inserted between the pastry ribbons. For the final layer, a ribbon is lightly folded over the top before baking, and before this magnificent creation is tasted.

Cake baked on a spit

It looks like a sugar mountain, an edible Christmas tree! The spit-baked cake is made from a pancake batter rich in eggs, butter and sugar. The mixture is baked over a wood fire on a wooden, cone-shaped spit which is turned by hand. More and more batter is added gradually with a ladle. Each spoonful coats the spit with a further layer of batter, which is cooked as it turns towards the heat of the fire. Gradually a thick sponge crust forms, covered in a rough texture of misshapen lumps. When all the batter has been used up, the cake is

The Alléluia of Castelnaudary

Practising Christians always enjoy celebrating the end of Lent and the arrival of Easter, and for everyone else it is the joyous coming of spring.
In the 19th C. the pâtissiers of Lauragais devised a bread flavoured with lemon for this occasion. It is said that Pope Pius VII baptised it *alléluia* (hallellujah) when on a visit to Castelnaudary. It is full of candied fruits and is religiously eaten at breakfast, with or without jam.

allowed to cool, then it is removed from its support and stood upright on the table.

Bricks, cannonballs and paving-stones

Don't worry, these regional specialities won't lie heavily in your stomach! Les Briques du Capitole, a speciality of Toulouse, are made of nougat. The cannonballs (*boulets*) of Montauban are in fact delicious toasted hazelnuts coated with sugar and dark chocolate. The Pavé du Quercy is a paving-stone eaten between Moissac and Montauban, and is also lighter than you might think. It consists of a delicious cake containing almonds, walnuts, raisins, candied cherries and vanilla.

The violets of Toulouse

Since the 1940s, a family firm in Toulouse has been making these famous violets, using a recipe brought from Italy by Napoleon. These candies are delicately made from whole violets encased in a crystallised coating of sugar. The same process is used to produce sweets with the subtle flavours of lilac, acacia and rose. The Candiflor Dedieu company is the one company in the world which makes real crystallised flowers and it exports its products to every continent. You will find its wares in all the gift shops and speciality food stores of Toulouse.

The little fruits of the Pyrenees

Wild berries picked beside mountain paths, including strawberries, raspberries and bilberries, create the flavours of fruits of the forest. They are made into *eaux-de-vie* (spirit made from fruit), homemade jams, jellies, liqueurs and preserved in syrup. They are used to flavour vinegar, tarts and berry pancakes. Pick your own as you wander through the countryside, or take some preserved berries away and enjoy them throughout the year.

Markets

Specialist markets selling garlic, foie gras and honey thrive throughout the region. Even if you don't arrive with a shopping list, markets are lively places to visit, where you can sample local produce from the stallholders and soak up the atmosphere.

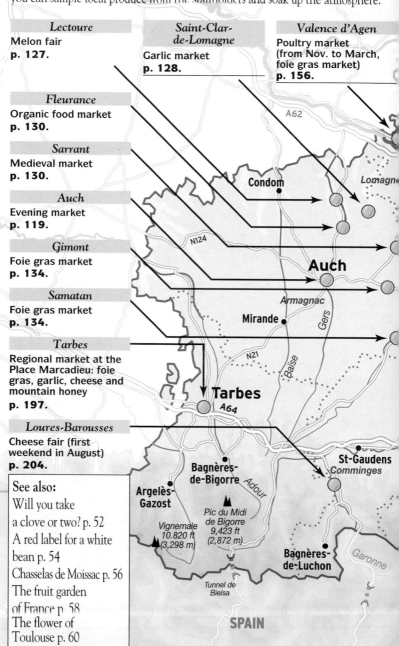

Lectoure
Melon fair
p. 127.

Saint-Clar-de-Lomagne
Garlic market
p. 128.

Valence d'Agen
Poultry market (from Nov. to March, foie gras market)
p. 156.

Fleurance
Organic food market
p. 130.

Sarrant
Medieval market
p. 130.

Auch
Evening market
p. 119.

Gimont
Foie gras market
p. 134.

Samatan
Foie gras market
p. 134.

Tarbes
Regional market at the Place Marcadieu: foie gras, garlic, cheese and mountain honey
p. 197.

Loures-Barousses
Cheese fair (first weekend in August)
p. 204.

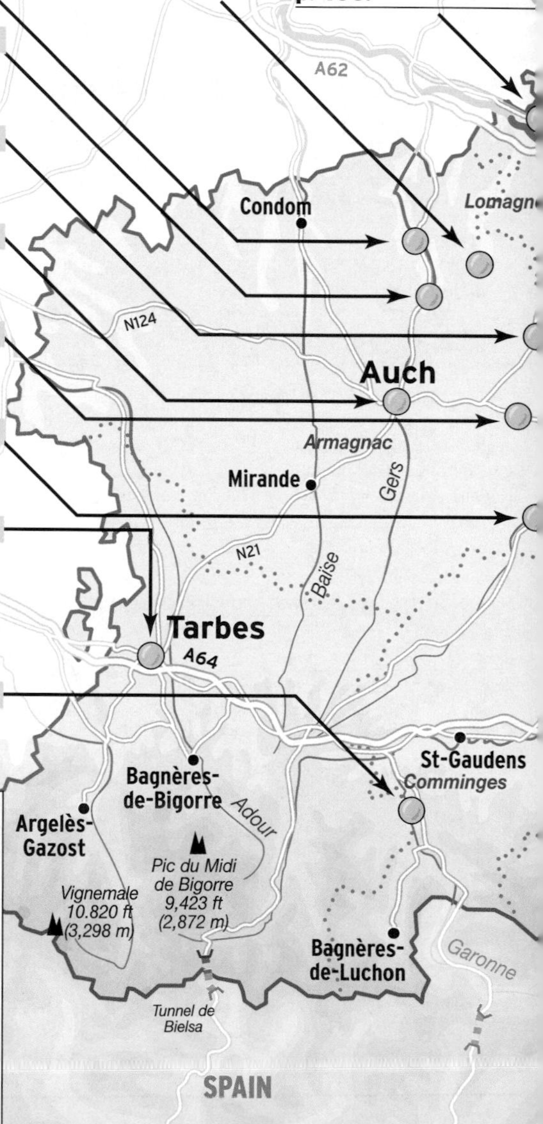

See also:
Will you take a clove or two? p. 52
A red label for a white bean p. 54
Chasselas de Moissac p. 56
The fruit garden of France p. 58
The flower of Toulouse p. 60

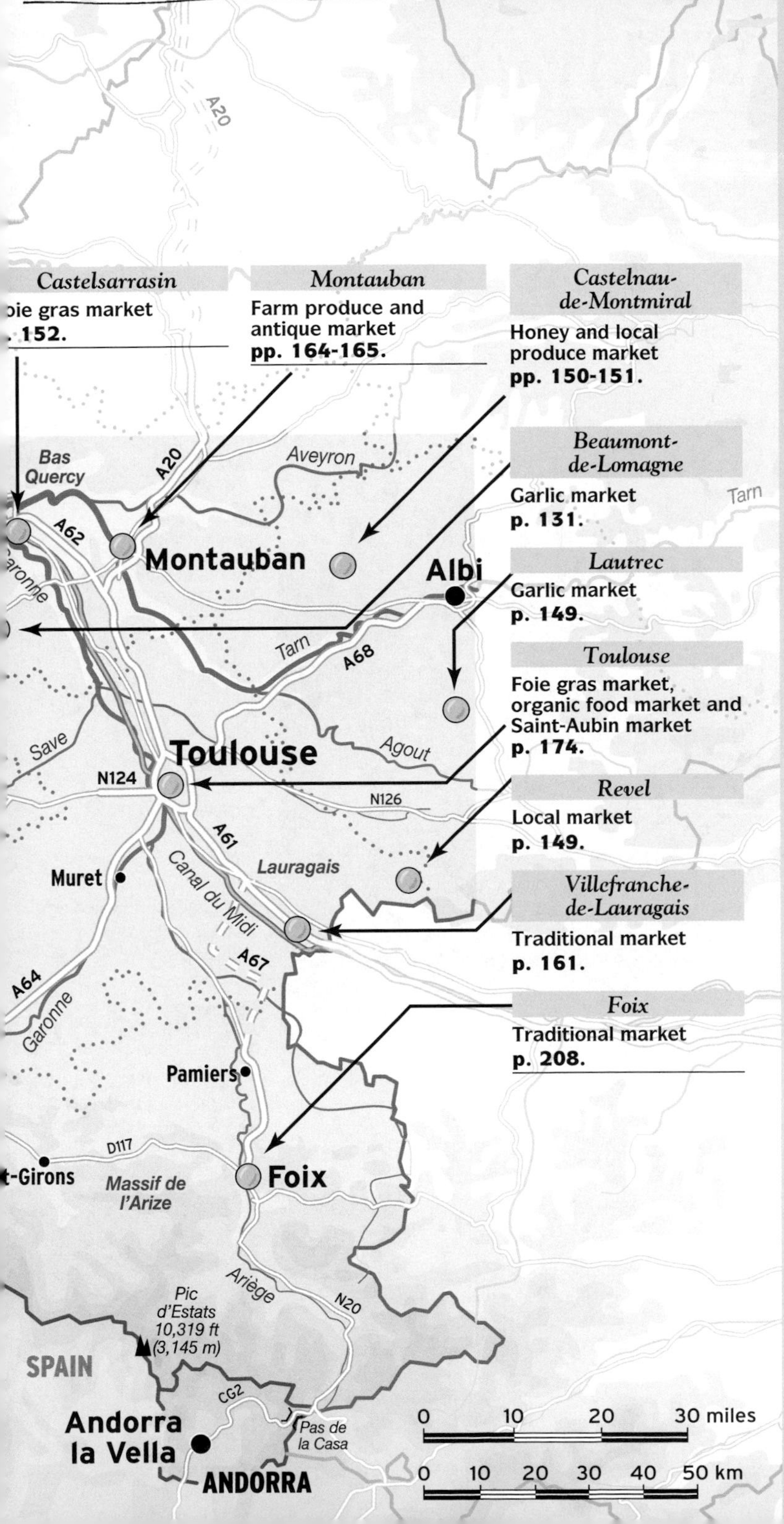
Castelsarrasin
oie gras market
. 152.
Montauban
Farm produce and antique market
pp. 164-165.
Castelnau-de-Montmiral
Honey and local produce market
pp. 150-151.
Beaumont-de-Lomagne
Garlic market
p. 131.
Lautrec
Garlic market
p. 149.
Toulouse
Foie gras market, organic food market and Saint-Aubin market
p. 174.
Revel
Local market
p. 149.
Villefranche-de-Lauragais
Traditional market
p. 161.
Foix
Traditional market
p. 208.
A20
Bas Quercy
Aveyron
A62
Montauban
Albi
Tarn
aronne
Tarn
A68
Save
Toulouse
Agout
N124
N126
A61
Muret
Lauragais
Canal du Midi
A67
A64
Garonne
Pamiers
D117
t-Girons
Massif de l'Arize
Foix
Ariège
N20
Pic d'Estats 10,319 ft (3,145 m)
SPAIN
CG2
Andorra la Vella
Pas de la Casa
ANDORRA
0 10 20 30 miles
0 10 20 30 40 50 km

Will you take a clove or two?

Lomagne is the land of white garlic. Out of every three heads of garlic eaten in France, one of them comes from Lomagne. The 'stinking rose' originated from the steppes of central Asia, but found its true home here, thousands of years ago. This typically southern flavouring, used in every cuisine worthy of the name, also has valuable medicinal properties.

The heritage of the Crusades

The bulb of the plant, which is divided into segments with a strong smell and peppery flavour, was brought back from the East in the Middle Ages by the Crusaders. In Lomagne, garlic found the ideal growing conditions. The climate was favourable and the soil was a healthy clay, rich in limestone and humus which would compost in spring and favour the development of the bulbs. Since then, white garlic has become the dominant variety.

Garlic by the ton

An area of 17,297 acres (7,000 ha) is devoted to garlic cultivation in Midi-Pyrénées, representing an annual harvest of 29,527 tons, i.e. 65% of the total French production. Lomagne is by far the largest growing area, accounting alone for a quarter of the crop. The centre is at Saint-Clar-de-Lomagne, where garlic fields cover 9,885 acres (4,000 ha).

White, pink or red

The white variety is the most heavily produced and consumed in France, but there are at least two other varieties which are cultivated in the Midi-Pyrénées, the red garlic of Cadours, in Haute-Garonne, and the pink garlic of Lautrec, in Tarn, known for its flavour and storage properties. The best varieties can be identified by their red label.

LE TOURIN À L'AIL (GARLIC SOUP)

Serves 4: 1 tbsp duck fat, 1 onion, 1 head of garlic, thyme, salt, pepper, 1 egg (separated), 1 tbsp wine vinegar, slices of bread.

Melt the duck fat in a deep saucepan and fry the finely chopped onion. Add the peeled garlic cloves, 3½ pt (2 l) hot water, thyme, salt and pepper, and simmer for 15 to 20 min. Add the egg white while continuing to beat the mixture. When ready to serve, add the egg yolk and vinegar. Arrange a few slices of bread in a soup tureen and pour the Tourin over them.

Consume without moderation!

Garlic soup, aïoli sauce, and crushed garlic seasoning are all typical of the foods you will find in the south of France, where garlic is an indispensable ingredient in cooking. It is used mainly for the characteristic flavour it gives to dishes but Garlic is also a valuable medicinal plant and extracts of it are used as an ingredient in a number of medicines. Many people take it daily in the form of a capsule. Garlic is known to kill parasitic worms, but it also has antiseptic properties. It has even been discovered to be beneficial in reducing blood pressure and cholesterol levels and is thus a protection against heart disease.

A red label for a white bean

The Tarbes bean (*haricot tarbais*) is loved for its thin skin, melting flesh and delicate flavour. Yet it nearly disappeared altogether from French plates. Thanks to the persistence of a few growers, the cultivation of this exceptional bean is once again becoming widespread, which is fortunate as it is an essential ingredient in local cuisine. It has even gained a red label of quality.

Bigorre, fiefdom of the *mounjete*

The haricot bean was a staple of the Aztec diet, and reached Europe in the holds of Christopher Columbus' ships. It appeared in the Tarbes region in the early 18th C., at the same time as maize. Bigorre seemed to have the right soil for growing this variety, and Tarbes became the main market for this type of haricot or French bean. It thus became known as the *haricot tarbais*, though in Gascon it is called *mounjete*.

The end of French beans?

In 1891, 45,714 acres (18,500 ha) of the beans were grown, but production slumped in the 1950s due to the introduction of herbicides and hybrid varieties of maize. By the 1970s, only 25 acres (10 ha) of Tarbes beans remained. The crop was revived in the 1980s thanks to a group of enthusiastic growers. Current production is estimated at 98 tons (100 tonnes) of dried beans and 98 tons (100 tonnes) of semi-dried or fresh beans a year.

The complicity of maize

The haricot bean is a climbing plant and the Tarbes variety was traditionally grown on maize plants. It would climb up the maize in order to reach the light. This proximity favoured a symbiotic relationship between the two plants. Nowadays, in

order to ensure even growth, the bean plants are trained over stakes and netting.

An exclusively local bean

The *haricot tarbais* has a typically very thin skin and melting, creamy, delicate flesh. It is known to absorb water readily, and thus cook faster, retaining its shape and firmness well. Every attempt to introduce this variety into other parts of France have failed. It only flourishes in the soil and weather conditions of Bigorre. The climate it

prefers combines the sea influences of the Gulf of Gascony and the land influences of the Toulouse district.

Picked with care by hand

The high price of the *haricot tarbais* (50 F for 2 lb 4 oz (1 kg)) is justified not by the rarity of the vegetable itself, but because of the care with which it is harvested. Picking, sorting, grading, packing and preparation for the table are all performed exclusively by hand. Furthermore, the *haricot tarbais* is protected from insect pests by being subjected to very low temperatures, a process which avoids the use of any chemical treatment and keeps the bean organic.

A worldwide reputation

As an indispensable ingredient in *cassoulet* and *garbure*, the *haricot tarbais* has an important place in the region's culinary heritage. Its fame extends far beyond the growing area and it is considered by connoisseurs to be the best of the 224 varieties of bean cultivated in France. Today it is exported to places as far afield as the United States, Japan and Australia!

GARBURE WITH *CONFIT*

Serves 4-6 people: 1 small green cabbage, 1 bunch of pearl onions, 4 potatoes, 4 turnips, 1 red pepper, 4 garlic cloves, 1 bouquet garni, 1 ham bone, 5½ oz (150 g) piece lightly salted bacon, 1 dried sausage, 1 lb (500 g) fresh *haricots tarbais*, 4 pieces preserved goose (*confit d'oie*) (wings and thighs), 4 slices day-old wholemeal bread .

Cut the cabbage into quarters, remove the thickest stalks, shred the leaves and blanch them in boiling water. Peel the onions, turnips and potatoes. Cut open the pepper, discard the seeds and slice it into strips. Peel and crush the garlic. Heat two knobs of goose fat from the confit in a saucepan and fry the onions. Add the vegetables, garlic, bouquet garni and ham bone. Add salt and pepper and moisten with 3½ pts (2 l) cold water. Bring to the boil and simmer for 30 minutes. Add the bacon and sausage, and cook for 3 minutes. Shell the beans, add them and cook for 30 minutes. Add the *confit* and cook for 10 minutes. Discard the ham bone and bouquet garni before serving. Arrange the meat and vegetables in a dish and serve with toasted wholemeal bread.

Chasselas de Moissac
a very special grape

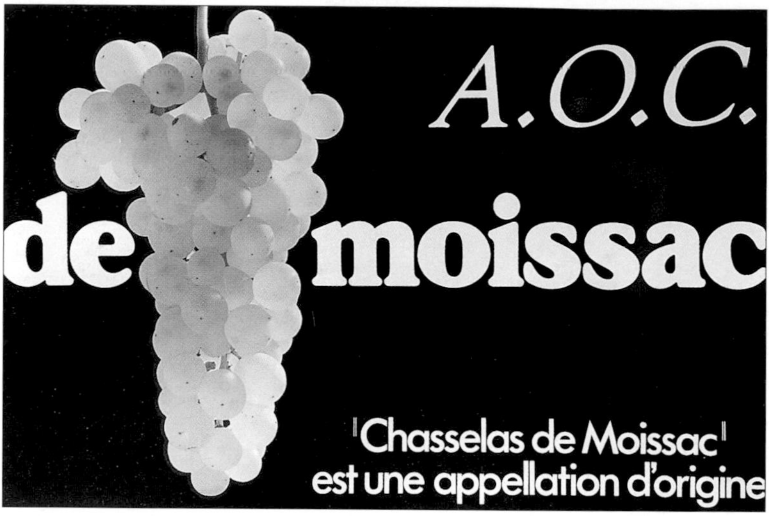

The golden and delicately fragrant Chasselas de Moissac is the fruit of a very special soil and microclimate. Nearly two thousand growers cultivate this table grape, and all work is done exclusively by hand. The grapes are grown over an area of 6,500 acres (2,600 ha) of sunny slopes. The traditional harvest in the autumn is well worth seeing.

Recognising the grape

Chasselas de Moissac forms long, hanging bunches. The grapes themselves are round, regular and translucent, milky white and slightly golden. In the shops, they are very easy to recognise thanks to the red ribbon which must be used on all packaging. The presentation of Chasselas is standardised. The grape is packed in a tray, wrapped in a bed of tissue paper. Each tray is numbered and bears the name of the grower. Unfortunately, Chasselas are only in season in September and October. It is best to buy only a small quantity at a time and, above all, to avoid storing the grapes in the refrigerator.

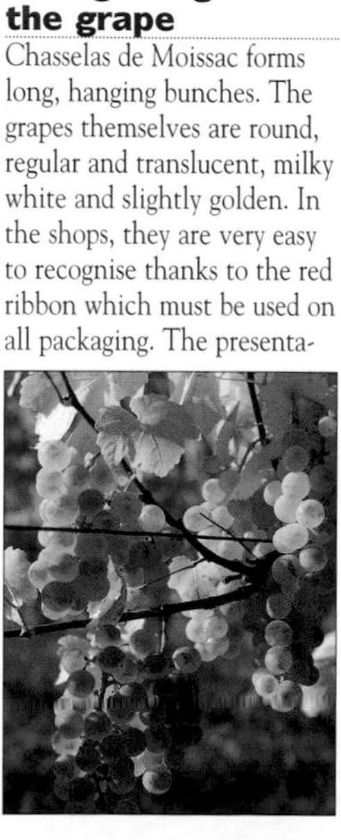

An Appellation d'Origine Contrôlée

Chasselas de Moissac was the first fruit ever to receive an AOC. Since 1953, the area of production has been very precisely defined. It covers the plateaux and slopes of Bas-Quercy, in the north of the département of Tarn-et-Garonne between Lauzerte, Moissac and Montauban, and a small area by the river Lot. The nature of the soil, the grape varieties and the techniques of cultivation are strictly regulated. The grapes may not be harvested until they reach an optimum sugar content of 16%.

Three types of trellising

The Chasselas vine has a long stem which is trained or trellised. By following the Chasselas route from Moissac to Lauzerte, you will easily recognise the three types of trellising used. These are vertical trellising (the most common and the only one which permits some mechanisation), V-shaped trellising and trellising in the form of a lyre. All three are designed to give the grapes maximum exposure to the sun.

Vertical trellising

Lyre trellising

CLAFOUTIS AU RAISIN (GRAPE PUDDING)

To serve 6: 1 lb 2 oz (500 g) Chasselas grapes, 1 tbsp kirsch or marc, 1 oz (30 g) butter, 2 oz (60 g) flour, pinch of salt, 5 oz (150 g) icing sugar, 3 eggs, 18 fl oz (½ l) milk.

Separate the grapes from the stalks, wash and pat them dry. Put them in a bowl to soak up the kirsch or marc. Preheat the oven to 325°F (180°C) gas mark 3. Melt the butter in a pan over low heat. Sift the flour into a bowl. Add the salt, half the icing sugar, the melted butter, and beaten eggs. Mix well, pouring the milk in gradually to make a smooth batter. Butter a deep flan dish. Put in the grapes and pour the batter over. Bake the pudding in the oven for 30 minutes. Sprinkle the clafoutis with the rest of the sugar then return to the oven for 15 minutes or until it is golden-brown on top. Serve warm.

A family business

The care needed to grow Chasselas is not suited to large-scale cultivation. Eighty per cent of production comes from family plots whose vineyards cover no more than 5 to 10 acres (2 to 4 ha). Currently, 1,670 families earn their living from Chasselas, producing 21,653 tons (22,000 tonnes) of grapes on 6,425 acres (2,600 ha). This represents 6% of the French production of table grapes.

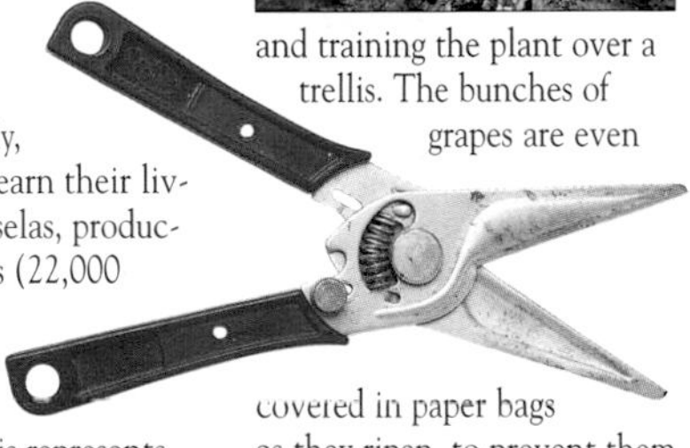

The hand-reared grape

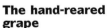

To cultivate the perfect grape, each process is carefully performed by hand, from pruning to picking, including removing buds, thinning the shoots and training the plant over a trellis. The bunches of grapes are even covered in paper bags as they ripen, to prevent them being burned by the sun. They are picked and laid out on racks, then the stalks are carefully trimmed. Any blemished grapes are removed with pointed grape-scissors.

Over a thousand years of history

The Chasselas grape has been grown since the Middle Ages, and owes its popularity to the monks of the Abbey of Moissac. In the early 19th C., the grape was exported by river to Bordeaux and thence by sea to Great Britain and even as far as Sweden. But it was the coming of the railways in 1850 which enabled the cultivation of the Chasselas table grape really to come into its own.

The fruit garden of France

Apples, pears, plums, peaches, melons, figs, hazelnuts, kiwi fruit, cherries ... Midi-Pyrénées is one huge orchard. Six thousand growers harvest 472,440 tons (480,000 tonnes) of fruit a year! Thanks to the important fruit-growing areas of Tarn-et-Garonne, the region is one of the main producers of fruit in France, supplying the whole country and with a thriving export market.

A century of fruit-growing

The Garonne valley constitutes a most favourable environment for fruit-growing, due to its soil and microclimate. In the 19th C. only two types of fruit were grown commercially, the plum and the grape. All other fruit was grown mainly for local consumption. However, in 1955, new varieties of fruit were introduced and intensive fruit-farming and orchards were developed. This was largely due to an influx of farmers from North Africa, who emigrated as the former French colonies gained independence.

The queen of plums

Midi-Pyrénées is the biggest producer of fresh table plums, representing 43% of the French harvest. The most celebrated variety is the greengage. This green plum is grown mainly in Tarn-et-Garonne and Lot. It is a traditional variety of plum, which has been cultivated for 500 years. The French name for the greengage, *reine-claude*, refers to the wife of King François I. The golden-green colour makes it instantly recognisable and the flesh is soft and sweet. But the pleasure is short-lived, as greengages are only in season during August! The bloom on greengages and other plums is not a chemical residue, it is a natural reaction of the fruit, a sort of protective film to shield it from the hot summer sun.

Eating apples

The apple orchards of Midi-Pyrénées are the third largest in France, producing a harvest of 242,125 tons (246,000 tonnes) of apples, including most of the well-known varieties. In addition

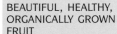

to the famous Golden Delicious, Granny Smith, Reinette and Chantecler, the region is the major French producer of Royal Gala and Fuji apples. A traditional local apple, the Bertanne, is also grown here. More than half the harvest is exported.

Melons grown in the open air

One melon out of four comes from the Midi-Pyrénées. Tarn-et-Garonne has even won the title of leading producer of melons in France, beating the Vaucluse. Production is mainly confined to two districts, Quercy and the Lectoure region of Gers. Although the Cavaillon melon, which ripens early, is the best known in France, the melons of the Midi-Pyrénées have a reputation for impeccable quality. They are grown in the open air and only picked when completely ripe. They are characterised by their fragrant red flesh which is juicy and very sweet. The season lasts from June to mid-October.

BEAUTIFUL, HEALTHY, ORGANICALLY GROWN FRUIT

The fruit-growers of Tarn-et-Garonne were the first to develop new methods of integrated crop protection devised by organic farming. In order to reduce the use of pesticides in the orchards, they have cultivated predator insects which protect the fruit from pests. It is easy to recognise the fruit grown in this way because the packaging is marked *Plaisirs de Cocagne*. This label guarantees the healthiest fruit for the consumer, as well as greater respect for the environment.

The flower of Toulouse

The violet was well-known in ancient times, the Greeks and Romans claiming it had medicinal virtues. The violet was used as an adornment and for skincare in the Middle Ages. In 1854, it became an important crop of the market gardens north of Toulouse. Until 1960, the 'love-flower' was to be found all over the city, in bouquets and candies, the leaves were used in perfume and the dried flowers were used to make infusions. However, setbacks caused production of the flower to decline and it is currently the subject of a rescue plan.

Habit de Parfumeur

Violets, lovely violets!

Bunches of violets were sold in the streets of Athens in 400 BC. The Greeks used to braid them into circlets to wear as a cure for a hangover headache. In the Middle Ages, they were to be found in the gardens of abbeys and a few centuries later, Henri IV and Louis XIII used their sweet scent as a perfume. Napoleon's supporters chose the violet as a rallying sign when the Emperor returned from the Island of Elba.

The violet arrives in Toulouse

The violet was first cultivated in Grasse, and reached Saint-Jory, near Toulouse, in 1854. The flower thrived due to the special nature of the soil and the amount of light in winter.

For a century, violets from Toulouse were exported all over northern Europe. These beautiful specimens were unrivalled, and the industry flourished. The growers, who were market-gardeners, found this additional source of revenue very profitable.

The height of popularity

In 1945, the Coopérative des Violettes et des Oignons de Toulouse was formed to regulate the market. An official was appointed to define the price of violets in points and ran a sort of stock exchange. From October to May, Toulouse station was bathed in the heady perfume of violets and it was considered good form in Toulouse society to present a bunch of violets as a token of affection, or as an apology for an absence or late arrival at a dinner party.

The decline

In the 1950s, the seedlings were attacked by an unexpected wave of insect pests and plant diseases. It was a disaster. Moreover, the violet now had to compete with a number of new plant species, and in particular with the fashion for pot plants. The terrible winter of 1956 was the last straw. The market-gardeners, who had grown violets as a sideline, abandoned them and reverted to vegetable-growing. Of the 400 or so growers earlier in the century, fewer than 10 violet-growers are now left in the Toulouse region.

The rescue plan

In 1986, a rescue plan was launched to revive the fortunes of the violet. The first objective was to find the reason for the degeneration of the plant in order to encourage horticulturalists to start growing it again. A specialist laboratory took charge. The second objective was to devise a new production and processing system for the flower, one which would be more efficient. The École Nationale de Chimie was set to work to solve the problem.

Initial results

A new violet variety was launched in 1992, and it looks very promising. It was tested by a grower in Toulouse and is now the plant on which the city has pinned all its hopes. The flowering period has been extended from five to eight months without interruption and the annual yield has been multiplied by 15! This violet has revived a Toulouse tradition and given it a future, so the market can develop once again.

THE RENAISSANCE OF THE VIOLET

The famous Violettes de Toulouse perfume, created in 1902, which won international renown, can now be reborn. As before, a staggering 5,500 lb (2,500 kg) of flowers will be needed to make only 2lb 4oz (1 kg) of pure essence. At present, all violet-scented toiletries and perfumes sold in perfumeries and souvenir shops in Toulouse are made from violets imported from Italy or the Côte d'Azur. But soon this will no longer be the case.

Arts and crafts

Brickwork, earthenware and wool from the Pyrenees are some of the crafts of the region, many of which are unique to the area.

① *Earthenware and ceramics*

Saint-Vincent-Lespinasse: Christian Pradier, sculptor and potter
p. 159.

② *Earthenware and ceramics*

Dunes: Nicole and Alain Morellini's pottery
p. 158.

③ *Miscellaneous*

Moissac, Rue Moura: including glass-blowing and lacemaking
p. 162.

④ *Wool*

Au Villar, Cap-du-Pech farm: mohair wool and knitted garments
p. 157.

⑤ *Wool*

Penne, Valeyres farm: mohair wool and knitted garments
p. 151.

⑥ *Earthenware and ceramics*

Frausseilles: Marie Coste ceramics
p. 141.

⑦ *Miscellaneous*

Saint-Juéry, Philippe Merloz: blown glass
p. 139.

⑧ *Leather*

Graulhet: Maison des Métiers du Cuir
p. 147.

⑨ *Earthenware and ceramics*

Giroussens: ceramic workshops and pottery market
p. 146.

⑩ *Miscellaneous*

L'Isle-Jourdain, En-Bladé farm: *béjouets gascons*
p. 135.

⑪ *Perfume and cosmetics*

Toulouse, the Berdoues factories: scented soaps and violet water
pp. 178-179.

See also:
The land of ancient crafts, p. 64
The leather-workers of Graulhet p. 66

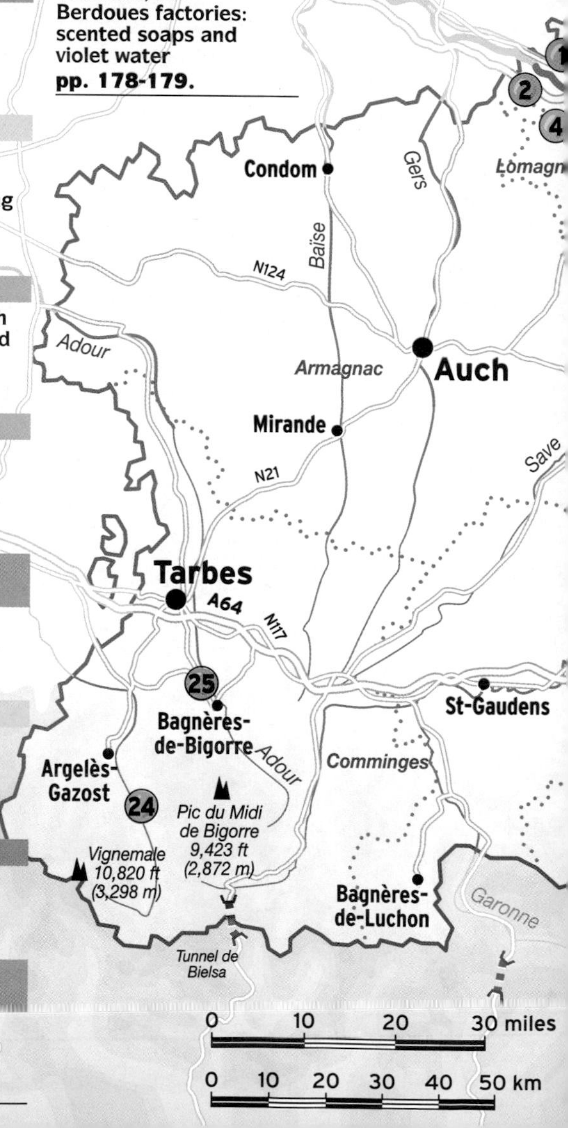

2 Perfume and cosmetics

Iontaut,
soutique de l'Écureuil:
oaps and cosmetics
nade with hazelnut oil
. 217.

3 Woodwork

Revel: Conservatoire
es Métiers du Bois
. 149.

⑭ Miscellaneous

Dufort, Chaudronnerie
Vergne: copperware
p. 149.

⑮ Earthenware and ceramics

Martres-Tolosane:
Faïenceries du Matet
p. 203.

⑯ Miscellaneous

Toulouse,
Maison Giscard:
ornamental brickwork
p. 176.

⑰ Miscellaneous

Lesparrou,
the Azêma factory:
horn combs
p. 215.

⑱ Wool

Fougax-et-Barrineuf,
Maurice and
Véronique Birebent:
natural mohair wool
p. 214.

⑲ Wool

Niaux, Jean-Jacques
Laffont mill: wool
and knitted garments
p. 223.

⑳ Miscellaneous

Saurat,
Sylvain Cuminet:
sharpening stones
p. 222.

㉑ Perfume and cosmetics

Castelnau-Durban,
Asinerie du Feillet: soaps
made from asses' milk
p. 211.

㉒ Woodwork

Audressein:
Catalat clog factory
pp. 206-207.

㉓ Earthenware and ceramics

Moulis,
Jean-Marie Mathon:
santons (figurines)
p. 219.

㉔ Wool

Luz-Saint-Sauveur,
the Lafonds factories:
wool from the Pyrenees
p. 185.

㉕ Earthenware and ceramics

Pouzac,
the Cazals factories:
ceramics

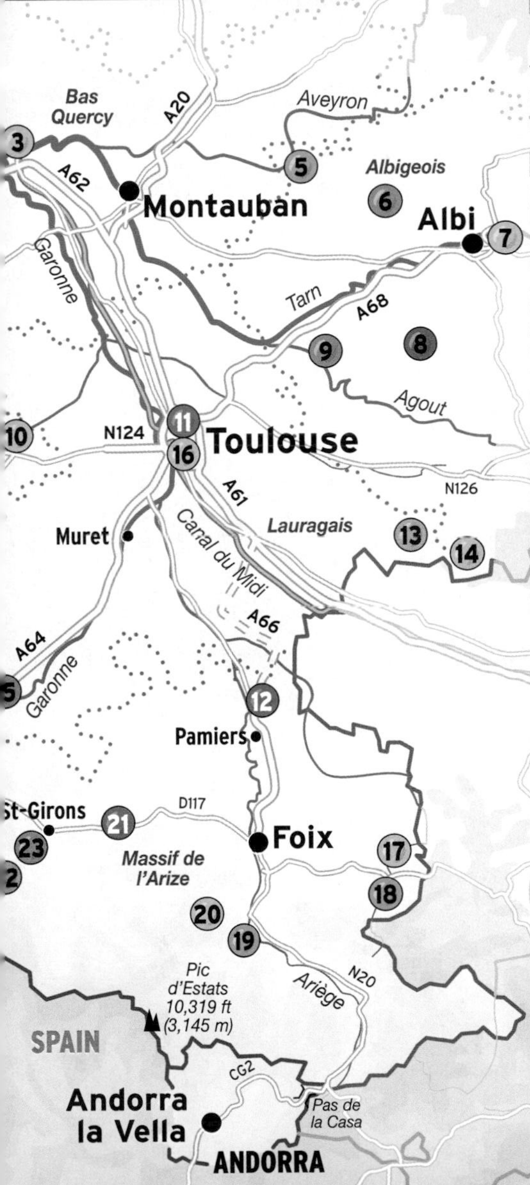

The land of ancient crafts

Do you have an irresistible desire to own a piece of marquetry? Or some decorative pottery? Do you need a horn comb? Or a pair of clogs? The place to find all these is in Midi-Pyrénées where you will find unique crafts made by talented local craftsmen. Local crafts are now actively being revived to ensure these traditional skills continue to flourish.

The marquetry of Revel

This fortified town in Haute-Garonne has a reputation for producing fine furniture, and it is all thanks to love. The master craftsman Alexandre Maunoury left Versailles and settled in Revel in the late 19th C., following his marriage to a local girl. He trained many furniture makers in the art of marquetry in his workshop and developed a special skill in copying antique furniture. The reputation of Revel continues to this day.

The pottery of Martres Tolosane

This little town in Haute-Garonne took advantage of its nearby clay deposits to become an important pottery centre. At the very moment when Bernard Palissy was inventing *faïence* (17th C.), it was well positioned to attract the first makers of this tin-glazed earthenware. For three centuries, the tradition

has continued. Decoration on the enamel was always performed by hand, using brushes made from cow's ears! *Faïence* is still fired twice, first at 1,760°F (960°C) and then at 1,620°F (900°C).

Horn combs

Combs made of horn originated from Ariège. When the Edict of Nantes was revoked in 1685, the Huguenots, who specialised in the technique, fled the area. It was only when they were able to return that the craft was revived.

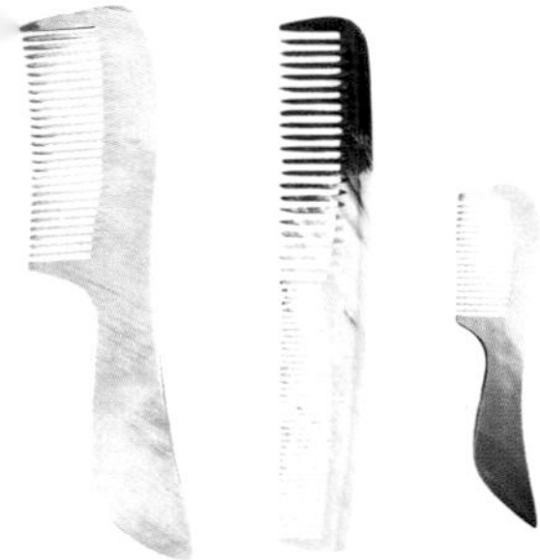

Wooden combs were already being made, but combs made of local animal horn soon flooded the market. The invention of an indentation machine in 1846 gave a further boost to the market, but it was wiped out by the emergence of plastic in the 1950s. Today, only two workshops continue to produce combs and they use horn imported from Africa! But the craftsman's skill still remains.

The clogs of Bethmale

These extraordinary clogs have a long, curved point. This is due to the Moors who invaded this little village in the Ariège in the 9th C. At the time, the men of the village hid in the woods to evade capture. One of them was betrayed by his sweetheart, who preferred a Moor. When he returned to the village he began to carve clogs which were full of bitterness… The toe of the clog was shaped into a pointed crescent and was decorated with nails in the shape of a pierced heart, that of his beautiful betrayer! Since then, clogs made at Bethmale are decorated with nails in the same design.

The coppersmiths of Durfort

Durfort, near Revel, is famous for its *dinanderie*, the copper-smelting works. The art is said to have been imported by the English during the Hundred Years War. This may be a myth, but what is certain is that the French name comes from the village of Dinant, a Belgian village on the river Meuse, which was known for its copper-smelting. At any event, Durfort has been making copperware since the 14th C. and produced many of the fine sets of copper pots which graced the kitchens of old. As a sign of the times, copper is now more often used for decorative rather than for utilitarian purposes. The flowerpot holders, saucepans and pitchers bought at Durfort are more likely to finish up hanging on a wall without ever being used for making jam or stew.

Bricks from Toulouse

The pink city owes its colour to its brickwork, and to the brick-makers of the Midi-Pyrénées. Handmade bricks are no longer produced in vast quantities, as new building materials have come into use, but the craft does survive in a few workshops. These brick-makers have preserved the old traditional craft and have adapted it to make some attractive decorative items, such as oval and rose-windows, balustrades and other ornaments.

The leather-workers of Graulhet

Nubuck, hide, velvet or grain side, Graulhet is familiar with leather in all its forms. Calfskin, cowhide, buckskin, goatskin and lambskin hang beside the skins of bison, kangaroos, lizards and ostriches. The skins are dyed in a range of colours from bright red to navy blue through to pastels, iridescent and patent leathers, as well as the traditional brown, beige and black. The leather-workers of Graulhet are heirs to a long tradition who do much of their work for French haute couture houses. They export belts, clothing and handbags all over the world.

The home of leather

Graulhet has been famous since the Middle Ages for its tanneries and today it is the French, and even the European, capital of leather dressing. The modern industry was born in 1851, at the same time as the wool-scraping industry at Mazamet in the Montagne Noire. The sheepskins scraped at Mazamet were sent for tanning to the workshops of Graulhet. Since 1950, this town in Tarn has also become the focus of the leather market. Leather-dressers comb the world for good leathers to tan, from China to Argentina, via Australia and New Zealand. Many foreign traders have also settled in Graulhet as a result.

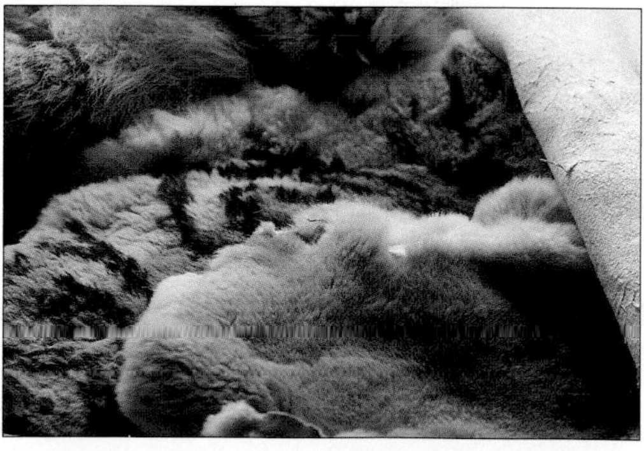

Focus on fine leather goods

With the emergence of industrial tools, numerous leather dressers converted their workshops to the production of fine leatherwork. In order to compete with

fierce competition from abroad, they specialised in luxury goods. Every variety of leather has been worked at Graulhet and a multitude of creations have emerged from their workshops. There are 50 or so small companies employing nearly 500 people, yet even with these small numbers the Graulhet leather industry is responsible for 4% of French turnover in leather goods!

The grain of the skin

No two skins are alike. Each description covers a very specific treatment and a characteristic finished product, as stated on the label. Thus, **velvet leather** indicates a pounced skin finished on the flesh side, a treatment that gives it a velvety look. **Undressed leather** is obtained by splitting the leather in half through the thickness. **Nubuck leather** is pounced on the grain to obtain a velvety texture. **Dipped leather** is only dyed after tanning. **Aniline leather** has a natural look which is visible through a finish that is transparent and colourless.

Keeping leather at its best

You can iron creased leather by placing lining fabric between the leather and a warm iron. To clean stained leather, rub it with a rag impregnated with soapy water. Brush it gently with a suede brush. Remove grease spots with Fuller's Earth or powdered pumice. If you get rain spots on velvet or nubuck, wait for the garment to dry then rub the marks against each other. Above all, never use surgical spirit, turpentine, wax polish or stain-remover! Also avoid exposing leather to a heat source and don't use a perfume spray on or near it.

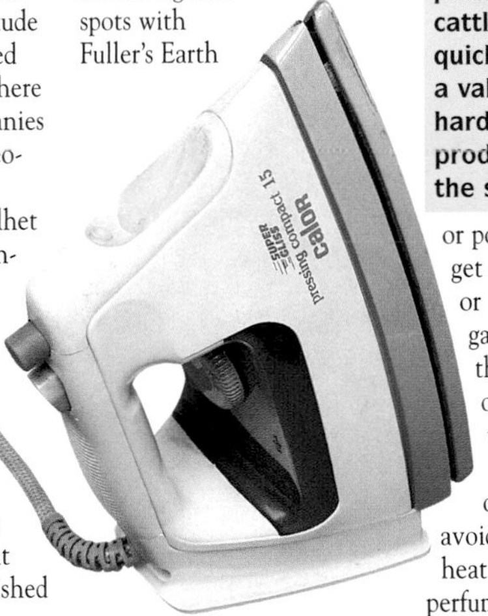

A little glossary

Délainage: scraping wool from a hide.
Tanning: treating the leather of large mammals (horses, calves, cows and bulls).
Mégie: alum-dressed and bleached leather.
Mégisserie: 'tawing' or dressing small skins (sheep, lamb, goat, pig).
Basane: a local speciality, tanning leather with an extract from an Argentinian tree called the *quebracho*.
Cuirot: a skin from Mazamet, in the Montagne Noire, known as slat, which has been scraped and sold for dressing at Graulhet.
Garouille: a special tannin prepared from oak root bark, used in the Middle Ages by the shoemakers of Graulhet. This tannin permits large hides of cattle to be tanned quickly. The result is a valuable and hard-wearing leather produced from the skins.

The history of the region, from prehistory to the present day

Shelters under rocks or in painted caves, ancient sanctuaries, castles and fortresses – the region retains a magnificent heritage of its tumultuous past at the crossroads of southern France.

① *Prehistory*

Aurignac:
Musée de la Préhistoire
p. 202.

② *Prehistory*

Dolmen of the Cap-del-Pouech (Neolithic) and prehistoric caves and cemetery of Mas-d'Azil.
pp. 210-211.

③ *Prehistory*

Aventignan, Gargas caves: rock paintings and animal carvings
p. 205.

④ *Prehistory*

Tarascon-sur-Ariège:
Parc Pyrénéen de l'Art Préhistorique
p. 220.

⑤ *Roman history*

Éauze,
Musée du Trésor:
Gallo-Roman treasure
p. 116.

⑥ *Roman history*

Montmaurin:
Roman villa
p. 202.

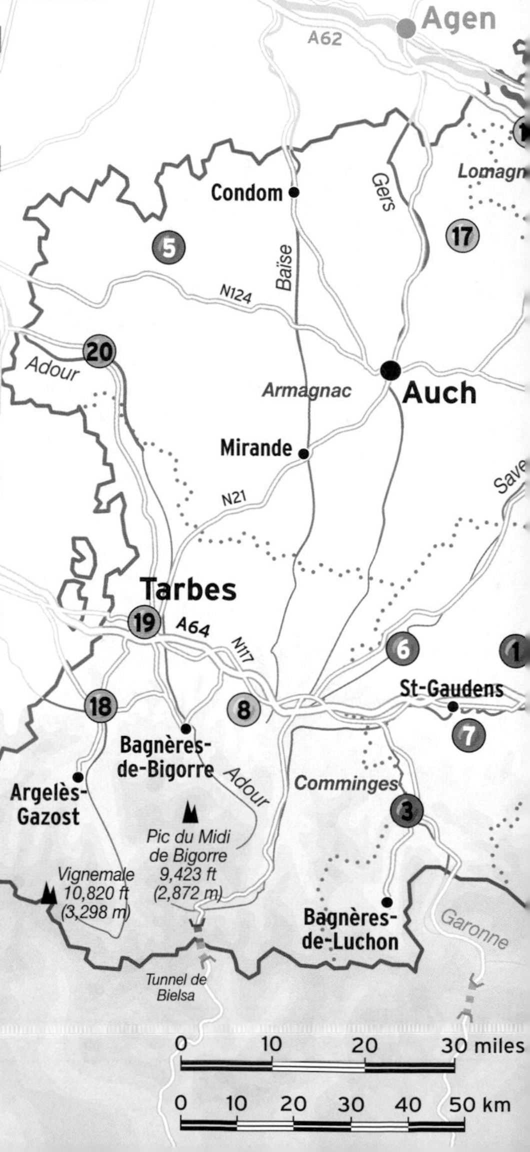

See also:

In the footsteps of prehistoric man p. 70
The revolt of the Cathars p. 72
Miracles, great and small, at Lourdes p. 74

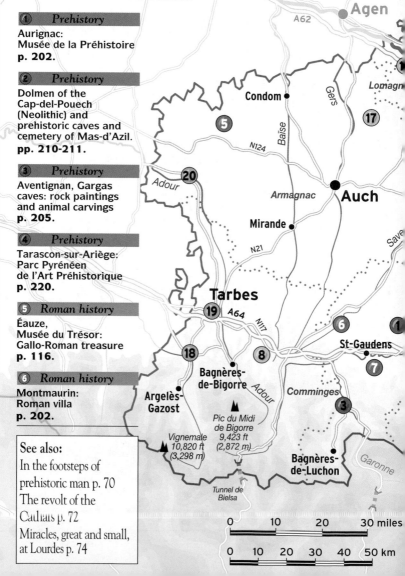

) Roman history

alentine:
allo-Roman villa
. 202.

) Castles and fortresses

ronghold of Mauvezin
nd Musée de
lachines de Guerre
. 182.

9 Castles and fortresses

Fortress-castle
of the Comtes de Foix
p. 208.

10 Castles and fortresses

Ruins of the Cathar
castle of Lagarde
p. 213.

11 Castles and fortresses

Lavelanet:
Ruins of the Cathar
castle of Montségur
p. 214.

12 Castles and fortresses

Leychert: Cathar
trail and ruins of the
Château de Roquefixade
p. 215.

13 Castles and fortresses

Château de Saint-
Geniès-Bellevue
p. 154.

14 Castles and fortresses

Château de Gaudiès:
costume museum
p. 216.

15 Castles and fortresses

Le Pin: Château
de Saint-Roch
p. 157.

16 Castles and fortresses

Château de Larra
p. 154.

17 Castles and fortresses

Saint-Clar-de-Lomagne:
Château de Gramont
pp. 128-129.

18 Miscellaneous

Lourdes: Basilica,
sanctuary and
Massabielle caves.
Musée Grévin:
the story of Bernadette
Soubirous
pp. 190-191.

19 Miscellaneous

Tarbes: the house where
Marshall Foch was born
p. 196.

20

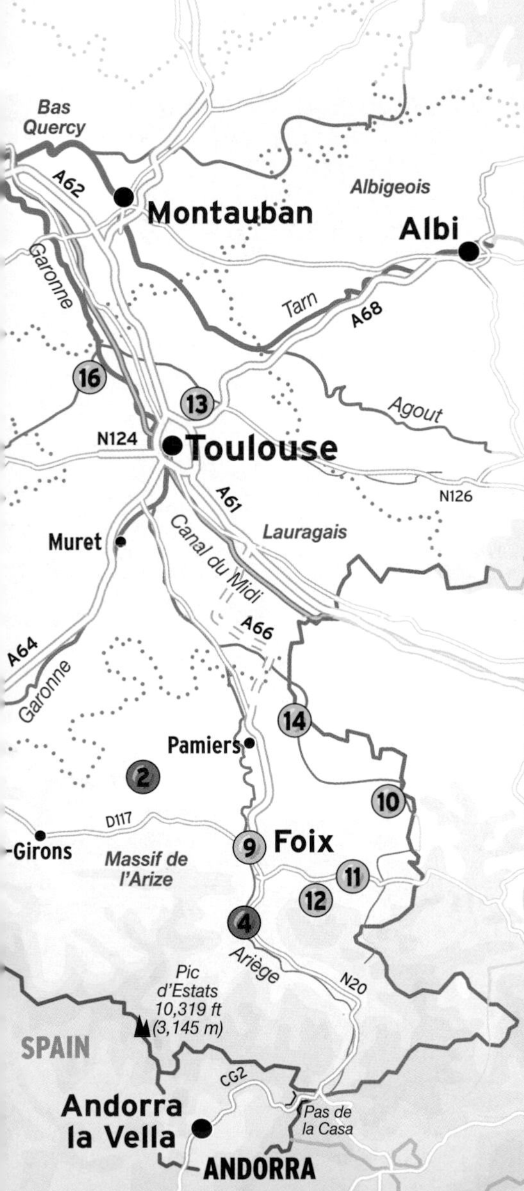

In the footsteps of prehistoric man

Thirty thousand years ago, this region was a land of rocks, glaciers and boulders. There was nowhere to shelter except in the rocky crevices cut into the mountainsides by the erosion of wind and water. Yet Cro-Magnon man survived in this environment and learnt to express himself creatively. In each of these caves, he has left traces of his existence, which tell his own story.

The early use of flint

Homo sapiens sapiens (or Magdalenian man) developed a real industry of flint tools in the region. This is irrefutable proof of his progress towards civilisation. Some of these tools and hunting weapons were honed in the Grotte de la Vache, near Tarascon-sur-Ariège. A complete armoury has been found in this cave, including arrowheads, harpoons, throwing-spears, needles, gouges, awls, etc.

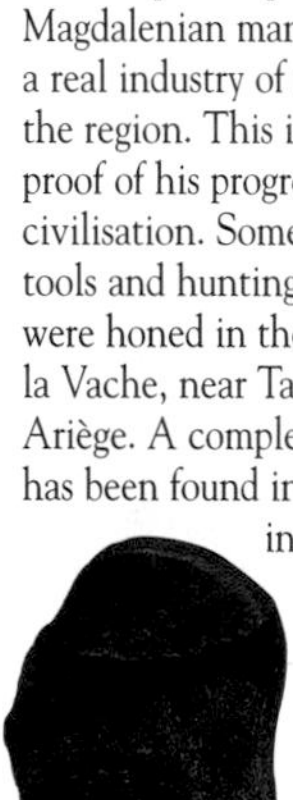

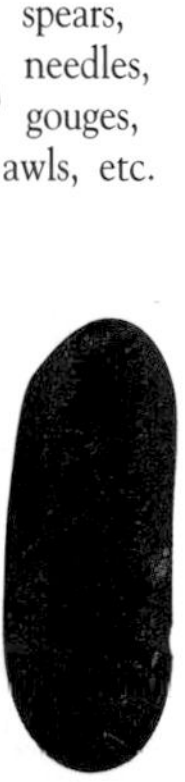

Working with bone and ivory

At the same time, progress was being made in the working of bone and ivory, two other raw materials which were available to Cro-Magnon man in the Paleolithic Era. This was yet another opportunity for artistic expression and religious sentiment which was already clearly marked. The ivory 'Venus' of Lespugne has come down to us intact from that era. It was discovered in the pretty village of Lespugne in the Haute-Garonne.

Mural art

Stone Age civilisation flourished less than 20,000 years ago. These craftsmen and artists left behind much evidence of their presence in Périgord, as well as some superb examples of their art in Midi-Pyrénées. The cave-dwellers created marvellous paintings on the walls of the caves they inhabited (cave art). Whether symbolic or figurative, this art is at its finest in the cave known

as the Grotte de Gargas (Hautes-Pyrénées).

The Azilian culture

Azilian culture succeeded Magdalenian culture about 10,000 years ago. After the great glaciations, the climate became warmer and this marked a turning point in the way of life of the prehistoric peoples. They no longer hunted reindeer and there were no more great migrations linked to the movements of herds of wild animals. The wildlife (deer, snails, etc.) and food sources thus became similar to those of the present era. The cave of Mas-d'Azil, in Ariège,

The Musée de la Préhistoire, in the cave of Mas-d'Azil

contains a wonderful re-creation of Neolithic art, produced by the most modern of the prehistoric peoples.

Natural beauty of the caves

Stalagmites and stalactites, needle-like rock formations, create splendid, mysterious, disturbing shapes in the deepest caves. They are formed when the limestone content of the water which flows underground or drips from cave ceilings is deposited and forms accretions. The droplets which fall from the ceiling deposit a little limestone before they fall, and this creates the stalactites. The droplets fall constantly in the same place, day in day out, year in year out, and gradually build up an accretion on the cave floor, a long, tall spur which resembles a church candle. This is a stalagmite. Other minerals will colour the limestone.

THE PROBLEMS OF PRESERVATION

Some caves are closed to the public or there is only limited access. This is because constant visitors bring the warmth of their bodies into the cave, together with the warmth of their breath, their germs and carbon dioxide. All of this could irreparably damage these magnificent works of art, which have only been preserved for thousands of years thanks to their isolation. In order to protect our heritage, scientists have calculated the annual number of visitors which a cave can withstand. In some caves, which are threatened with irreparable damage, you will just find reproductions of the original paintings. The only consolation is that some museums do not even display the real paintings of the old masters, but only faithful copies – so that the genuine works of art will still exist to be admired by our great-great-grandchildren!

The revolt of the Cathars

The Cathars, or Albigensians, called themselves 'The Perfect'. In Midi-Pyrénées, the Cathars were brutally persecuted by both the King of France and the Church. They were heretics who belonged to a religious movement that swept through south-western France in the 13th C. The terrible Wars of Religion, which eventually wiped them out, actually served to create the basis for a unified France.

Ruins of the Château de Montségur

Catharism

Catharism, or Albigensianism, was a Manichean doctrine, an extremely demanding form of Christian worship. For the Cathars, the world was divided into good and evil, the latter being incarnated by the visible world, that is to say everything which was on earth. Cathars had, at all costs, to avoid the temptations of earthly attractions and the pleasures of the flesh, by living chastely, not eating meat and mortifying themselves daily. The devout believers (the 'perfect')who followed these rules were the clergy, while mere believers venerated them.

The birth of the movement

The Cathar movement emerged in France in the early 11th C., the earliest adherents including the nobility of the counties of Toulouse and Foix, then the viscounts of Carcassonne and Béziers. For reasons which were largely political, they disliked the royal power of the king of France and that of papal Rome. Later, during the 12th C., the common people followed their example in large numbers and whole villages converted to Catharism. They did so for the same reason, namely, opposition to the king and consequently to Roman Catholicism.

A dual threat

The clergy, who were often perceived as being corrupt at the time, soon realised that the advent of Catharism could cause a deep rift in Christian unity. At the time, the machinery of the feudal system was threatened with collapse. The King of France and the Pope were equally worried by the rise of Catharism. Their concern increased when the King of Spain supported the Count of Toulouse (a Cathar) at the Battle of Muret in 1213. Languedoc risked becoming a Spanish province.

The king's reaction

In 1209, after a long period of peaceful co-existence, King Philippe Auguste of France launched the first counter-attack against the Cathars (the famous 'Albigensian Crusade'). The royal armies came down from the north along the Rhône valley. They captured Béziers, their orders being: '*Kill them all, God will recognise his own!*' Then the Crusaders, led by Simon de Montfort, invaded Narbonne, Carcassonne and Toulouse … Twenty years and numerous massacres later, military victory was won.

The reaction of the Church

In 1215, after the Lateran Council, the Church decided to send the Inquisition into the region, to 'reinforce' the armies of the king. The inquisitors subjected the Cathars to 'questioning' and offered them a terrible ultimatum – freedom for those who denied their faith, burning at the stake for the rest. There were some unforgettable scenes of 'the Perfect' throwing themselves into the flames and becoming the martyrs of Catharism.

Resistance and the end

In 1229, the war ended with the surrender of Toulouse. But Catharism was not yet dead. Cells of resistance were organised everywhere, encouraged by the local nobility who secretly supported the heresy. The Perfect hid in the woods and continued to preach. They were subjected to manhunts by the forces of the Inquisition, which continued to terrorise them in the towns and in the countryside. The death blow was dealt to Catharism in 1255, the date of the fall of the Château de Montségur, the final bastion of Catharism.

King Philippe Auguste (1165-1223) initiated the Albigensian Crusade

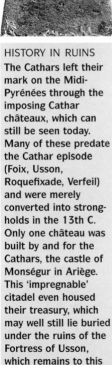

HISTORY IN RUINS

The Cathars left their mark on the Midi-Pyrénées through the imposing Cathar châteaux, which can still be seen today. Many of these predate the Cathar episode (Foix, Usson, Roquefixade, Verfeil) and were merely converted into strongholds in the 13th C. Only one château was built by and for the Cathars, the castle of Monségur in Ariège. This 'impregnable' citadel even housed their treasury, which may well still lie buried under the ruins of the Fortress of Usson, which remains to this day inviolate.

Miracles, great and small, at Lourdes

In only 140 years, Lourdes has become the most popular place of pilgrimage in the Christian world. At the famous grotto where Bernadette Soubirous saw visions of the Virgin Mary, more than five million pilgrims from all over the world come every year to meditate – and wait for a miracle. Yet few know the full story of the young shepherdess, who had daily meetings with the saintly woman in white.

A simple shepherdess

Bernadette was born in 1844 into a poor miller's family. She spoke the local patois known as Bigourdan, but had a lot of difficulty in mastering French, which caused wagging tongues to whisper that she was 'simple-minded'. She always wore the traditional costume of the Pyrenean shepherdess, the *capulet*, a cape of thick cloth which fell behind her.

Dogged by poor health, her asthma attacks persisted until her death in 1879.

The miracle cave

The Grotto of Massabielle has changed a great deal since the days of Bernadette's visions.

At the time, it served a rather different purpose for the villagers. It was here that the local swineherd brought his herd of pigs to graze, as the place was damp and grassy. In hot weather, the men bathed in the nearby stream and came to laze in the grotto for long afternoons.

Visions of the Virgin

Bernadette was 14 years old at the time of her first 'meeting', on 11 February 1858. It was a harsh winter and she had gone to search for kindling. While in the grotto, she heard a noise.

She turned her head and saw a woman in white, a magnificent vision who appeared to her 17 times, until 16 July, and who 'spoke' in Gascon to the young shepherdess. She taught her a prayer, and told her to dig in the ground at a specific spot to make a spring burst forth. She asked the young

girl to convince the local priests to build a chapel and organise processions.

The crowds move in

An apparition of the Virgin? At first, few people believed it. On 19 February, only 30 curious people crowded

around Bernadette in the grotto. On 20 February, there were 80 of them, and 100 the next day... Enthusiasm and curiosity in the village grew as the vision manifested itself daily to the girl. The story caused great excitement. Four years later, in 1862, the promise Bernadette had made was honoured. A place of worship was constructed and in 1864 the first procession was organised.

A booming business

Lourdes has become a popular shrine for the devout and the sick, and has done very well out of this 'manna from heaven'. Five million visitors a year descend on this town of 18,000 inhabitants, which now has more than 300 hotels (the second largest number of hotels in France after Paris, now that's a miracle). The streets are lined with shops selling religious artefacts – phosphorescent Virgins, bottles of holy water in the shape of the Virgin, sequined basilicas, rosaries of all kinds, lighters, pens, badges… A nice little earner!

Honouring Our Lady

Lourdes and its disconcerting 'bazaar of the faith' should not obscure the strong religious traditions of the region. The cult of saintly healers and sacred springs have always been dear to the Pyreneans. Many churches in the region honour the Virgin by dedicating touching statues in stone or painted wood. A mother rather than a disembodied saint, Mary is represented either holding an infant in her arms or weeping over the body of her son (*pietà*). High in the mountains, the *estive* (when the shepherds took their flocks up to the high mountain pastures in the summer) was the occasion for pilgrimages honouring the Virgin whose statues graced the little mountain chapels.

When the vision revealed her identity

On 25 March 1858, the day she saw her 16th vision, Bernadette Soubirous dared to ask a question which had long been burning on her lips. She asked the Lady to reveal her identity and heard the reply; 'I am the Immaculate Conception...' At the time, this doctrine was merely debated in the Church by a few theologians. That is why Bernadette's priest was moved to ask her: 'But what is the Immaculate Conception?' The answer, of course was the Virgin Mary.

Historic churches

From Romanesque cathedrals to painted churches in small, remote mountain village you will be surprised by the ecclesiastical architecture of the region. These places (worship are evidence of the spirituality which is entrenched in Occitan culture.

① *Albi*
Sainte-Cécile cathedral
p. 136.

② *Argelès-Gazost*
Saint-Savin Romanesque abbey-church
p. 187.

③ *Barran*
Church of St. John the Baptist: spiral steeple
p. 120.

④ *Bonnemazon*
Escaladieu Cistercian abbey
p. 182.

⑤ *Pamiers*
Pamiers cathedral
p. 216.

⑥ *Engolaster*
Sant Miquel Romanesque church
p. 228.

⑦ *Foix*
Saint-Volustien church
p. 208.

⑧ *La Romieu*
St-Pierre collegiate church
p. 125.

⑨ *Lavaur*
The Jacquemart (automaton) at the cathedral
p. 146.

⑩ *Lombez*
Sainte-Marie cathedral
p. 134.

⑪ *Luz-Saint-Sauveur*
Saint-André church, Romanesque abbey-church
p. 187.

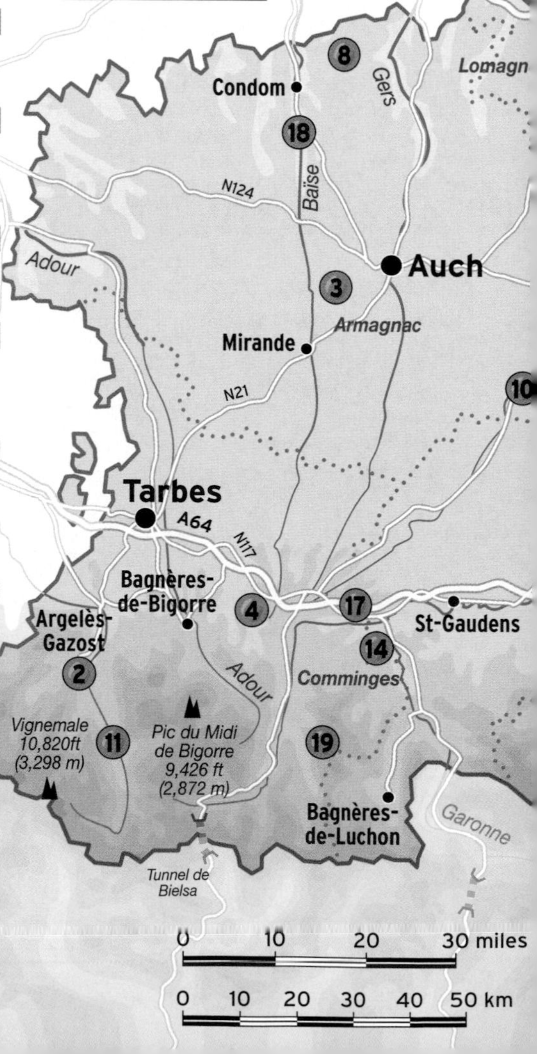

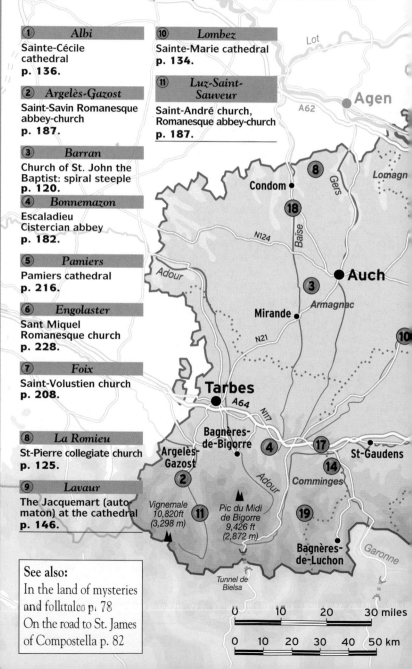

See also:
In the land of mysteries and folktales p. 78
On the road to St. James of Compostella p. 82

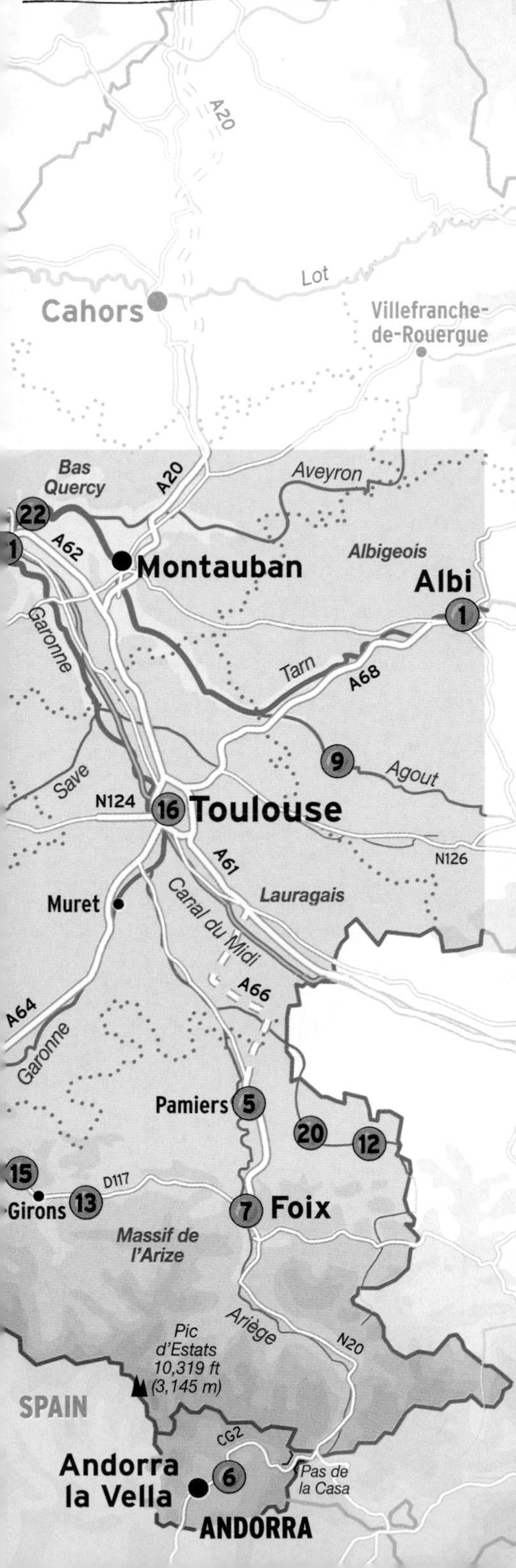

⑫ *Mirepoix*

Saint-Maurice Gothic cathedral
p. 212.

⑬ *Rimont*

Combelongue Romanesque abbey
p. 210.

⑭ *Saint-Bertrand-de-Comminges*

Romanesque cathedral
p. 204.

⑮ *Saint-Lizier*

Romanesque cathedral and bishops' palace
p. 218.

⑯ *Toulouse*

Saint-Sernin basilica: monuments and museums
pp. 170-179.

⑰ *Valcabrère*

St-Just Romanesque church
p. 205.

⑱ *Valence-sur-Baïse*

Cistercian abbey of Flaran
p. 125.

⑲ *Louron Valley*

Vielle-Louron, Estarvielle and Mont: painted churches
p. 198.

⑳ *Vals*

The church in the rock with Catalan frescoes
p. 216.

㉑ *Castelsarrasin*

Saint-Sauveur church (Southern Gothic)
p. 152.

㉒ *Moissac*

Romanesque cloister of St-Pierre abbey-church
p. 162.

In the land of mysteries and folktales

In the Midi-Pyrénées, mysteries and folk legends have always had an important role to play. The area has proved to be a rich source of rituals, myths and strange tales. The Cathar episode encouraged and entrenched this wild spirit. There is constant talk in the villages of strange creatures, bogeymen, good giants, fairies, demons and witches. So be on your guard, the subject may well arise unexpectedly in conversation!

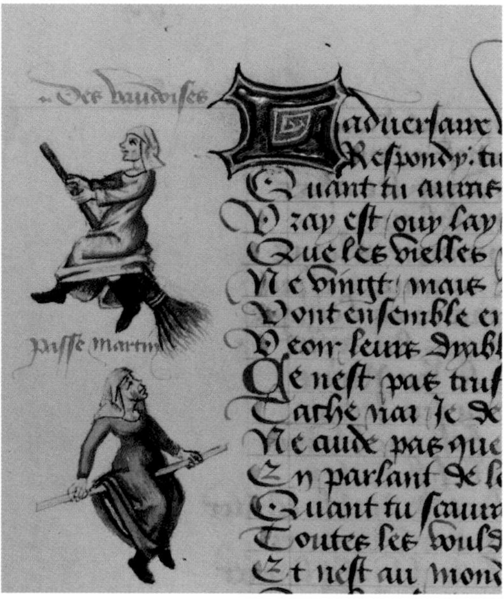

The miraculous tooth

At Lézat-sur-Lèze, in Ariège, a strange procession makes its way to the church from the village every month. It is reserved exclusively for young infants (accompanied by their parents) who suffer from toothache. They come to beg for the favours of St. Appolonia, a local saint, by touching her old pointed canine tooth which rests in a silver box! This yellowing relic is said to have the virtue of alleviating the pains of teething. The whole village resounds to grateful testimonials from every generation!

The Sun god

Like the Incas, the inhabitants of the upper valleys of the Ariège long considered themselves the worthy children of the Sun god. Even today, the sun is the object of veneration. The mountains known as the Pics du Midi (Bigorre and Ossau) are still associated with the sun because they pinpoint the meridian, that is to say, the highest position of the sun in the sky. Similarly, in the valleys, when the sun disappears in the evening, it is not said to set, but to 'pass to the other side'. Children's counting rhymes chanted in the evenings often begin with the words 'Blessed be the sun'.

Saint Fris

The basilica of Bassoues in Gers contains a strange treasure. In the crypt, there is a sarcophagus containing the perfectly preserved body of a local hero, St. Fris. This

soldier died in a battle in 732, and was buried at the spot where he fell. Three centuries later, at the same place, a peasant noticed that one of his cows was

behaving strangely. She never ate, but merely licked a stone. The peasant scraped away the soil, found the sarcophagus and dug it out intact. A fountain welled up and there was a succession of further miracles – St. Fris began to speak and God appeared.

The *follet*

The *follet* is a sort of elf or hobgoblin of the Pyrenees who is very popular in the

mountains. He was said to run through the valleys pursuing nubile young women. He and his accompanying gusts of wind were said to be the 'wind of fertility'. To protect themselves from his advances, young girls were supposed to throw grains of sand or maize at him, as the *follet* had to stop and count them before he could make a play for them. Is the *follet* still around? To be on the safe side, young girls should bring some sand with them when they go up into the mountains!

A special menhir

A standing stone near the village of Poubeau in the Valley of Larboust (Comminges) has long been the subject of much conjecture. In the past, it was used for rituals at carnival time. Young people would light a fire and dance around its phallic silhouette as a prelude to the festivities. As recently as a hundred years ago, women would rub themselves against the stone to make themselves fertile and men would do the same to maintain their virility.

LAND OF THE *CAGOTS*

This marginal group has left many traces of its presence in the Midi-Pyrénées. The *Cagots* were members of an unfortunate cast. They were the objects of derision, and were rejected on the grounds that they brought bad luck and defiled anyone they approached. These so-called 'descendents of lepers' were denied public service employment and could not enter religious orders or guilds. In the churches, they had to enter by a special door and use a special font. They were not allowed to touch food they wanted to buy, and only had the right to work with wood. They lived in exclusion on the outskirts of towns and villages. Many places still bear their name. There is a happy ending however, because their segregation came to a definitive end in the 19th C.

The blue of Lauragais

In Renaissance times the Lauragais became the land of plenty. The cultivation and processing of woad (*pastel* in French, hence the name of the crayon) revolutionised the region. The leaves of the plant produced a deep blue dye which became very popular throughout Europe. Merchants and bankers in Albi and Toulouse amassed colossal fortunes which they used to build magnificent mansions. But this golden age was short-lived. A century later, woad was replaced forever by indigo from the Antilles.

A very sought-after blue

Isatis tinctoria, or woad, is a yellow-flowered plant belonging to the cabbage family. It may have been imported into France by the Saracens. At any event, the plant has been known since ancient times, and has been used since then to produce a valuable blue pigment used in painting and fabric dyeing. In the 14th C., this indelible blue was particularly sought after by drapers and dyers in northern Europe, and the peasants of the Lauragais began to grow woad on a commercial scale.

The golden age of woad

In the mid-15th C., a technique was discovered of preserving the leaves and the pigment, which made the fortune of the people of the Lauragais. As many as 100,000 people were involved in growing and processing the woad. In the early 16th C., Toulouse became the European centre of the woad trade. The blue gold was exported via Bordeaux to Bilbao, Hamburg, Antwerp and

London. In a short space of time, the families of the traders in woad managed to amass considerable wealth. They created dynasties whose names still remain attached to the most elegant of the Renaissance mansions in Toulouse. They are names such as Bernuy, Assézat, Boissonchevry, Delfau and Delpech.

Making woad in the land of plenty

The woad leaves are first pulped in windmills, then dried. The pulp is shaped by hand into little dark-green balls, which are called *coques* or *cocagnes*. These balls are left to dry for 4 or 5 months to harden them. They are then crushed and crumbled into pieces the consistency of gravel, from which the dye is extracted after fermentation. The drier the *coque* or *cocagne*, the more expensive it is, because the blue obtained will be denser and deeper. There is a French proverb: 'In the land of plenty, the longer you sleep the more money you make.'

Indigo replaces woad

After its meteoric rise to fame, woad was subjected to a decline which was as rapid as it was final. From the second half of the 17th C., the situation deteriorated. The Wars of Religion, speculation and a deterioration in quality contributed to a collapse in the price, at the same time as the appearance of a competitor, indigo, which was to deal it the death blow. This new blue vegetable dye from the West Indies and Americas was cheaper and easier to use. It supplanted woad despite the protectionist measures taken to preserve the market.

HOPE OF A REVIVAL

For several years, the Gobelins tapestry factory has been using woad as a blue dye, and scientists are interested in some of its properties which could be used in pharmaceutical products. This work contributed to developing industrial uses for the plant. You may well be using it without knowing. Since 1991, beauty products containing linoleic acids have been made from extracts of woad seeds. Some 148 acres (60 ha) on the slopes of the Lauragais are now devoted to growing woad.

On the road to St. James of Compostella

Romanesque art flourished in the Midi-Pyrénées in the 11th and 12th C., and has left its mark everywhere. Large religious monuments such as cathedrals, churches and abbeys, and small ones, such as little chapels, hospices, fountains, fortifications and feudal castles, make it possible to trace its development. If you only see one example, make sure it is the basilica of Saint-Sernin in Toulouse, the largest Romanesque building in Europe.

Interior of the cathedral of Saint-Maurice at Mirepoix (Ariège)

First simplicity . . .

In the 11th C., the Romanesque churches of South West France were examples of the earliest southern Romanesque art. They were built of ashlar crushed with a hammer, a technique imported from Italy. The ground plan was simple: a single nave and a rectangular choir, which soon became semi-circular. The only adornment were *bandes lombardes*, narrow friezes, though sometimes the window embrasures were decorated with scrollwork.

Brick bell-tower at Rieux-Volvestre

Then complexity

The ground plan became more complex in the mid-11th C.: two side chapels were added to a semi-circular apse, and the choir opened on to three naves. The vaulted ceilings, which had consisted hitherto merely of rafters, became cylindrical semi-circular arches, supported on very thick walls with few openings. A campanile (a square, multi-storeyed bell-tower) adjacent to the southern end or attached to the cross of the transept was an almost standard feature.

ROMANESQUE HALTS ON THE ROAD TO ST. JAMES OF COMPOSTELLA

Modern pilgrims on their way to the shrine of St. James of Compostella still break their journey at the great Romanesque churches along the route to St. James. Saint-Jacques, Saint-Sernin in Toulouse, the church of Saint-Just de Valcabrère in the Haute-Garonne, Saint-Lizier in Arlège, the abbey of Escaladieu in the Hautes-Pyrenees and numerous little chapels, monasteries and hospices were welcoming their predecessors 11 centuries ago. This pilgrimage declined in popularity in the 16th C., but is being revived and the 'walkers of God' once again flock to the Romanesque churches. They are identifiable because they wear the traditional scallop shell.

Expansion

Towards the end of the 12th C. and at the beginning of the 13th C., advances in stone-cutting made it possible to develop the architecture. This is the second era of Romanesque art. The buildings became larger. A vast apse was surrounded by an ambulatory with numerous radiating chapels, side-aisles flanked the nave and high galleries were added. It is in this period that some of the largest building projects began, such as Saint-Sernin in Toulouse, Sainte-Foy at Conques and Saint-Pierre at Moissac.

Sculpture

The great innovation of the 12th C. was the introduction of sculpture into smaller buildings. It appeared on the outside of windows and in the choir. Two figures were particularly popular, the lion,

showing the influence of the Toulouse workshops and the face of the bear, emphasising the mythical importance of this resident of the local mountains. The notable exception were the Cistercian monasteries of the late Romanesque period, which were very austere and lacked interior and exterior decoration of any kind.

The *bastides*

Between the 11th C. and the 14th C., *bastides* flourished in the Midi-Pyrénées. These were new towns designed to become home to 'colonists' who were to fight the Cathar heresy. They were usually situated on hilltops and heavily fortified. A market square stood in the centre; it was usually square or rectangular and surrounded by covered arcades. The surrounding street plan was very regular. The first inhabitants were attracted by extending privileges to them. They had individual freedom, their spouses were equal and they had the right to own property. This made the *bastides* very prosperous and inviting places. With time, Gothic buildings were added (16th C.) as well as middle-class residences (18th C.).

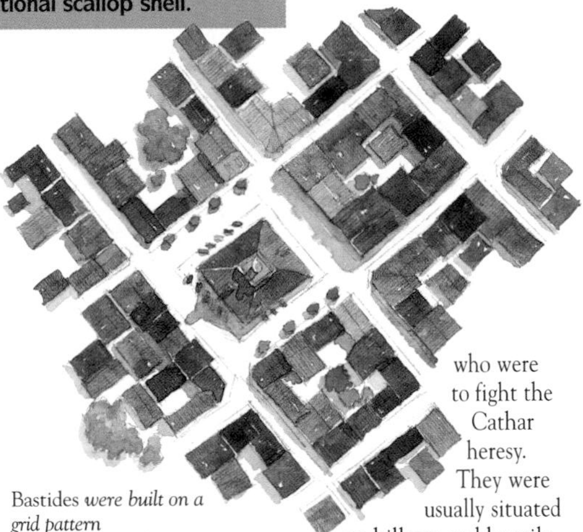

Bastides *were built on a grid pattern*

Old towns and pretty villages

Walled towns, hilltop villages or those nestling in a hollow are among the picturesque sights of a region which has retained so much traditional architecture.

1 *Auch*
Old town
p. 118.

2 *Auvillar*
p. 156.

3 *Bassoues*
Covered market, half-timbered houses and castle keep
p. 133.

4 *Dunes*
Walled town
p. 158.

5 *Mirande*
Walled town
p. 132.

6 *Mirepoix*
Central arcaded square and half-timbered houses
p. 212.

7 *Mazères*
Medieval walled town
p. 216.

8 *Penne-du-Tarn*
Walled town
p. 151.

9 *Revel*
Walled town
p. 149.

See also:
Mountain dwellings and country homes p. 86
Traditional use of bricks and tiles p. 88

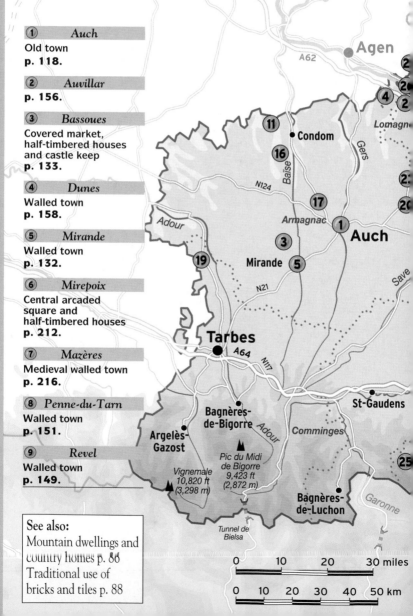

⑩ Le Mas-d'Azil
ledieval walled town
ith market and houses
ith wooden eaves
. 210.

⑪ Fourcès
Valled town
. 124.

⑫ Castelnau-de-Montmiral
p. 150.

⑬ Castelsagrat
Medieval walled town
p. 159.

⑭ Cologne
Walled town and picturesque corn market
p. 130.

⑮ Cordes-sur-Ciel
Walled town
p. 140.

⑯ Larcssingle
p. 123.

⑰ Lavardens
p. 121.

⑱ Lisle-sur-Tarn
Pountets (inhabited bridges)
p. 145.

⑲ Madiran
Ancient fortified village
p. 113.

⑳ Mauvezin
p. 130.

㉑ Montauban
Pink brick-built town
p. 164.

㉒ Montjoi
Listed village
p. 159.

㉓ Brignemont
18th C. windmill
p. 155.

㉔ Rieux-Volvestre
Medieval houses and cathedral
p. 169.

㉕ Seintein
Walled town
p. 206.

㉖ Valence-d'Agen
Walled town, washhouses
p. 156.

㉗ Ordino
p. 225.

㉘ Camon
Fortified village
p. 213.

㉙ Puycelci
p. 150.

㉚ Rabastens
p. 145.

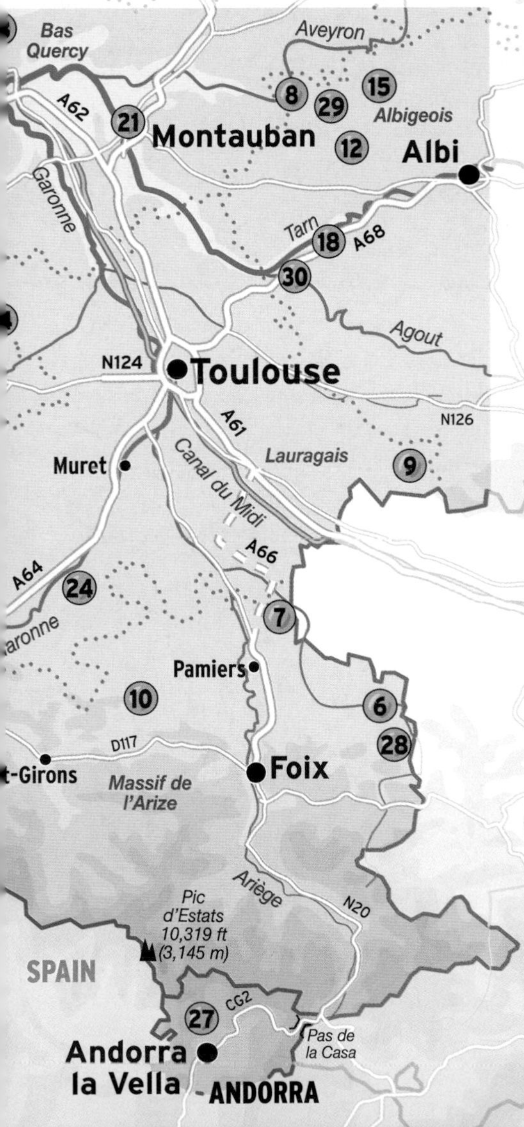

Mountain dwellings and country homes

In every part of the Midi-Pyrénées, a different type of solution has been found for building homes. In most places, a choice had to be made between good materials and plenty of space. In the mountains, there are plenty of stones and pebbles but there is little land that is suitable for building. On the plains around Toulouse, stone is hard to find but there is plenty of material for brick-making and lots of suitable land. In Quercy, in the north, the balance is finally achieved and the district has some of the loveliest country houses in France.

The Ariège house

In the mountains, the materials used for building are whatever can be found locally – granite, limestone, shale, slate or pebbles, plastered with a mixture of limestone and sand which gives the houses their typical pale yellow or grey colour. They often have a small bulge at the side of the house, a bread oven opening directly into the kitchen. On the plains, the houses are brick-built and the roofs are covered with channelled tiles from Toulouse. The gardens are also much bigger, thanks to the availability of space.

The *orris*, a shelter for shepherds

The name comes from *horreum*, the Latin word for a loft. These little drystone huts for shepherds had turf roofs and were built without wood or mortar. They are to be found in the heights of the Vicdessos district, in the Ariège, and particularly in the valley of Soucem. Some are still inhabited and are surrounded by *mazucs*. These underground storage chambers, marked with mounds, were used as food-safes or cellars for ripening cheeses.

DOVECOTES AND PIGEON LOFTS

In Gers, every farm had its dovecote or pigeon loft, which may have been part of the farm or a separate building. The Gascon style is square, built of lovely dressed stone and with a four-angled sloping roof covered in flat tiles. The Toulouse style has a single sloping roof on two parallel levels, covered with channelled tiles. Whatever the style, the pigeonholes through which the birds fly always face the east or the south.

The imposing Gascon house

The so-called block house, which combines living quarters with a workshop, is the most typical form of Gascon house. The house is often arranged in a

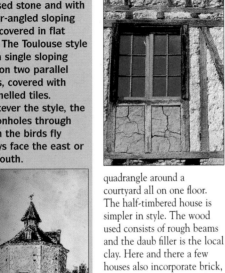

quadrangle around a courtyard all on one floor. The half-timbered house is simpler in style. The wood used consists of rough beams and the daub filler is the local clay. Here and there a few houses also incorporate brick, stonework or pebbles in the spaces between the wooden struts. It all depends on what building materials were available locally.

The attractions of Quercy

The Quercy house had a feature which adds much to its charm, a covered terrace or *bolet*. The living quarters were on the first floor and were reached via a wide staircase leading to the terrace. Behind the front door, the main room had a huge fireplace in which a man could stand upright. Beneath it, on the ground floor, all the rooms were used for work. There were stables, coach-houses, store-rooms and wine-cellars. The roof was covered with channelled tiles in the south and slates or flat tiles in the north.

Pink or yellow around Toulouse

Brick reigns supreme here. Whether baked or mud-bricks, yellow or pink, they are used everywhere in the regional capital. In the east, towards Bram and from Villefranche, walls are built entirely of brick. In the west, it predominates around Montauban but disappears at the approach to Agen.
All the houses in the Albi region are of red or pink brick in the north, but in the south, between Saint-Félix and Toulouse, a few pebbles are sometimes added for variety. The low-pitched roofs are always covered with channelled tiles.

Traditional use of bricks and tiles

Lacking stone, the builders of the Toulouse region of the Midi turned to local resources – sand, pebbles and the soil of the Garonne, baked or unbaked. The bricks and tiles of ochre, pink or red are typical of the whole region. Even such huge edifices as the handsome cathedral at Albi, the Roman-style towers of Toulouse and whole towns such as Gaillac, Montauban and Rabastens are built of the pink and red brick and tiles, giving a beautiful pink glow to the landscape.

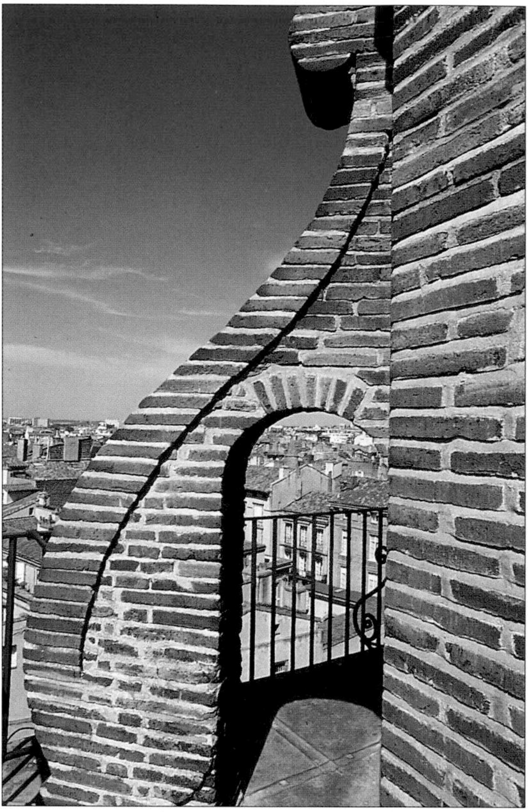

Bricks are everywhere!

From the Roman era to the end of the 19th C., brick was the most widespread construction material in the Toulouse district. Its warm, luminous tones were typical of secular and religious architecture. Brick was inexpensive and easy to use and, what is more, it combined well with decorative stonework. Similarly, the architecture of farmhouses and homes in the suburbs used brick with pebble decoration, an attractive combination.

Sun-baked and fired

Brick was long used unbaked, fired bricks being reserved for large public buildings, châteaux and the homes of the wealthy. From the 19th C. onward, fired bricks began to be used more frequently. At first they were used alternately with mud-bricks, but they later became so widespread that they monopolised the urban landscape. Unbaked or badly baked bricks were used for protected walls, facings and outbuildings. The most heavily fired bricks were used for buildings for the nobility or walls subject to bad weather.

An ancient technique

As the descendent of the Roman brick, the building bricks used in southern France were made by hand

in mobile workshops set up close to the major building sites. The clay was crushed and kneaded by foot and by hand and once it was smooth it was poured into a mould then dried for several weeks before being fired. The kiln was large enough to contain as many as 20,000 bricks, which were first heated gently in order to prevent breaking and cracking. The temperature was then raised to 1,832 °F (1,000 °C) for 2 days. Each firing produced several qualities of bricks depending on the position in which they had been loaded into the kiln.

WALL DECORATIONS

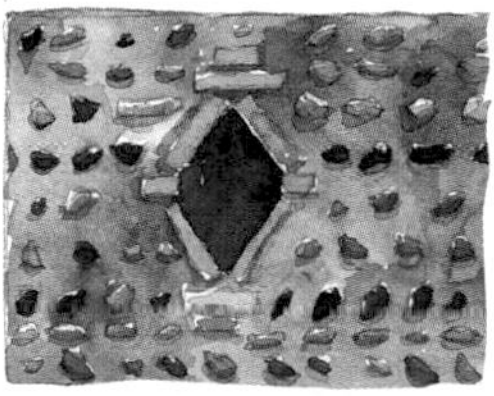

Embedded pebbles in a fishbone pattern.

Half-timbered houses. The spaces between the wooden slats are filled with mud and brick.

Wall made of briques foraines.

The *foraine* brick

In the 17th C., only well-baked bricks were entitled to be called *foraine*. These were positioned around the edge of the kiln where the high temperature started vitrification. These bricks were particularly hard-wearing and therefore expensive. The improvement in manufacturing and firing techniques in the 19th C. made it possible to achieve much more consistent production quality. The term became generalised and the *brique foraine* became the standard for brickmaking. The brick produced was flatter and wider – 16½ x 11 x 2 in (42 x 28 x 5 cm) than those used in northern Europe.

A profusion of statues and friezes

Friezes, sculptures, arcades, ogival ceilings can all, or almost all, be made of bricks manufactured by traditonal methods. Bricks can easily be cut and shaped. By inventing a moulding technique for fired clay which would avoid the back-breaking work associated with stone-cutting, Auguste Virebent revolutionised architectural decoration in 1830. His mouldings were extremely successful. Fluted false columns, cariatids, cherubs and animal and vegetable friezes decorated the mansions of Toulouse.

THE CHINESE CHANNELLED TILE

The channelled tile which now covers the roofs of Languedoc, Gascony and Provence actually originates from China. Roofs were covered in bamboo until terracotta was discovered in 2700 bc. Bamboo was gradually replaced by tiles which had the same fluting as the bamboo. In the 8th C., the tiles were exported to Baghdad, then through Spain to North Africa. The pattern finally reached France in the 11th C. where they gradually came to replace the Roman tile.

Festivals in the Pyrenees

Jazz, classical music, street theatre, but also wine and bread festivals, the Gascony-Pyrenees region is fond of celebrations.

① *Moissac*

Vibrations of the Voice: music festival
p. 163.

② *Montauban*

Fête du Goût et des Saveurs: tastings
p. 167.

③ *Vaour*

International Burlesque Festival
p. 151.

④ *Cordes*

Fêtes du Grand Fauconnier: medieval fair
p. 141.

⑤ *Gaillac*

Wine festival
p. 143.

⑥ *Lautrec*

Garlic festival. Fête du Pain at the Salette mill
pp. 148-149.

⑦ *Toulouse*

The Garonne Festival: music, theatre and exhibitions
p. 179.

⑧ *Canal du Midi*

D'Écluse en Garonne festival: concerts and dances
p. 161.

⑨ *Saint-Félix-du-Lauragais*

Old-fashioned fair
p. 149.

⑩ *Rieux-Volvestre*

Fête du Papogay
p. 168.

⑪ *Mirepoix*

Festival de la Marionnette
p. 212.

See also:
Bullfighting in the Landes pp. 92-93

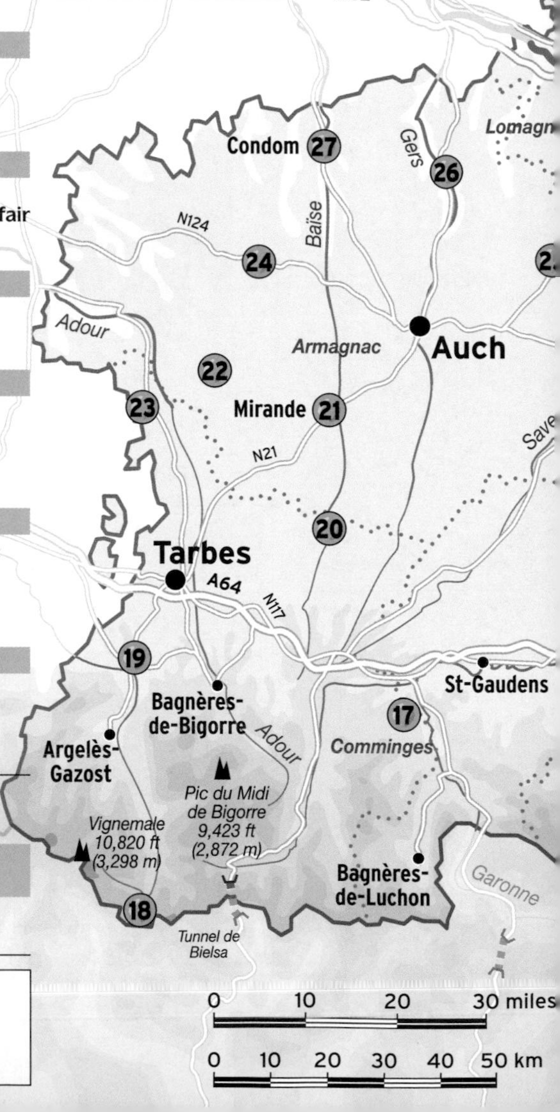

2) Foix
ledieval festival
. 209.

3) Engolaster
he Legend of the Lake
ıasquerade
. 227.

⑭ Escaldes-Engordany
International jazz festival
p. 227.

⑮ Vallée d'Ordino
International music festival
p. 227.

⑯ Saint-Lizier
Classical music festival
p. 219.

⑰ Saint-Bertrand-de-Comminges
Religious music festival
p. 204.

⑱ Gavarnie
Festival de Gavarnie: festival of theatre and music
p. 185.

⑲ Lourdes
Religious music festival
p. 191.

⑳ Trie-sur-Baïse
Pourcailhade: pig festival
p. 183.

㉑ Mirande
Country music festival
p. 132.

㉒ Marciac
Jazz festival
p. 115.

㉓ Madiran
Wine festival
p. 113.

㉔ Vic-Fezensac
Festival Salsa Tempo Latino.
Féria de Pentecôte: bull-fighting festival
p. 117.

㉕ Sarrant
Medieval festival
p. 130.

㉖ Lectoure
Photographic festival
p. 126.

㉗ Condom
Festival de Bandas y Peñas: band festival
p. 123.

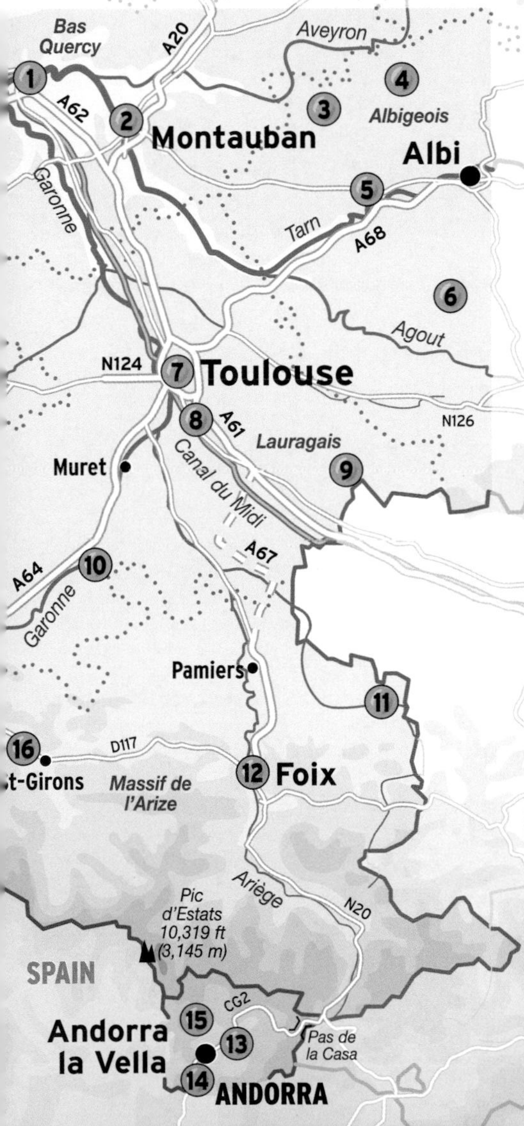

Bullfighting in the Landes
la course landaise

The traditional sport of Gascony, *la course landaise*, remains the main event in village festivities. It is fairly close in spirit and atmosphere to the *corrida* or bullfight but without the bloodshed. This form of bull-running is a game of courage, a unique and fascinating one, as well as a colourful spectacle which brilliantly expresses the *joie de vivre*, impetuosity and daring of the Gascons. The bullrings of Gers attract thousands of spectators every year.

An unchanging ritual

A run lasts for two hours in a Landes-style bullring, which consists of a rectangle within a semi-circle, or the Spanish circular ring. It always begins with a parade (*paseo*) of the side-steppers (*ecarteurs*) to the music of a triumphal march, played by the band who provide musical accompaniment throughout the performance. Each team (*cuadrilla*) tackles 10 animals and consists of seven ***écarteurs*** in boleros and four men in white: the ***sauteur***, two ***entraîneurs*** and the ***cordier***.

The rope

In the Spanish and Portuguese bullfights, the bull dies in its first fight. It could not be allowed to fight again because its instinct would lead it to charge at the man and not the lure. But for the cows of the Landes, the solution is not so drastic. However, after they have been in the ring several times, they are held by a rope. This makes it possible to control them and avoid accidents.

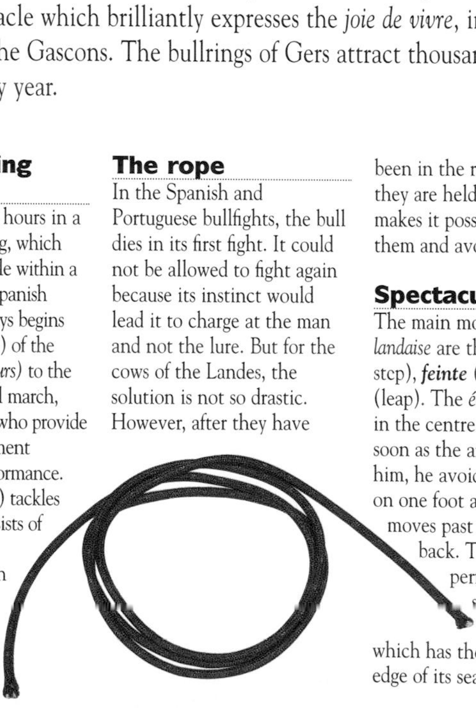

Spectacular moves

The main moves in the *course landaise* are the ***écart*** (side-step), ***feinte*** (feint) and ***saut*** (leap). The *écarteur* stands in the centre of the ring. As soon as the animal charges him, he avoids it by pivoting on one foot and the animal moves past the small of his back. The *sauteur* performs various spectacular leaps over the bull which has the public on the edge of its seats. These

THE *CORRIDA*

Bullfighting reached France from Spain in the mid-19th C. The rules remain the same. Six *toros* (bulls) are fought during a *corrida*, and always to the death. Some people find this appalling, others admire the movements of the matador as a wonderful ballet which contrasts with the naked aggression of the bull. Bullfighting is not widespread in the Midi-Pyrénées, but there is a bullring at Vic-Fezensac, in the Gers.

include the angel leap, the running leap, the perilous leap and the leap with feet in a beret!

A strictly codified sport

At one time the *courses landaises* were largely improvised, but they have been regulated by a federation since 1830. A jury marks all the moves: 1 to 5 for side-steps and feints from the other side of the rope, 1 to 7 for so-called inside side-steps which are much more dangerous. Everything is taken into account: presentation, elegance and precision of movement, danger and ground conceded to the animal. The move is most appreciated if the rope touches the bolero of the side-stepper. The way the cow behaves also gives it a right to a mark (out of 10).

The long life of the Landes cow

The Landes cow is a wild animal, the female version of the Spanish bull. Although once a purely local breed, today cows are imported from Spain, Portugal or the Camargue. Her career begins at the age of three and ends at about 14. She can live for more than 20 years and weighs between 660 and 880 lb (300 and 400 kg).

The perilous leap

The angel leap

Ancient origins

The *course landaise* is one of the most ancient bullfighting sports. In the Middle Ages, oxen were allowed to run through the village square. The first recorded spectacle dates from 1289. Edicts, papal bulls, decrees and all types of ban multiplied, but nothing would stop the Gascons from testing their courage against cows and sometimes even bulls. It was Napoleon who finally gave them 'the freedom to have themselves killed', but only in a bullring!

The feet together leap

The step aside

The *bandas*

The *bandas* are the local bands which always play for the bullfights, whether they are *corridas* or *courses landaises*. They sometimes include jazz and South American music in their repertoire, and carry on playing well into the night, once the *féria* is over, for the pleasure of the revellers.

Leisure and relaxation

There are lots of enjoyable things to do in this region, from donkey-riding to helicopter flights, to say nothing of boat trips on the river Garonne and its tributaries, or taking a cure in one of the region's famous spas.

① *Condom*
Boat cruises on the river Baïse
p. 123.

② *Encamp*
The National Car Museum
p. 226.

③ *Gaillac*
Minature railway network
p. 143.

④ *La Massana*
Flying over Andorra in a helicopter
p. 227.

⑤ *Montclar-de-Quercy*
Water sports at the leisure centre
p. 167.

⑥ *Malause*
Lou Malaousenc: river cruises on the rivers Tarn and Garonne
p. 159.

⑦ *Mauroux*
À Ciel Ouvert: astronomy courses
p. 129.

⑧ *Montauban*
Mini-cruises on the river Tarn
p. 164.

⑨ *Bagnères-de-Luchon*
Thermes
p. 200.

⑩ *Prat-Bonrepaux*
Orpaillage dans les rivières de l'Ariège
p. 219.

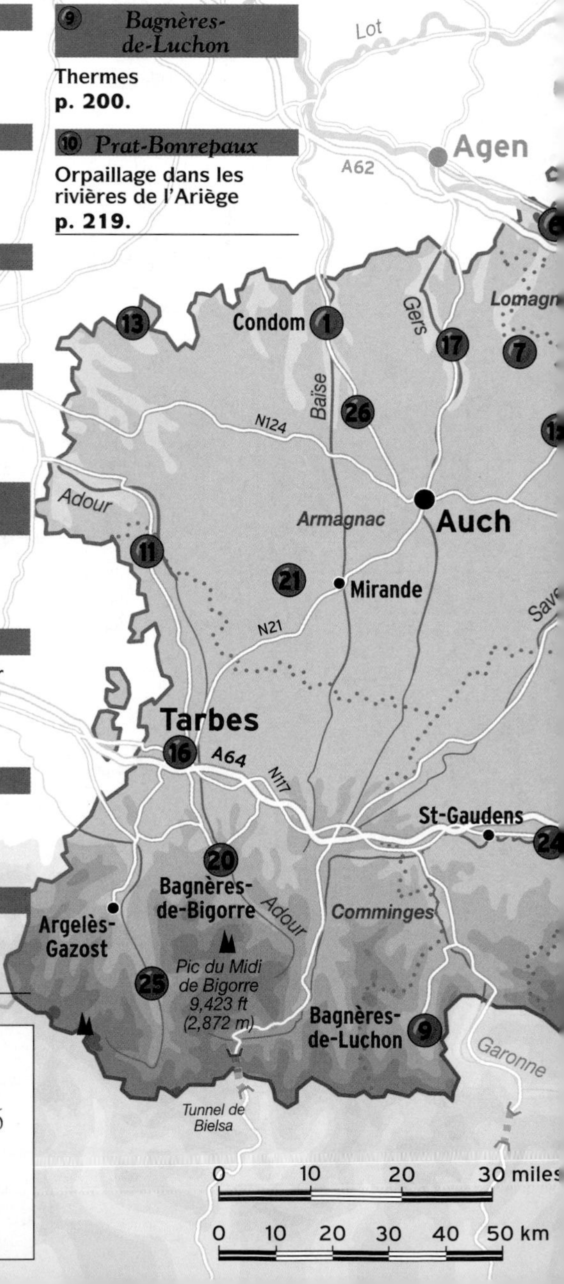

See also:
A paradise for fresh-water fishermen p. 96
Big game for experienced hunters p. 98

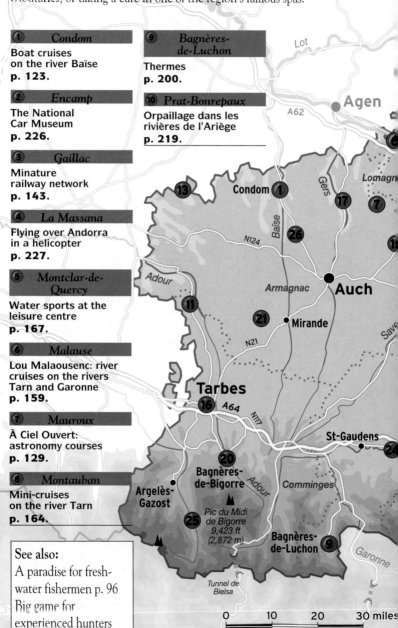

) Castelnau-Rivière-Basse

›nkey rides along the
ınks of the river Adour
113.

) Saint-Lieux-lès-Lavaur

eam locomotive
ps
147.

⑬ Barbotan

Thermal baths
p. 116.

⑭ Saint-Nicolas-de-la-Grave

Watersports, swimming and cycling by the lake
p. 163.

⑮ Sarrant

Ferme de l'Ange: donkey rides
p. 129.

⑯ Tarbes

National stud farm
p. 197.

⑰ Lectoure

Watersports centre
p. 127.

⑱ Toulouse

Les Bateaux Toulousains, cruises on the river Garonne
p. 172 .
Société Dune: hired boat trips on the Canal du Midi
p. 177.

⑲ Albi

Barge cruises on the river Tarn
p. 137.

⑳ Bagnères-de-Bigorre

Healthy workoutrs at the Grands Thermes spa
p. 181.

㉑ Bars

Guided tour of a *ganaderia*
p. 133.

㉒ Ax-les-Thermes

Thermal baths
p. 221.

㉓ Aulus-les-Bains

Thermal baths
p. 206.

㉔ Salies-du-Salat

Thermal baths
p. 203.

㉕ Luz-Saint-Sauveur

Thermal baths
p. 188.

㉖ Castéra-Verduzan

Thermal baths
p. 121.

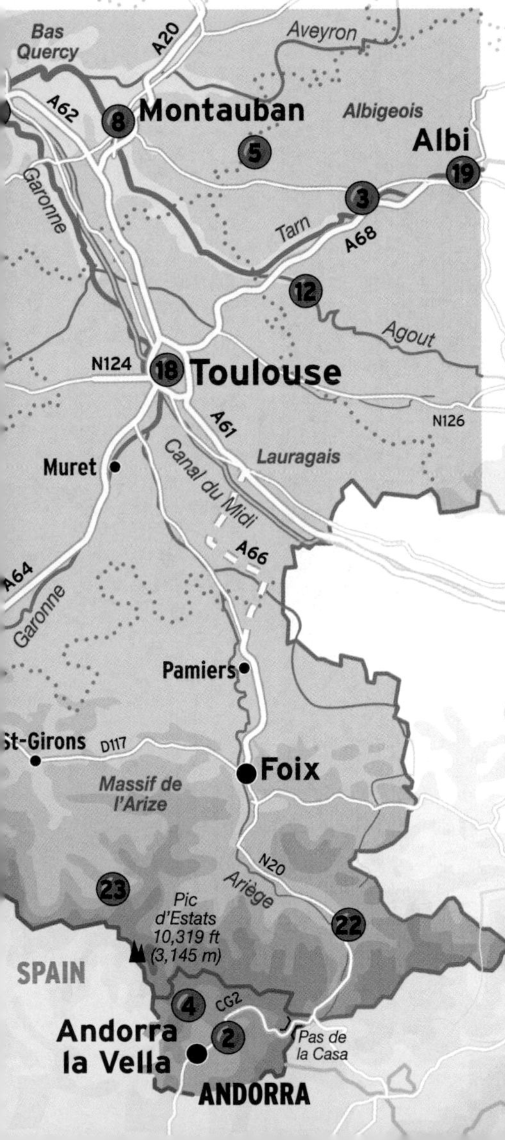

A paradise for freshwater fishermen

Whether you are a coarse fisherman or a fly-fisherman, an experienced angler or a Sunday fisherman, you are sure to have some great catches here! With more than 1,560 miles (2,500 km) of waterway and more than 1,000 lakes, the Midi-Pyrénées is an angler's paradise! You can tease a trout in the rushing waters of the mountain streams, or try your luck in the rivers of the plain and the large lakes which are well-stocked with carp, perch-pike, pike and shad.

Trout

Rainbow trout and brow trout are to be found in most of the mountain streams, mountain lakes and major rivers. *La pêche au toc*, fishing with a sinker, is a Pyrenean tradition which is practised on all the major waterways – the Ariège, the Garonne and the Neste d'Aure. Fly-fishing is also popular, especially in the medium-sized rivers. It is best to use composite flies, classics such as the grey fly with a yellow body or the red fly with a red body. These will always give the best results.

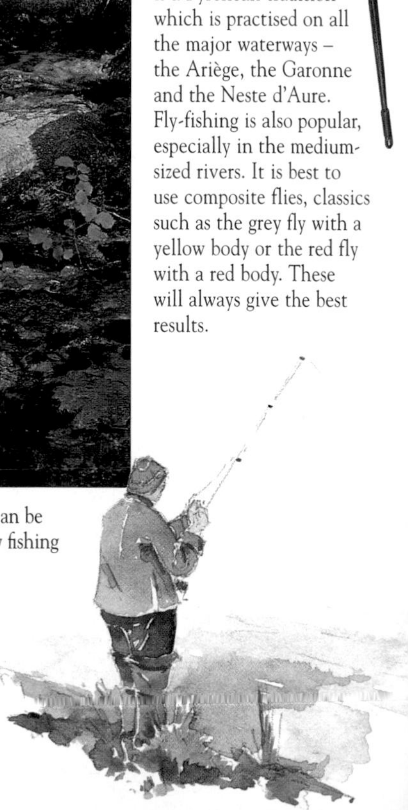

Fishing à la carte!

For those who like fishing but don't get much of a chance to do so, the French fishing federations have a special fishing licence. The *Vacances* card costs 150 F, and permits every type of fishing for 15 consecutive days between 1 June and 30 September on first and second class rivers. The licence can be bought in any fishing tackle shop.

GÎTES FOR ENTHUSIASTS

Hotels and campsites registered as Relais Saint-Pierre supply services which are adapted to the needs of fishermen. They are always situated next to an interesting waterway and have a hire shop for tackle, a live bait tank and the right to issue fishing licences. There is plenty of information about the best spots to fish and the local rules. Food is even prepared for the morning fisherman. (A list of the *gîtes* is available from the Centre Régional du Tourisme, ☎ 05 61 13 55 55.)

Perch-pike

Moissac is proud of being the capital of the perch-pike, but this very popular fish also swims in the Canal du Midi, in the Adour near Riscle, and in the Garonne between Toulouse and Valence-d'Agen, as well as in the Tarn between Aveyron and Albi. The Lot also contains some fine specimens. There are many lakes which contain perch-pike, such as Astarac, Pessoulens and Bure. In the Aveyron district, the best catches are to be found at Castelnau-Lassouts and Golinhac.

Perch-pike

Carp and coarse fish

The Midi-Pyrénées is the favourite region in Europe for carp-fishing, which is becoming more and more popular. Anglers come from far and wide – the United States and even Japan! The Garonne, the Lot, the Tarn and the lakes of Marciac and Uby are the best places. The hilltop lakes of Gers are excellent places for fishing a position. The lake of Beaumont-de-Lomagne, yielded a carp weighing 74½ lb (34 kg)!

Shad

This migrating fish is caught by casting or fly-fishing between 20 May and 15 June. Local enthusiasts practise fishing with a taut line weighted with a pebble. They will show you the hatcheries where the shad breed in season. It is an amazing sight! The two spots to remember are Lamagistère and Saint-Nicolas-de-la-Grave (Tarn-et-Garonne).

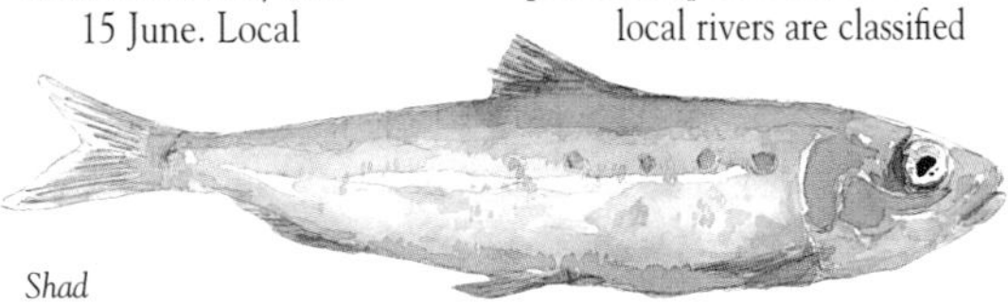

Shad

Pike

The best pike run in the South-West is between Puy-l'Évêque to Cajarc, on the Lot. It is easy to get to because the road runs beside the river on at least one of its banks. The popular places are at the bend of the Ile Saint-Vincent, Cahors, Labéraudi, Saint-Géry, Tour-de-Faure and the Luzech lake. The Sarrans and Pareloup lakes are also popular.

Pike

The return of the salmon

Since 1980, fish-ladders have enabled migrating fish to leap over the dams of the Garonne. In 1994, 55 salmon managed to swim up as far as Toulouse. Major efforts have been made to reintroduce this protected species and several local rivers are classified as 'salmon rivers'. In order to encourage salmon to breed, here is an important piece of advice; avoid catching grilse, the young salmon who have not yet taken their return trip to the sea. Unfortunately, some anglers mistake them for trout!

Big game for experienced hunters

The Midi-Pyrénées is considered a hunting region by the local people. The woods and undergrowth harbour a diverse and abundant fauna which attracts hunters in search of deer, wild boar and woodpigeon. Traditional hunting has now become a separate tourist and economic activity. In the absence of natural predators, hunting also makes it possible to regulate the wildlife population which is constantly increasing.

Large game

Over 10 years, there has been a real population explosion in the number of roe-deer, and the hunting plans (the number of kills allowed during the season) has multiplied by 20 since 1980. Simultaneously, the wild boar, who do so much damage to crops, have doubled their numbers, as have the deer in the large forests since 1970. For this reason, hunting is very much encouraged!

HUNTING WITH A LICENCED GUIDE

The Office National des Forêts (☎ 05 62 73 55 00) runs an interesting scheme. A hunter can benefit from a guide who knows the territory and the game well, and who shares his enthusiasm and experience. With the guide's knowledge, the hunter can therefore go after all the large game, tackling an animal which is approaching or fleeing, or he can also creep up silently on his prey.

The izard, a Pyrenean celebrity

The izard is a mountain goat which is smaller than its Alpine cousin, the chamois, but it is also more agile. The numbers of this goat, which were threatened by excessive hunting in the first part of the 20th C., are now increasing thanks to an energetic policy of nature reserves. However, the mouflon is another story. Despite strenuous efforts at reintroduction they remain few and hunting them is strictly forbidden. In all cases, contact the local hunting association or the departmental federation responsible for managing culls.

Rare birds

The snow partridge is a most unusual bird. In the winter, its plumage is white as snow, but it later takes on the fawn, grey and black colouring of the surrounding rocks. It was once very numerous, but the numbers have fallen considerable. The other favourite game bird is the grey partridge which lives mainly in the Pyrenees. Unfortunately, they are becoming increasingly rare because the reduction in flocks of sheep is depriving them of their favourite food – sheep droppings. The hunting plans are thus very reduced. The red grouse or cock of the woods is also in decline.

The wood pigeon

Small game

Even though it has been subjected to pressure from farming in lowland areas, small game is the staple of hunters and is very much in evidence due to the vast areas of nature reserves. Wild rabbits, pheasants, red partridges, hare and woodcock have been the subject of specific management measures and are regularly released into the wild.

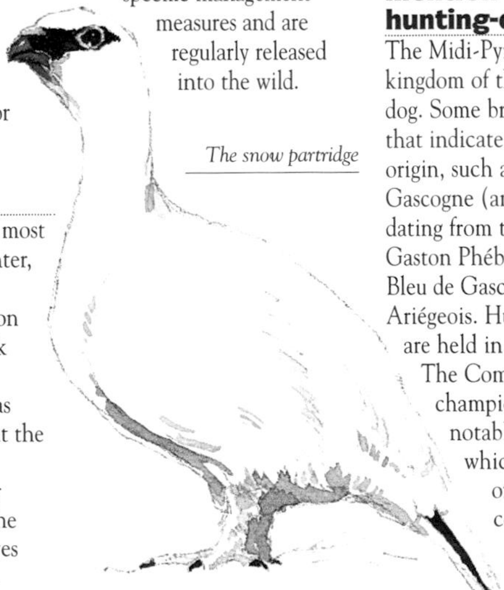

The snow partridge

Wood pigeon

In the Midi-Pyrénées, the wood pigeon or ring-dove is traditionally caught in nets, by lying in wait for it, but more rarely in traps as in Aquitaine. Some hunters wait for it to fly over certain peaks in the Pyrenees. But for the last few years, the wood pigeon has been getting the better of the hunter. In the winter, there are major flights, but the hunting season only lasts from October to mid-November. Some do not even migrate. In 80% of the communities in Tarn, the birds find food on the spot and build their nests!

Water-fowl

The region is on the edge of the great migration routes and this enables hunters to get a good bag. Mallards are the most important game, but there are also teal, sheldrake and coots in the hilltop lakes. The valleys of the Garonne, Lot and Tarn also have many favourable spots for migrating birds.

A special mention for the hunting-dog

The Midi-Pyrénées is the kingdom of the hunting-dog. Some breeds bear names that indicate their place of origin, such as the Bleu de Gascogne (an ancient breed, dating from the time of Gaston Phébus), Petit Bleu de Gascogne or the Ariégeois. Hunting trials are held in their honour. The Comminges championship is a notable show at which rival packs of hounds compete – though no guns are present.

Sporting holidays

Quiet walks or adrenalin-pumping bungee jumps, family relaxation or outdoor adventures, the region offers a vast choice of sporting activities accessible to everyone.

① *Skiing*
Peyragudes-Balestas
p. 198.

② *Skiing*
Val-Louron
p. 198.

③ *Hang-gliding*
Vieille-Aure, École de la Vallée d'Aure
p. 199.

④ *Water sports*
Aignan, Lac de Lupiac
p. 115.

⑤ *Kayaking rafting*
Andorra la Vella, Federacio Andorrana de Canoa-Caiac: hydrospeed and whitewater canoeing, and kayaking along the Valira del Nor
p. 228.

⑥ *Walking*
Auvillar: rambling and hiking
p. 157.

⑦ *Water sports*
Barbotan, Lac de l'Uby
p. 116.

⑧ *Water sports*
Castelnau-de-Montmiral: Vère-Grésigne leisure centre
p. 151.

⑨ *Water sports*
Canal du Midi, Le Bivouac, Bassin Saint-Férréol
p. 160.

See also:
Cross-country skiing of all kinds p. 102
Air and water sports p. 101
'Le rugby' in South West France p. 106

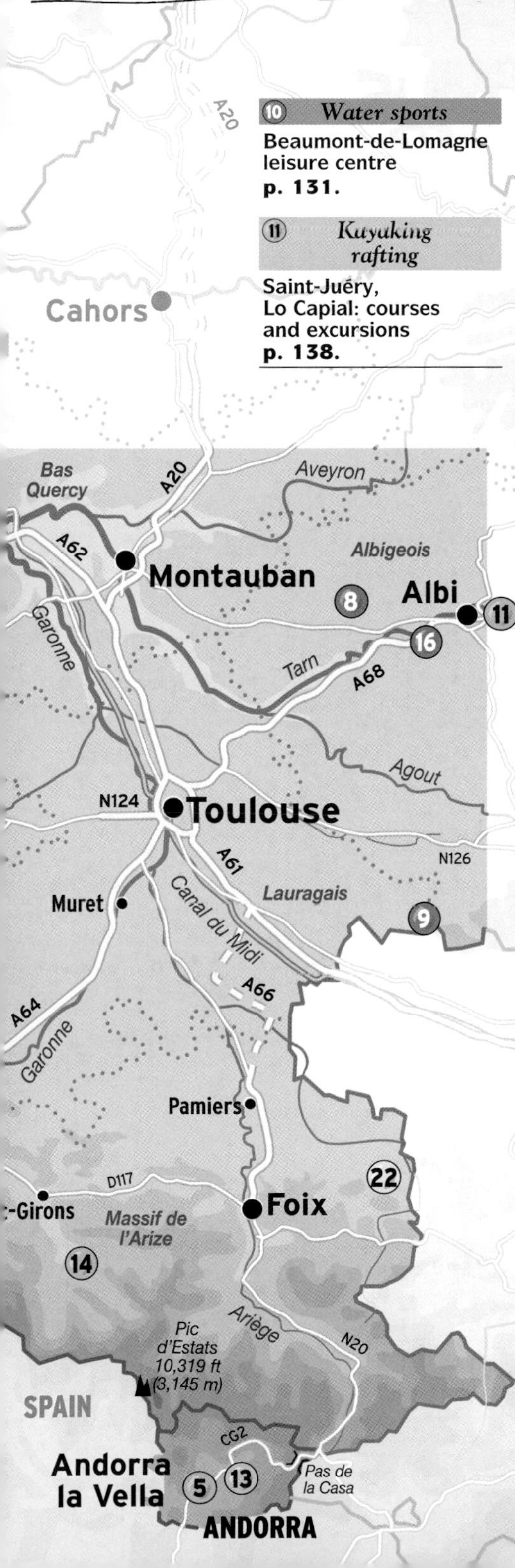

⑩ *Water sports*

Beaumont-de-Lomagne leisure centre
p. 131.

⑪ *Kayaking rafting*

Saint-Juéry, Lo Capial: courses and excursions
p. 138.

⑫ *Water sports*

Castéra-Verduzan leisure centre
p. 121.

⑬ *Walking*

Hiking trails around the Lac d'Engolaster
p. 228.

⑭ *Kayaking rafting*

Ercé, L'Escalusse: kayaking, rafting and hydrospeed
p. 207.

⑮ *Miscellaneous*

Esterre, Elastic Pacific: bungee jumping
p. 188.

⑯ *Water sports*

Aiguelèze leisure centre
p. 138.

⑰ *Water sports*

Lectoure, Lac des Trois Vallées leisure centre
p. 127.

⑱ *Kayaking rafting*

Luz-Saint-Sauveur, Pierre Maystre: rafting and kayaking
p. 188.

⑲ *Kayaking rafting*

Saint-Lary-Soulan, École Pyrénéenne des Sports de Montagne: rafting and canyoning
p. 199.

⑳ *Skiing*

Superbagnères
p. 201.

㉑ *Walking*

Valence-d'Agen: circular walks
p. 157.

㉒ *Miscellaneous*

Mirepoix, Kart'Are: karting track
p. 212.

Cross-country skiing

of all kinds

Since 1990, more and more facilities for cross-country skiing, as an alternative or complement to downhill skiing, have been opening up in the Pyrenees. Most of the ski resorts, such as Barèges, Cauterets, Hautacam, La Mongie, Luz-Ardiden, Saint-Lary-Soulan and Nistos, have maintained, signposted routes. Val-d'Azun is exclusively devoted to cross-country skiing and deserves a commendation, with its 81 miles (130 km) of routes between an altitude of 4,500 and 5,000 ft (1,350 and 1,500 m). There are various types of cross-country skiing, ranging from easy to endurance.

Cross-country skiing on a piste

This is practised on pistes prepared or traced in advance (and often signposted). The layout often has short, easy loops for beginners as well as long stretches of 2 to 9½ miles (3 to 15 km). The routes are always on smooth ground at medium altitude (less than 6,000 ft (1,800 m). There are level, uphill and downhill stretches, but there are no steep gradients – in principle!

Off-piste

Cross-country skiing can also be practiced on virgin snow in the winter, but only on condition of 'leaving a trace' so that you can find your way! There are three types, called *promenade*, *randonnée* or *raid* (see below). Uneven ground is not suitable for this type of skiing, and it is quite impossible to make any progress in deep snow, especially if it is only freshly fallen or powdery. It is also important not to go cross-country skiing if the surface snow is icy.

Promenades

This is the easiest type of 'off-piste' skiing. You take short 'walks' on skis in the immediate vicinity of a resort or village, following a level or slightly sloping route or crossing fields covered in snow. The route can also take you further afield, along roads or forest paths. But the ground is always smooth, such as valleys, pastures or thin forests and the gradient is small. Some experience of mountain conditions is necessary.

Nordic skiing

Nordic skiing, or *randonnée*, is different from *promenade*, cross-country skiing because it involves much longer excursions, lasting about a day. It also involves much more difficult routes. These cross-country skiing excursions must only be

In the early days of winter sports

tackled by seasoned skiers, with experience of mountain skiing in winter.

Nordic endurance tests (*raids*)

This is reserved for the real experts. The skiing trip lasts for two or more days, staying overnight at a shelter or lodge. The Pyrenean *raid nordique* often covers two neighbouring valleys. There is always plenty of excitement but you must always be accompanied by a professional guide.

The equipment

Shaggy or scaly? You will have to answer this question when choosing cross-country skis!

So-called 'shaggy' skis (*peluches*) grip the snow better, unlike scales (*écailles*) which slide. Your choice of skis must also prevent you sliding back down a slope you are climbing. A *système antirecul* on your skis is a good idea, but it has its disadvantages because the more effective it is, the less easy it is to slide on the skis over the easy stretches! One piece of advice is to choose skis than can be waxed, *skis à farter*, which will be a compromise solution, helping you to grip but also making for a smooth run on the level and downhill.

Advice to beginners

No particular technique is involved in cross-country skiing. It is simply a matter of transferring ordinary walking movements to the skis. 'It is just a transfer' according to instructors.

A skier in 1913

But there is still a slight difference because of the sliding time which intervenes between taking two steps. Start on a very gently slope, to find and feel your balance. Within a maximum of two days, you will have learned the rhythm and movements of the 'sliding walk'.

Snow-shoes on ice

Wherever snow falls heavily (and there is no lack of it in the Pyrenees!), walks wearing snow-shoes offer a new way of enjoying the mountains in winter. No specific technical level is required for this sport. All you need to know is how to walk – and have some resistance to rounding bends. (Find out more at the Tourist Office in each valley).

Air and water sports

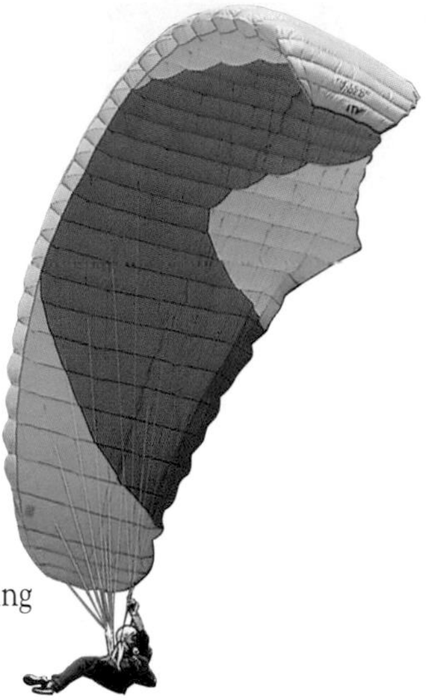

In the Midi-Pyrénées, the waterways offer many possibilities of travel and exploration – gently, if you sail down the Canal du Midi or hair-raisingly, if you are negotiating the whitewater torrents of the higher slopes of the Pyrenees. Choose between canyoning, rafting and kayaking. There are even greater thrills from hang-gliding and deltaplaning!

Boating on the Canal du Midi

Although barges have become rare on this ancient canal in the Languedoc, the beauty of the landscapes and old-fashioned charm of the locks make them a tourist attraction of the first order. The British happen to have been the pioneers who showed the French the joys of river tourism. You can rent out a motor-boat or flat-bottomed boat for excursions lasting one day, one week or even more. Don't forget to bring your bicycle which is indispensable for exploring once the boat is moored. It is an ideal leisure pursuit for those who love a tranquil place.

Canyoning

This sport consists of exploring a waterway in three different ways: hiking, swimming and rock-climbing. The Hautes-Pyrénées is a canyoning paradise, and the sport is practised in the upper valleys of Luz and Gavarnie. If you are really bitten by the bug, try the Spanish canyoning sites of Sierra de Guara, in upper Aragon, and the southern slope of Mount Perdu. Be aware, however, that it really requires an excellent mastery of the three sports.

Whitewater rafting

This is a family leisure pursuit. Eight or ten people are crowded onto a single raft guided by a boatman, who takes you down a raging torrent. If you hold on tight, there is no

THE BEST RIVERS

Four rivers in the Hautes-Pyrénées are unbeatable for those who love whitewater sports. They are the Arros, the Gave de Pau, the Adour and the Neste d'Aure. The Arros (Baronnies) is in a lovely setting but can only be negotiated by canoe or kayak in the spring. The Gave de Pau has 114 miles (182 km) of a wide variety of types of water for every level of skill throughout the year. The Adour, which is a mountain torrent until it reaches Tarbes, is navigable for small craft when the snow melts and, above Tarbes, it is good for peaceful family outings. Between Saint-Lary-Soulan and Arreau, you can navigate the Neste d'Aure throughout the year, with a choice of canoe, kayak or raft.

danger, but the experience is unforgettable and you get a unique view of the countryside. The **mini-raft** is even more exciting and much harder work. It takes four to five paddlers over the rapids. Under the watchful eye of an instructor, you have to negotiate the highest waves! It's easy to capsize.

Hydrospeed

This is a solo race over the surface of the water. You wear a wet-suit and lie on a surfboard, guiding and propelling yourself along with your hands. An amazing experience!

Kayaking and hot-dogging

Absolute freedom. In a single or two-person kayak or an inflatable canoe (called a hot dog), you glide through the water, keeping to your course and trying not to capsize. Surfing on the wave-tops of this whitewater is incredibly exciting, especially because as soon as you start paddling, you will find that the craft obeys your slightest command. There is no danger, although you could find the exhilaration intoxicating!

Freefalling

A **deltaplane** is an ultralight hang-glider with a featherweight structure hanging from a single sail 460 to 635 sq ft (13 to 18 m^2) in size. Only the weight of the pilot suspended underneath can direct the movements of the delta. Beginners should start with the **delta wing**, which is simpler, before graduating to long distance flights by deltaplane. **Paragliding** is

based on parachuting. The parachute is segmented and divided into cells. With a few pounds in weight in a rucksack you will take off, sitting under the sail and pulling on the controls manually. However, you need training from a recognised establishment!

'Le rugby' in South West France

Most of France's rugby fans are to be found in the Midi-Pyrénées region. For some, it is almost a religion. Rugby appeals to the conviviality of the people of this area, their love of contact as well as their tendency for exaggeration, belligerency and solidarity. The soul of the region is felt in the crowd at a rugby stadium, whether watching Rugby Union or Rugby League.

Born in 1823

It is all the fault of an English schoolboy. William Webb Ellis, a poor football player, invented the principle of rugby unintentionally when he picked up the ball and ran with it. Only ten years later, c. 1835, the new sport reached France and spontaneously took root in the South, where it became a hugely popular regional sport.

The team

The players are all amateurs in France (there is no such thing as a professional) in order to keep the game spontaneous. However, professionalisation, which has overtaken the other rugby-playing nations, is only a matter of time. The 15-man Rugby Union side consists of 1 back, 4 three-quarters, 1 opening half, 1 scrum half and 8 forwards.

The 15-aside game

This is the French equivalent of Rugby Union. The teams need to score as many points as possible by carrying or kicking the oval ball. The match lasts for 80 minutes and is divided into two halves with a five minute break. A **try** (5 points) is scored when a player gets the ball over the opposing team's line and plants it on the ground. When he kicks the ball over the two opposing goal posts,

THE SPIRIT OF COMPETITION

In rugby, the concept of contact is legitimised. Action is primarily based on confrontation. However, any aggression, violence or brutality is not within the spirit of the game. This sport, which is played in a spirit of rivalry, is based on the desire to dominate the opponent 'healthily'. The physical element, which is always intense, should never be combined with brutality or aggression.

he scores a **goal** (3 points). If a try is **converted** into a goal, that is an additional 2 points.

The scrum

This spectacular formation is one of the distinctive features of the game. It can take place, for example, when a player commits the foul of passing the ball forward (the 'forward pass'). Immediately, the forwards (who are usually the most stocky team-members) of the two teams butt their heads together. The half-scrum then throws the ball into this human mass. By pushing and shoving, the players try to move the ball out to the advantage of their own team.

The 13-aside game

This game is the French equivalent of Rugby League which is played with only 13 men (6 forwards instead of 8). This alternative version of the original French game was created in 1934 by Jean Galia, after he was left out of the French national team. In Rugby League, the scrum is held whenever the ball is offside. It is very popular in certain parts of the region, particularly in Saint-Gaudens, in Haute-Garonne, and in Languedoc (Narbonne, Saint-Estève, Carcassonne), where it has been nicknamed 'rugby of the heretics' or 'rugby of the Cathars'.

The Pyrenees and Gascony in detail

Gascony 112

The Albi district 136

La Vallée de la Garonne 152

The Pyrenees 180

Comminges 198

Ariège 206

Andorra 224

The Pyrenees and Gascony in detail

In the following pages, you will find details of the most interesting places to visit in the Pyrenees and Gascony. The region has been divided into tourist zones, and a colour code allows you to find the area you are looking for at a glance.

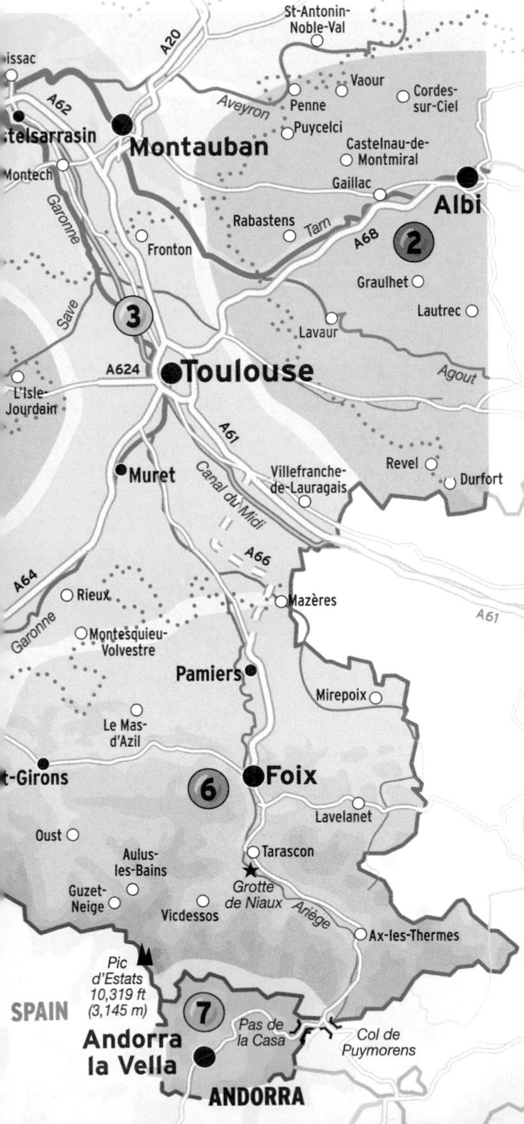

St-Antonin-Noble-Val
A20
issac
A62
Aveyron
Vaour
Penne
Cordes-sur-Ciel
Puycelci
telsarrasin
Montauban
Castelnau-de-Montmiral
Montech
Gaillac
Albi
Garonne
Rabastens
Tarn
A68
2
Fronton
Graulhet
Save
3
Lautrec
Lavaur
A624
Toulouse
Agout
L'Isle-Jourdain
A61
Muret
Canal du Midi
Villefranche-de-Lauragais
Revel
Durfort
A66
A64
Rieux
Mazères
A61
Garonne
Montesquieu-Volvestre
Pamiers
Mirepoix
Le Mas-d'Azil
t-Girons
6
Foix
Lavelanet
Oust
Aulus-les-Bains
Tarascon
Grotte de Niaux
Guzet-Neige
Vicdessos
Ariège
Ax-les-Thermes
Pic d'Estats 10,319 ft (3,145 m)
SPAIN
7
Pas de la Casa
Col de Puymorens
Andorra la Vella
ANDORRA

Le Val d'Adour
in the footsteps of d'Artagnan

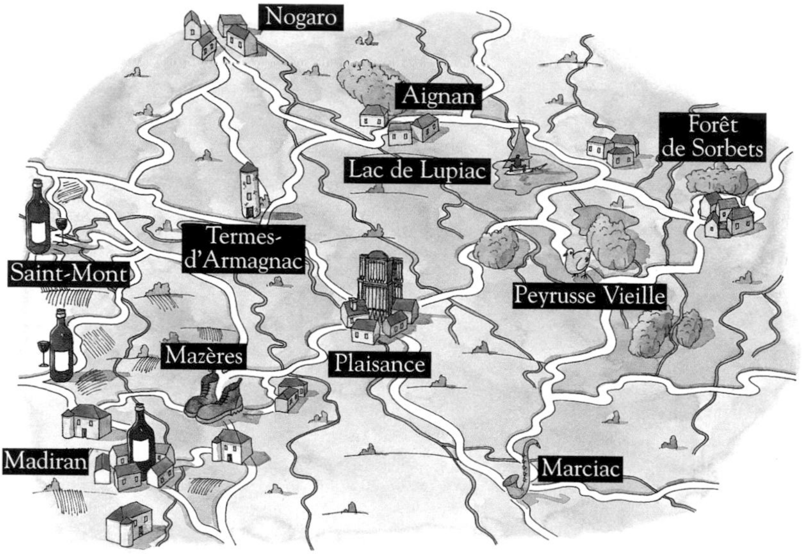

Between Aire-sur-l'Adour and Tarbes, the cobbled streets in the Adour resound to the exploits of the sons of Gascony. The most famous musketeer was born here. The lands of d'Artagnan are a stronghold of culinary tradition. The gentle landscape is dotted with villages where the finest foie gras has been made for generations, and on the hillsides, the oldest families of grape-growers produce the wine of Madiran and the Côtes de Saint-Mont.

Saint-Mont

La cave coopérative des producteurs Plaimont

Route d'Orthez
☎ 05 62 69 62 87.

Open daily, 8.30am-noon and 2-6.30pm; out of season, closed Sun. and holidays. Although less well-known than Madiran, the Côtes de Saint-Mont is nevertheless a pleasant surprise. The wine-makers produce 12 million bottles of red, rosé or white, including the famous **Colombelle**, a fresh young white with the scent of wild flowers. In the Saint-Mont cellar, you can discover wines costing between 15.50 F and 50 F a bottle. **Monastère de Saint-Mont** 1995, at 75 F a bottle, will keep for up to 12 years! For those who would like to know more, the cooperative also offers an introduction to wine-tasting and guided tours of the cellars.

ON THE BANKS OF THE ADOUR

Ferme des Flâneries Castelnau-Rivière-Basse, hamlet of Mazères
☎ 05 62 31 90 56.
Open by appointment.
The Ferme des Flâneries is the place for a really relaxing family stroll. The farm provides a pack-donkey to carry your picnic and any provisions along the signposted path that runs beside the banks of the Adour. The excursion is a 3 hours round trip on level paths. You can also visit the Lac de Préchac, which is suitable for swimming and has a children's playground. Anyone who would like to stay longer can take advantage of the guest rooms at Les Flâneries.

Viella

Vic Bilh wine tasting

Domaine de Berthoumieu,
☎ 05 62 69 74 05.
Open daily, 8am-noon and 2-7pm (Sun., 3-7pm).
Vic Bilh, the old country, is the name given to the Terroir du Madiran and Pacherenc. This little vineyard of only 2,965 acres (1,200 ha) produces a strong red wine. Pacherenc, dry or sweet, is an unusual white wine which is a blend of several local grape varieties. Pacherenc, produced at the Domaine de Berthoumieu is among the best-known (55 F). Enjoy wine tastings at the vineyard, where you can buy wines to drink now or lay down for future consumption.

Madiran

The old town and Gascon cuisine

This ancient fortified village with its ochre-coloured houses roofed with tiles is the home territory of Madiran, a strong, tannic red wine which keeps very well. The village boasts a lovely wooden market hall and the beautiful 12th C. abbey church. The priory opposite has been turned into an attractive **hotel** and offers a **cuisine which is typical of the best of Gascony**, including pigeon with Madiran, fresh liver with fruits in season, *garbure*, foie gras, etc. (Le Prieuré, ☎ 05 62 31 92 50; menus from 100 F.)

The wine festival

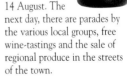

Information at
☎ 05 62 31 98 09.
Free admission.
Every 14 and 15 August, Madiran celebrates its wines. This spectacular series of events, worthy of anything produced by the most seasoned professionals, is a unique opportunity for acquiring some decent bottles of the wine and getting well acquainted with it. The highlight is an open-air feast on 14 August. The next day, there are parades by the various local groups, free wine-tastings and the sale of regional produce in the streets of the town.

A tour of the vineyards

To explore Madiran and Pacherenc, begin at the **Château de Perron** (☎ 05 62 31 93 27), then go on to the magnificent classified wine store (*chai*) of the

Spotcheck

A2-A3

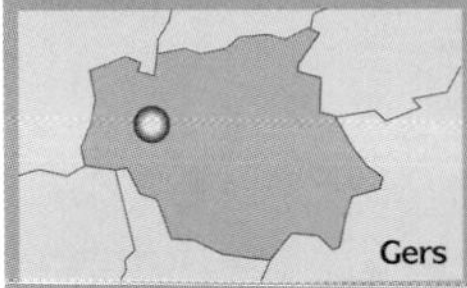

Things to do

- Madiran and Vic Bilh wine tastings
- Jazz festival at de Marciac

With children

- Lac de Lupiac
- Forêt de Sorbet

Within easy reach

Mirande, p. 132
Auch, p. 120
Vic-Fézensac, p. 117

Tourist Office

Marciac:
☎ 05 62 09 30 55
Plaisance-du-Gers:
☎ 05 62 69 44 69

Château de Montus (☎ 05 62 31 93 27), both at the edge of the village of Madiran. At Maumusson-Laguian, visit the biggest underground wine-store in Europe and the Jardin des Senteurs, a scent garden celebrating the vine and wine of the **Domaine de Bouscassé** (☎ 05 62 69 74 67) where Alain Brumont's Madiran is considered to be the best.

JAZZ IN MARCIAC

Jazz in Marciac has become a tradition: every August, the countryside around Gers starts to swing. Marciac repeats the magic formula which has made its reputation: there are unique concerts, with jazz legends of yesteryear, great contemporary artists and up and coming musicians. The programme is always excellent (Ray Charles, Dee Dee Bridgewater, Herbie Hancock, Michel Petrucciani, The Count Basie Orchestra, etc.) and improvised gigs late into the night contribute to the reputation of this festival. (Information on ☎ 05 62 09 33 33. Admission charge.)

Termes-d'Armagnac

Musée du Panache Gascon

☎ 05 62 69 25 12.
Open daily except Tues. am, June-Sept., 10.30am-noon and 3-8pm; open daily except March, Oct.-May, 2-6pm.
Admission charge.

For a superb **panorama** over the valley of the Adour, the Pyrenees and the slopes of Armagnac and Madiran, climb the 150 steps of the spiral staircase in the tower of Termes-d'Armagnac. The **Musée du Panache Gascon** at the foot of the tower provides an attractive glimpse of local history and tradition. The various rooms are decorated with period furniture and artefacts as well as figures in traditional costume, including D'Artagnan and the three musketeers.

you with the most delicious and surprising dishes in his extensive repertoire, including goat with nettles, lamb sweetbreads with *ceps* in pastry, and *pastilla* of lobster with foie gras. Greatness and originality. (Dishes from 80 F; full menu from 250 F.)

The Musée du Panache Gascon at Termes-d'Armagnac

Plaisance-du-Gers

The cuisine of Maurice Coscuella

Hôtel Ripa Alta, Place de l'Eglise,
☎ 05 62 69 30 43.
Open daily.

Plaisance-du-Gers is a delightful walled city (*bastide*) which houses one of the wonders of French cuisine, **the culinary skills of Maurice Coscuella**. Without breaking the bank, this chef will serve

Daniel Birouste's organ

This immense musical instrument, built in 1980, was the mad scheme of an organmaker. The body is made from solid oak, there are four keyboards, 43 stops, 3,135 pipes which work inside it representing a total of 2,000 hours work! Daniel Birouste will also show you inside his workshop, **Facture Instrumentale** (☎ 05 62 69 31 64). A tour organised by the tourist office

WOOD PIGEON WATCHING

Contact the Fédération des Chasseurs du Gers (Route de Toulouse, 32000 Auch, ☎ 05 62 68 28 30) if you fancy a spot of wood pigeon watching, as this bird is becoming ever more numerous and overwintering in Gers. Armed only with a camera and a pair of binoculars, you can visit the facility where the birds are ringed at Nogaro or watch birds on the Magnan reserve and the Lac Saint-Jean, at Peyrusse-Vieille. The trip (180 F) lasts a day and includes a visit to an Armagnac and a Saint-Mont cellar, including a real Gascon meal!

takes you right through the town, ending with an organ concert.

Marciac

Territoires du Jazz

Place du Chevalier-d'Antras,
☎ 05 62 09 30 18.
Open daily, April-Sept., 9am-noon and 2-6.30pm; out of season, closed Sat., Sun., Mon., Tues. and public holidays.
Admission charge.

Marciac is famous for its jazz festival and has even opened a **Jazz Museum,** telling the story and legends of jazz. From the African roots of Louis Armstrong, Miles Davis and Bernard Lubat via New Orleans (Dixieland), the blues and spirituals, each great period in jazz is presented in a separate room. The visit is accompanied musically, as each visitor is given a set of headphones. You are even allowed to sing along with the music!

Aignan

Lac de Lupiac

3m (5 km) E of Aignan via D37
☎ 05 62 09 26 13.
Open daily, 1.30-7pm.
This lake measures 32 acres (13 ha) and has every facility for supervised swimming, angling, sailing, windsurfing, canoeing, kayaking and

Château de Castelmore, near Lupiac

rowing. Alternatively, you can laze on the **fine sandy beach** for a few hours. The most famous Gascon hails from this area. Charles de Batz, Count d'Artagnan, was born very near here at Castelmore, 2½ miles (4 km) from Lupiac. Even though the Château de Castelmore is not open to visitors, it is worth a glimpse from a distance.

Forêt de Sorbet

7½ miles (12 km) S of Aignan via D35
This beautiful 106 acre (43 ha) forest is a great place to study wildlife. There are 21 **panels** along the way, depicting migrating birds, animals, species of trees and the fungi that grow on them. Follow the sign-posted route which will lead you through the forest (time: 1½–3 hour walk). Perfect for a picnic in the shade.

The pale sands of Armagnac

The centre of the wine-growing area of Armagnac has a reputation for producing the finest vintages. Vineyards and oak forests can be seen for miles. The mystery of the flavour lies in the soil, which consists of pale-coloured sand, full of iron oxide. In this part of Gascony, dubbed Armagnac Noir, the passage of time is governed by the vine, the market, the migration of the wood pigeons, bullrunning and bullfights.

Cazaubon

7½ miles (12 km) from Éauze on the D626

Spas and water sports

Barbotan-les-Thermes, one of the oldest spas in France, is recommended for treating rheumatism and circulation problems. If you prefer water sports to mud-baths, the huge **Lac d'Uby** (198 acres (80 ha)) is a swimming lake. The **base de plein air** (☎ 05 62 09 53 92. Open daily, 10am-7.30pm. Admission charge) has a large, fine sandy beach with a children's play area. There is also windsurfing available (51 F/h) or you can hire a pedalo (22 F for half an hour) and even a canoe (38 F/h).

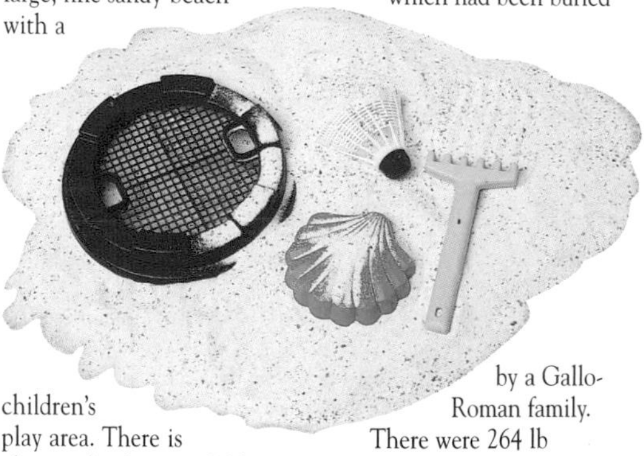

Éauze

Musée du Trésor d'Éauze

Place de la République
☎ 05 62 09 71 38.
Open daily except Tues., 10am-noon and 2-6pm; out of season, 2-5pm; closed public holidays and Jan.
Admission charge.

The capital of Armagnac was prosperous in Roman times. At least, that is what emerges from the fabulous **treasure** found in 1985 by two archeologists who found a fortune which had been buried by a Gallo-Roman family. There were 264 lb (120 kg) of gold and bronze coins in leather bags, as well as magnificent jewels encrusted with precious stones and pearls!

La Maison des Producteurs du Floc de Gascogne

Route des Vignerons
☎ 05 62 09 85 41.
Open daily except Sat., 8.30-noon and 2-6pm.

Floc is a typically Gascon aperitif, the result of a combination of fresh grape juice and Armagnac. It has had an Appellation d'Origine Contrôlée since 1977; the alcohol content is 16–18%. White

or rosé, it is drunk chilled or iced, but never on the rocks. It is enjoyed before dinner or as an accompaniment to foie gras or Lectoure melon. Try a tasting at La Maison du Floc de Gascogne (45 F a bottle).

The Domaine de Lagajan

Route de Sauboires, Éauze
☎ 05 62 09 81 69.
Open daily, 9am-6pm.
Gisèle and Constantin Georgacaracos will initiate you into the secrets of Armagnac. They will explain the distillation process and show you the copper still. You will discover a delightful **little museum** of everyday artefacts and tools, and you will taste some excellent Armagnacs (150 F for a bottle that is six years old; 1982 vintage 220 F a bottle). Also try the **eau-de-vie des Muses**, a white, fruity liqueur (110 F a bottle).

THE *FERIA* DE VIC-FÉZENSAC

The *corrida*, like the regional *course landaise*, is an integral part of Gascon culture. Every year, bull-fighting aficionados flock to the bullrings of Gers. The best known is the Pentecôte de Vic-Fézensac *feria*. It is also one of the biggest festivals in the South-west, lasting three days and nights. Revellers drink in one bodega after another, in an unforgettable atmosphere. However, accommodation is usually booked well in advance, and it can be hard to find lodgings during the *feria*! (For information ☎ 05 62 06 56 55.)

Vic-Fézensac

12½ miles (20 km) E of Éauze by the N124

Latin music festival

Information
☎ 05 62 06 56 66
or 05 62 06 34 90.
The Festival Salsa Tempo Latino invades the streets of Vic-Fézensac in late July. For three days and three nights, Vic la Gasconne vibrates to the frenetic rhythms of the salsa, the rhumba and the cha-cha. The best bands from Miami, Caracas and Havana flock to this little Gascon village, and there is a thriving fringe festival which stages many free performances and concerts.

Spotcheck

A2

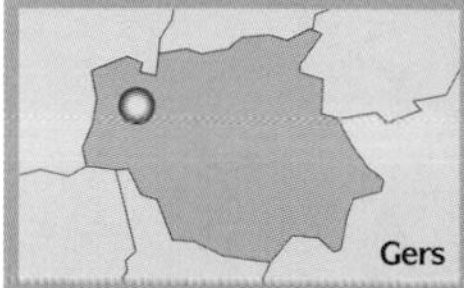

Things to do

- Water sports centre at Lac d'Uby
- Le Houga deer and wild boar

Within easy reach

Condom, p. 122
Plaisance-du-Gers, p. 114

Tourist Office

Éauze: ☎ 05 62 09 85 62
Nogaro: ☎ 05 62 09 13 30

Le Houga

3¾ miles (6 km) E of Nogaro

❀ Deer and wild boar

La ferme au Cerfs et Sangliers,
Route de Mont-de-Marsan, Le Houga
☎ 05 62 08 96 97.
Open daily except Mon., March-Oct. from 11am; out of season by appointment, Jan.-Feb.
Admission charge.
More than 500 stags, does, fawns, roebuck and wild boar roam freely in this unusual breeding-ground which is also a scenic place for a quiet walk. You can also buy delicious preserves and canned game. In July, the **Championnat du Monde des Roucoulaïres** is held here, a competition for wood pigeon imitators! This extraordinary event is followed by a delicious feast of spit-roast venison.

Le Pays d'Auch
in the heart of Gascony

Auch is a medieval city perched on a limestone hilltop, with pretty ochre-coloured houses and pink roof tiles. It has lovely old streets and a quiet charm. Auch is the former residence of the prelates and the Counts of Armagnac and reverberates with the history of the region. This southern city is elegant, discreet and a lovely place to live, where people can enjoy a civilised pace of life.

Auch

D'Artagnan, a typical Gascon hero

D'Artagnan, the hero taken straight from *The Three Musketeers*, welcomes you! The real-life model, Charles de Batz, was born quite close by, at the Château de Castelmore. His statue stands on the 19th C. **grand staircase** which leads from the river up to the Cathedral of Sainte-Marie. Climbing this massive flight of 234 steps is an excellent way to get to know the town. At the top there is a wonderful view of the town from the Place Salinis.

The *pousterles*

The old part of the town is built in a semi-circle on the left bank of the river Gers, and consists of a labyrinth of medieval streets, broken by flights of steps called ***pousterles***. These steps linked the upper town with the lower before the grand staircase was built. These picturesque alleyways, full of flowers and greenery which lead down to the Gers, are havens of peace only a step away from the town centre. Climb the steps of the **Rue Fabre-d'Églantine** up to the Porte d'Arton, then to the **Rue de la Convention**. This is rather an athletic way to sample the charms and secrets of the town, but well worth the effort!

The famous cakes of Collongues

21 Avenue d'Alsace
☎ 05 62 60 23 10.
Open daily, 8am-8.30pm.

This family of *patissiers* and confectioners have been established for several generations. It is really hard to choose between Armagnac-flavoured sweets, sugar plums and ***croustades***! The house specialities are ***pousterles***, flaky pastry flavoured with orange and chocolate (10 F for 3½ oz (100 g)) and **Germagnac**, a sponge cake with almonds and raisins soaked in Armagnac (31 F for a cake big enough for 4-5 people).

LE MARCHÉ À LA LANTERNE
2 Thurs. per month, July-Aug., 8.30pm-2am.
For information
☎ 05 62 60 27 35.
The town of Vic-Fézensac started the idea, which was soon copied by Auch (as well as Aignan, Solomiac and Lavardens). The idea is simple: hold an open-air market in the evening so that people can shop and then browse among the stalls. There are lots of food and craft stalls as well as the standard market produce and goods.

The Musée des Jacobins

4, Place Louis-Blanc
☎ 05 62 05 74 79.
Open daily except Mon. and holidays; from 1st Oct.-30 Apr., 10am-noon and 2-5pm; from 1st May-30 Sept., 10am-noon and 2-6pm.
Admission charge.
This museum in a former convent contains the most remarkable collection of **pre-Columbian art** in

St. Gregory's Mass (detail), in the Musée des Jacobins

Spotcheck
B2-B3

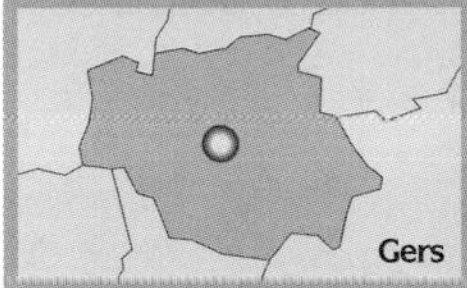

Things to do
- Climbing the *pousterles*
- Collection of pre-Columbian art at the Musée des Jacobins
- The twisted spire of Barran

With children
- The Castéra-Verduzan leisure park

Within easy reach
Mirande, p. 132
L'Isle-Jourdain, p. 134

Tourist Office
Auch: ☎ 05 62 05 22 89

France. There are more than 1,200 exhibits and a masterpiece that should not be missed, *St. Gregory's Mass*. This is a mosaic picture made with humming-bird feathers created in 1539 by local craftspeople under the direction of Franciscan monks, only four years after the discovery of the New World! The museum also contains collections of art and archaeology and regional wedding costumes.

La Maison de la Gascogne

Place Jean-David
☎ 05 62 05 12 08.
Open daily, June-Sept., 10am-1pm and 14.30-7.30pm.

In July and August, this former corn market becomes a showcase for Gers, displaying the very best of what Gascony has to offer: Armagnacs, wines, foie gras, *confits*, *croustades* and much more. There are free tastings, opportunities to meet local producers and traditional games. A visit to the Maison de la Gascogne is an excellent opportunity to learn about the local dishes and to pick up some good advice on buying the local produce as well as a few traditional recipes.

A walking tour

The Tourist Office (☎ 05 62 05 22 89), which occupies the half-timbered brick house by the cathedral, has a choice of two leaflets which will help you to take a walking tour of Auch. The two routes lead you through the town before you come to the signposted path which you follow to the **banks of the Gers**. From the river, there is a magnificent view of the upper town lit up at night.

The Hôtel de France restaurant

Place de la Libération
☎ 05 62 61 71 71.
Open daily.

Prepare your tastebuds: Auch is the capital of good living and good eating. The tradition is carried on by several excellent restaurants, of which the best known is the **Hôtel de France**. It is situated in a beautifully restored post-house, close to the cathedral, and is owned and run by the master chef Roland Garreau. Local foods are on the menu (cream of chestnut with *confit*, breast of duck baked in a salt crust, wood pigeon, breast of mallard in a floc-flavoured sauce, etc.) and there are many variations on a theme (such as the fish catch of the month cooked in numerous different and delicious ways). Menus from 170 F to 480 F. The hotel and restaurant are free for children under 10.

The Cathedral of Sainte-Marie

Place Louis-Blanc
☎ 05 62 05 22 89.
Open daily, 9am-noon and 2-6pm.
Admission charge to the choir stalls.

The Cathedral of Sainte-Marie is an imposing building. The nave is 350 ft (105 m) with an ogival ceiling 86 ft (26 m) high, and two towers 146 ft (44 m) high flank a superb façade. There are 113 **choir stalls** which were carved in oak by master craftsmen and depict more than 1,500 characters surrounded by elaborate patterns. The chapels boast 18 richly-coloured stained glass windows of the most stunning designs.

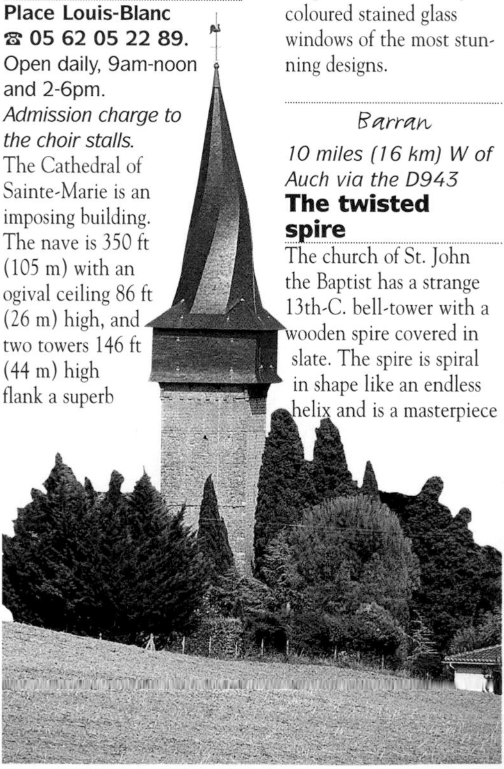

Barran

10 miles (16 km) W of Auch via the D943

The twisted spire

The church of St. John the Baptist has a strange 13th-C. bell-tower with a wooden spire covered in slate. The spire is spiral in shape like an endless helix and is a masterpiece of the carpenter's art. Yet according to local legend it was the wind that gave it its curious shape!

Castéra-Verduzan

12½ miles (20 km) NW of Auch via the D930

The water sports centre on the lake

Route de Saint-Puy

☎ 05 62 68 10 43.

Open daily, July-Aug. at weekends, June and Sept., 10.30am-7.30pm.
Admission charge.

The spa village of Castéra-Verduzan is like an oasis of green in the hills. You have a choice of taking the cure or relaxing by the lakeside waters. In addition to having a fine **sandy beach**, the leisure park is equipped for all types of water sports: windsurfing, 4-person boats (50 F for 2 hours) or sailing boats (40 F for 2 hours) and pedalos (25 F for half an hour).

Lavardens

12½ miles (20 km) N of Auch via the D103

The hilltop château

Lavardens is one of the prettiest villages in Gascony. The château, built on a rocky spur, has a **magnificent panorama**. Take a walk through the huge rooms where you will find that the flooring consists of beautiful stone and ornamental bricks laid in geometric patterns. Go for an evening stroll to see the castle lit up on a summers night. In September, the **Concours International d'Épouvantails à Moineaux,** a scarecrow competition, is held in the village! (Information at the Tourist Office, ☎ 05 62 64 51 20.)

Roquelaure

5 miles (8 km) from Auch

Ferme de la Gouardère

☎ 05 62 65 56 51.

Open daily, 9am-6pm.

Guy and Maryse Galbez will be delighted to give you a guided tour of their cannery. This is an opportunity to see how the ducks are reared as well as to taste and buy some specialities of the region. There are **foie gras** (135 F for a 6 oz (190 g) pot), ***confits*** (two thighs and two drumsticks: 66 F) and ***rillettes*** (23 F for a 6 oz (190 g) pot). This traditional duck-breeding farm is also a *ferme-auberge*, a farm-inn where good simple cooking is served at a very reasonable price.

Château de Lavardens

Condom
the queen of Armagnac

Condom is a little town deep in the valley of the Baïse, and is full of delights. If Armagnac is the main attraction here, that is no reason to neglect the elegant mansions which are evidence of the prosperity which gives the town its characteristic charm. In the surrounding countryside, there are hillsides and valleys containing many attractions, including some of the prettiest villages in France.

The 18th C. Hôtel de Cugnac

Condom

A tour of the *hôtels particuliers* (mansions)

In Condom, historic monuments are part of daily life. The town hall, local school and sub-prefecture are housed in veritable palaces! The Tourist Office (☎ 05 62 28 00 80), which is inside a handsome medieval residence, offers a tour of the great 18th C. mansions. The best of these, the Hôtel Polignac and the Hôtel de Cugnac, with their magnificent stone balconies, columns, ironwork and cornices are worth the walk alone!

Musée de l'Armagnac

Rue Jules-Ferry
☎ 05 62 28 31 41.
Open daily except Tues. and public holidays, 10am-noon and 3-6pm.
Admission charge.

This museum boasts a huge wine-press weighing 18 tonnes, as well as many tools which were once used for cultivating vines and making wine. There are old stills, hand-made bottles made by Gascon glassmakers, including a 31¼ pt (18.5 l) demijohn. Complete the visit with a little tour of the *chais* in which wine and brandy is aged at the **Maison Papelorey** (Rue des Carmes, ☎ 05 62 28 15 33. Open Mon.-Fri. 9-noon and 1.30-5pm; closed 1-15 Aug.). This Armagnac merchant is happy to welcome you.

❀ La Maison Ryst-Dupeyron

36, Allée Jean-Jaurès
☎ 05 62 28 08 08.
Open daily, July-Aug., 9am-noon and 2-6pm (until 5pm in Sept.); out of season, weekends only by appointment.
Free admission.

One of the best brands of Armagnac offers you a **guided**

tour (1 hour) of its *chais* with a **slide-show** explaining how Armagnac is made. There is also a small **museum** inside the house which contains figures in traditional costume and free **tastings**. You can buy Armagnac to take away (135 F a bottle for a VSOP Armagnac), as well as Floc (50 F a bottle), Crème de Mûres (mulberry liqueur) (90 F a bottle) and prunes in Armagnac (89 F a jar).

A festival of bands

On the second Sunday in May, Condom hosts the **Festival de Bandas y Peñas**, a festival of the bands that attend the *ferias*. About 15 bands play in the streets and bars of Condom throughout Saturday night (delicate ears should beware!), before the big competition on the Sunday. (Information ☎ 05 62 28 00 80. Admission charge.)

❀ Sailing down the Baïse

Gascogne Navigation, Quai de la Bouquerie
☎ 05 62 28 46 46.
River cruises daily except Sun., at 3pm and 4.45pm; Easter-Nov., Sun. at 11am and noon. Departure from Condom. Admission charge.

Ever since the old locks were restored, boats are again sailing up and down the river Baïse. The old barges have now disappeared, but the trip is still delightful. You can choose between a family outing on a little motor boat or take a trip on the *D'Artagnan* for a guided cruise (time: 1½ hours) passing through one lock (45 F/pers., 35 F for children aged over four). On Sunday, there are lunchtime cruises leaving from Condom (145 F/pers.) or trips as far as the Abbey of Flaran (time: 2½ hours; 60 F/pers., 40 F for children aged over four).

Spotcheck
B2

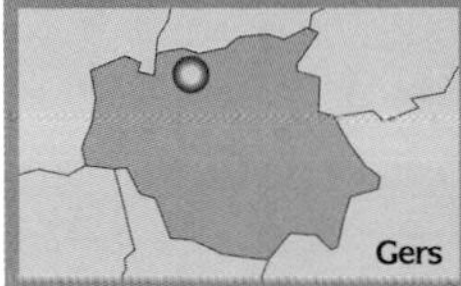

Things to do
- Armagnac tasting

With children
- Boat trip on the Baïse
- Medieval war machines

Within easy reach
Éauze, p. 116
Auch, p. 118

Tourist Office
Condom: ☎ 05 62 28 00 80
Montréal-du-Gers:
☎ 05 62 29 42 85

Larressingle

3 miles (5 km) W of Condom via the D15

A fortified town

Larresingle is a small but strong **fortress**. The imposing entrance, with its vaulted, machicolated tower opens onto narrow streets lined with delightful medieval houses. Extend this journey into the past at the **Halte du Pèlerin**: 50 characters tell the story of the village at the time of the Hundred Years War. (☎ 05 62 28 11 58. Open daily, 15 May-15 Oct., 10.30-noon and 2.30-6.30pm; out of season, weekends only, 3-6pm. Admission charge.)

❀ Medieval machines

Cité des Machines du Moyen-Age
☎ 05 62 68 33 88.
Daily shows, July-Aug.; May-June and Sept., Sun. at 4pm.
Admission charge.

Near the village of Larressingle is a 13th C. siege camp where various war machines for attacking and defending have been assembled. These ingenious

mechanisms have been authentically reconstructed and you can operate them yourself. The kids will love it!

Cassaigne

3¾ miles (6 km) S of Condom

❀ Le Château de Cassaigne

Route d'Eauze
☎ 05 62 28 04 02.
Open daily, 9am-noon and 2-7pm. Closed Mon., 15 Oct.-15 March and end of Jan. to mid-Feb.
Free admission.

The former residence of the bishops of Condom is now used for making Armagnac. Your exploratory visit should include the storage cellars (*chais*) and a visit to the château. There is a **slide show**, a **free tasting** and **shop** (95 F for a bottle of 3-star Armagnac, 192 F to 500 F for an Armagnac *hors d'âge* (see p.43), aperitifs, liqueurs and fruits soaked in Armagnac). Cassaigne is also famous for two other delicious speciality drinks, the **Esprit d'Armagnac**, a vanilla-flavoured Armagnac liqueur (163 F), and a peach and Armagnac **aperitif** (79 F).

Montréal-du-Gers

9½ miles (15 km) W of Condom via the D15

❀ Gallo-Roman villa of Séviac

☎ 05 62 29 48 57.
Open daily, March-Oct., 10am-noon and 2pm-6pm; July-Aug. 10am-7pm.
Admission charge.

This is the largest and most luxurious of the Gallo-Roman villas in the South-west. It is paved with wonderfully coloured and patterned **mosaics**. These beautiful floorings have infinite variations on the themes of vine branches, grapes, lotuses, figs, lillies and laurels, combined with geometric patterns. Pottery, jewellery and marble from the villa are exhibited at the Musée de Montréal (Information at the Tourist Office, ☎ 05 62 29 42 8; same opening hours as the villa).

Fourcès

The old village

This circular fortified village (*bastide*) was built around the ancient château and has some very lovely old houses with

Chapter house of the 12th C. Abbey of Flaran

stone or wooden arcades, grouped around a huge circular square shaded with plane trees. The proportions, the warmth of the materials, the vegetation and the presence of water make Fourcès a perfect stopping place. The biggest **flower market** in the region is held on the last weekend in April.

Gondrin

6¼ miles (10 km) W of Condom via the D931

❀ Le Domaine des Cassagnoles

☎ 05 62 28 40 57.

Open daily, 9am-6pm; by appointment on weekends and out of season. Gilles Baumann produces **Vins de Pays** des Côtes de Gascogne (15.50 F to 34 F a bottle), **Floc de Gascogne** (46 F a bottle) and fragrant **Armagnacs** aged 15 years (210 F a bottle, VSOP 130 F). The speciality of the house is a high-quality dry sparkling white wine (31 F a bottle). The domaine's wines and spirits regularly win medals.

Valence-sur-Baïse

5 miles (8 km) S of Condom via the D930

The Abbey Flaran

☎ 05 62 28 50 19.

Open daily, July-Aug., 9.30am-7pm; out of season, 9.30am-noon and 2-6pm.
Closed 15 Jan.-15 Feb.
Admission charge.

This Cistercian abbey, founded in the 12th C., is a masterpiece of harmony and elegance with its pale stones and the purity of its lines. The jewel of the abbey is the **chapter house.** Four groups of marble columns ascend into a mass of arches. There is also a garden of aromatic plants which is a pleasant place for a peaceful stroll.

La Romieu

7½ miles (12 km) NE of Condom via the D931

The Abbey-church of Saint-Pierre

Open Feb.-May and Oct.-Dec., 10am-noon and 2-6pm (until 7pm in June and Sept., noon-7.30pm in July-Aug.).
Closed Sun. morning and Jan.

This is another outstanding building, this one dating from the early 14th C.
To appreciate the tranquil beauty of the church, visit the cloister when the light floods the arcaded square and wander through the church, under the starry ceiling decorated with angelic musicians. Painted frescoes have been preserved in the sacristy.

The Birthplace of *Pousse-Rapière*

Montluc SA, Château de Montluc, Saint-Puy
☎ 05 62 28 94 00.
Open Tues.-Sat., 10am-noon and 3-7pm; Sun and public holidays, 3-7pm. Closed Jan.-Feb., 25 Dec., 1 May; Mon., Oct.-May.
The speciality of the Château de Monluc is *pousse-rapière*, a typically Gascon aperitif flavoured with a hint of orange (90 F a bottle). The recipe is a secret, but it is known to contain one volume of liqueur Armagnac to six volumes of Armagnac brut. It is both mild and strong. Begin by visiting the château and its wine-cellars before having a tasting. The domaine also makes Armagnac (145 F for a VSOP, 190 F for a *hors d'âge*), and Vins de Pays des Côtes de Gascogne. There is also *vin sauvage*, a dry sparkling white wine (120 F for 3 bottles) which is used in making *pousse-rapière*.

Lectoure the melon capital

The hot baths of Lectoure on the Cours d'Armagnac

Lectoure is famous for its delicious melons, and is also one of the loveliest towns in the Midi-Pyrénées. The capital of the district, known as La Lomagne, stands like an acropolis on its chalk escarpment. It has the charm and tranquillity of an Italian town, and the landscape, punctuated with cypress trees, houses of pale-coloured stone and terraced gardens, palm trees and fountains, provides a compelling reason to visit.

The old town

The attractions of the old town include the **Cathedral of Saint-Gervais** whose choir-stalls are sculpted with fantastic animals, the **Fontaine de Diane** with its double Gothic arch, the **Tour du Bourreau** and the **Musée Lapidaire**, which contains an impressive collection of the stone altars which were used by the Gauls to perform their sacrifices. The Bournaca footpath will take you through the town from one fountain to another. This is a two-hour tour, which is best done in the spring, when the acacias and sunflowers are in full flower. (Information at the Tourist Office, ☎ 05 62 68 76 98.)

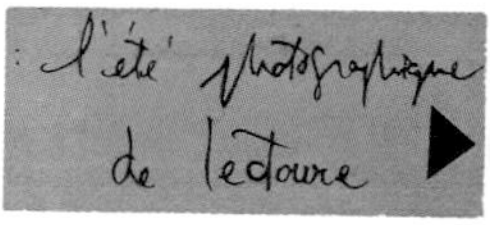

❀ Photography festival

Centre de Photographie de Lectoure
Association Arrêt sur Images
5 Rue Sainte-Claire
☎ 05 62 68 83 72.
Exhibition daily, mid July-Sept., 2-7pm (Sun, from 3pm).
Admission charge.

Photography enthusiasts should not miss this international event. It is held annually and is an opportunity to find out what is happening on the contemporary photography scene. There are many photography exhibitions, most of them unique, held throughout the summer

from July to September, and some of the great names in photography put in an appearance.

Musée Lapidaire

Town Hall, Place du Gal-de-Gaulle
☎ 05 62 68 70 22.
Open daily, 10am-noon and 2-6pm.
Admission charge.
This museum in the impressive setting of the vaulted caves of a former bishops' palace offers a collection of **pagan altars** that is unique in the world. The stones evoke the ancient rituals of the Gauls, during which bulls or rams were sacrificed to the goddess Cybele. The museum also contains huge fossils of mastodons, tortoises and turtles as well as sarcophagi, pottery and amphoras from the Gallo-Roman period.

THE LECTOURE MELON

This is a truly local fruit. Until very recently, local people grew their own melons for their personal consumption. Since the 1960s, melons have been grown by market gardeners with great success, because the local soil is especially suited to the melon. Melons are grown in open fields and are said to be sweeter than those of the rival Cavaillon. In Lectoure, the melon is celebrated in August, when an outdoor feast is arranged in the streets of the town. (Information ☎ 05 62 68 76 98.)

The woad workshops

Route de Condom
☎ 05 62 68 78 30.
Open daily, 10am-12.30pm and 2-7pm.
Woad is produced as a dye and colouring agent in the workshops inside this restored 17th C tannery. The leaves of the plant produce a brilliant blue pigment (the only one which does not run in a washing machine), which is used in fine art and the textile industry and from which a range of brilliant blue items can be produced. You can buy angora or silk scarves (from 95 F), crayons, inks, dyes and house paints, all of them extracted from woad.

Spotcheck

B2

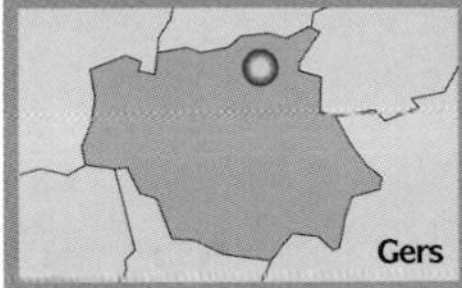

Things to do

- Photography festival
- Water sports centre of the Lac des Trois Vallées

Within easy reach

Condom, 10½ miles (17 km) W, p. 122
Saint-Clar, 6¼ miles (10 km) E, p. 128

Tourist Office

Lectoure: ☎ 05 62 68 76 98

Lac des Trois Vallées

Espardiagnes, Route d'Auch
The lake is accessible from Lectoure along the Cœur de Gascogne footpath (allow one hour). Once there, the **water sports centre** (☎ 05 62 68 82 33. Open daily, June-Sept., 9am-9pm;

April-May, until 6.30pm. Admission charge) offers beaches suitable for sunbathing and swimming, aquatic games for children and fishing ponds. When the weather is very hot, the bubble pool and water chutes are very much appreciated by young and old alike! You can also hire pedalos (from 45 F), canoes and kayaks (40 F) and even go for a plane ride (100 F for 15 minutes). This is highly recommended, especially the flight over the highest local peak, the Pic du Midi, which will cost 335 F for a flight lasting 1¾ hours.

The gentle valleys of the Lomagne

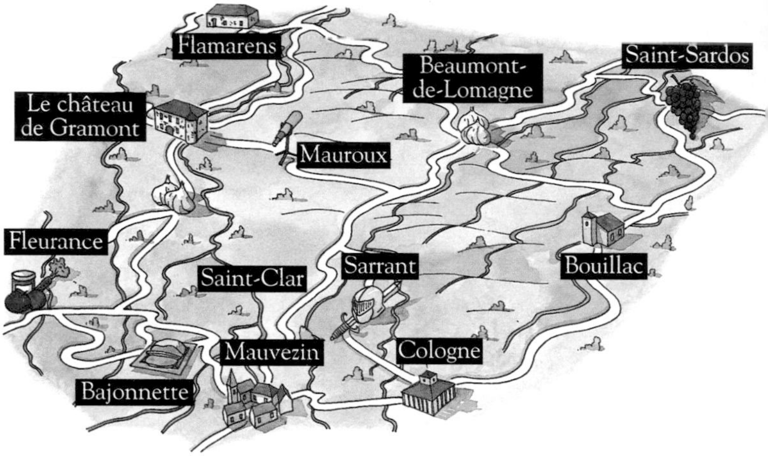

The rolling hills of the Lomagne district sit astride two départements, Gers and Tarn-et-Garonne. The landscape is dotted with fortified villages (*bastides*), hilltop châteaux and dovecotes. This is the garlic-growing district where the limestone outcrops are white in the morning sun and golden at sunset.

Flamarens

10½ miles (17 km) N of Lectoure via the D953

The Ecomuseum of the Lomagne

☎ 05 62 28 62 95.
Open daily, June-Oct., 9am-noon, 2-6pm
Admission charge.

A typical Lomagne farmhouse has been converted into a museum and displays the tools and artefacts which were used **in daily life by the Gascon peasants** before farming became mechanised and the tractor replaced the horse. The reconstruction of a Gascon tenant-farm (*métairie*) shows what life was like in the region in the late 19th C.

Saint-Clar

8¾ miles (14 km) SE of Lectoure via the D7

The garlic market

The reek of garlic will take your breath away! White garlic bulbs in bunches, in sacks, in heads or in bulk are sold in the market hall every Thursday morning.

The perfect place to stock up. Saint-Clar-de-Lomagne even holds a garlic festival on the second Thursday of August, with a **tasting of the traditional dishes made with garlic**. A fortnight later, a competition is held to build the best models with garlic. There are carriages, châteaux and Eiffel towers, all of them made of garlic! (Information ☎ 05 62 66 40 45.) Leave some time to explore the streets of Saint-Clar, one of the loveliest fortified towns of the South-west. There are narrow streets, half-timbered houses and lovely stone arcades. The lovely **covered marketplace** has open wooden arches which are covered with an ancient tiled roof.

❀ HEAD IN THE STARS

Au Moulin du Roi, 32500 Fleurance
☎ 05 62 06 09 76.
Open Wed. and Sat., July-Aug. 3-6pm.
Admission charge.
Take advantage of the clear skies of the Lomagne for an introduction to astronomy. This star-gazing farm, the brainchild of Hubert Reeves, invites you to discover the universe through its planetarium. Star-gazing with musical accompaniment is organised from June to September, as well as weekend courses run by expert astronomers. In August, there are one-day observations of the sky and short courses which will teach you how to build and launch a micro-rocket and how to make a sundial.

Gramont

3¾ miles (6 km) N of Saint-Clar via the D40

The château

☎ 05 63 94 05 26.
Open daily, June-Oct., 9am-noon and 2-7pm; out of season, 2-6pm. Closed Dec.-Jan.
Admission charge.

The Château de Gramont consists of a Gothic gatehouse and Renaissance wing. The interior architecture belies the fairly plain exterior and includes an amazing spiral staircase. It is fully furnished and exhibitions and a music festival are held there in the summer.

Spotcheck
B2-C2

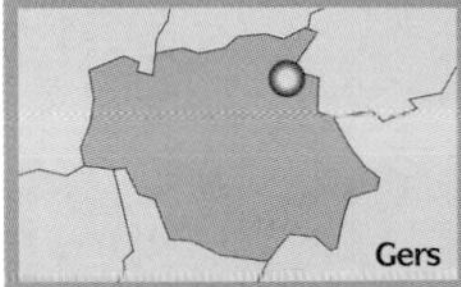

Things to do
- The garlic markets of Saint-Clar and Beaumont-de-Lomagne
- The medieval festivals of Sarrant

With children
- Ecomuseum of the Lomagne
- Donkey rides

Within easy reach

Castelsarrasin, p. 152
Auch, p. 118

Tourist Offices

Cologne: ☎ 05 62 06 99 30
Saint-Clar: ☎ 05 62 66 34 45

Sarrant

15½ miles (25 km) SE of Saint-Clar

Donkey rides

La Ferme de l'Ange, Sarrant
☎ 05 62 65 00 30.
Booking in advance advised.

At the Ferme de l'Ange, you can explore the region with the help of a pack-donkey to

Performers at the Sarrant medieval festival

carry your provisions or by riding a donkey (100 F for a half-day). You can also experience a ride in a donkey-cart (35 F/pers./h; minimum of five people). One of the routes takes you to the lovely Gascon dovecotes and châteaux to be found in the region of Sarrant. To return to the farm from the village, just follow the donkeys!

The Sarrant medieval festival

In this authentic setting, the locals dress up in period costumes for the annual medieval fair. The **Fêtes Médiévales de Sarrant** (third weekend in August. Information ☎ 05 62 65 00 34. Admission charge.) is a lovely excursion back in time. There is street theatre a medieval market, performances and tournaments, knights in armour, jugglers and acrobats, as well as concerts and shows of early music and dance.

Fleurance

6¼ miles (10 km) SW of Saint-Clar

Organic market

Fleurance has made a speciality of organic farming. Every Tuesday, the growers gather in this old fortified town. There are vegetables, fruit, cheeses, wine, honey, bread and eggs – everything produced organically. Fleurance is also home to Maurice Másségué who is a specialist in propagating wild herbs. (Information at the Tourist Office, ☎ 05 62 64 00 00.)

Bajonnette

7½ miles (12 km) from Fleurance via the D654

The Ferme de Laoueillée

☎ 05 62 06 84 39. Open daily, 9am-1pm and 2-7pm. Closed Sun. afternoon.

Françoise and Denis Bégué have the best that Gascony can offer: whole duck foie gras (110 F for a 6 oz (180 g) jar) and goose foie gras (76 F for a 3¼ oz (90 g) jar). Both have won medals at the Concours Agricole de Paris. You can also buy takeaway meals, duck breast and *confits*. You can go and see the farm's ducks and geese and help to feed them at any time of year.

Mauvezin

15 miles (24 km) S of Saint-Clar

The holiday village

This pretty fortified village is part of an interesting tourism experiment, a VVF (Village Vacances Familles – family holiday village) which encompasses the whole town! About sixty of the ancient houses built of golden stone have been converted into communal *gîtes*. The market hall, a magnificent wooden structure and the old parts of the town with their public wash-houses and fountains, have been beautifully restored.

Cologne

3¾ miles (6 km) E of Mauvezin via the D654

The old market hall

The old market hall, with its pillars of stone and wood occupies the centre of this fortified town. It has a small belltower and contains some very rare 15th C. grain measures cut into the stonework. The hall is surrounded by half-timbered houses with arcaded frontages built of wood, brick, stone and slaked lime.

❀ THE HONEY AND BEE MUSEUM

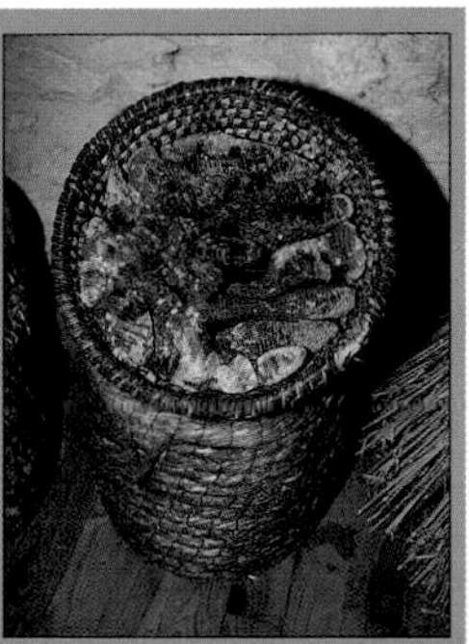

Musée du Miel et de l'Abeille, Moure, 82120 Gramont
☎ 05 63 94 00 20.
Open daily except Wed., May-Sept., 10am-noon and 2-6pm; out of season, by appointment.
Free admission and sampling.

Chantal and Émile Moles scour the world in search of artefacts linked to their occupation and exhibit their findings in their amazing museum. There is an Indonesian hive made of ferns, a Lomagne hive built of cow-pats, and the largest hive in the world (which may contain 1 million bees). Food-lovers will be able to watch honey sweets and old-fashioned gingerbread being made (30 F for 1lb 2oz (500 g)). The shop sells 12 different kinds of honey (from 15 to 30 F for 1lb 2oz (500 g)) and there are other homemade specialities: **dried fruit in honey** (15 F a 9 oz (240 g) jar), candles, **mead** (35 F a flask), **honey vinegar** (25 F for 12fl oz (35 cl)) and **honey tea** (20 F).

Beaumont-de-Lomagne

10½ miles (17 km) E of Saint-Clar

Beaumont garlic

Beaumont holds the largest **garlic market** in France (on Tuesday and Thursday mornings). After wandering around the vast market-hall, walk up the Rue du Presbytère to admire a pretty row of **mediaeval houses**, then take the Rue de l'Église, where there is a **15th C. mansion** with magnificently carved corbels.

½ mile (800 m) from the village

The pleasures of the water

Water sports centre
☎ 05 63 65 26 43.
Open daily, 8am-10pm.
Admission charge July-Aug.

This huge 70 acre (28 ha) lake has a **sandy beach** and exercise equipment, **games** and **water chutes**. Windsurfing boards, dinghies, canoes, kayaks and pedalos are available for hire (21 to 32 F for half an hour). On land, there are tennis courts and mountain bikes available for hire (40 F for half a day). Afterwards, relax in a Jacuzzi (30 F for half an hour).

9½ miles (15 km) E of Beaumont-de-Lomagne via the D3

❀ The Saint-Sardos wine cellars

☎ 05 63 02 52 44.
Open Mon.-Fri., 8am-noon and 2-6pm; Sat., 8.30am-noon.

Vine-growing was introduced by the monks of the Abbey of Grandselve, and has continued for a thousand years at Saint-Sardos. The *vin de pays* is red, rosé or white and bears the name of the village. There are tastings and sales at the cooperative (Gilles-de-Morban 1996, 17.70 F a bottle; Domaine-de-Grandselve 1996, 30 F a bottle).

Bouillac

9½ miles (15 km) W of Beaumont-de-Lomagne

The treasure of Grandselve

The chapel of the church at Bouillac contains the reliquaries (containers for holy relics) of the Abbey of Grandselve, the second most valuable gold church ornaments of the Midi-Pyrénées region. The reliquaries are made of wood covered in gold leaf and richly decorated with precious stones. Each one is in the shape of a miniature church. The oldest and most beautiful is the crucifixion reliquary.

Beautiful Mirande

With its grid pattern of streets and central marketplace surrounded by arcades, the capital of the Astarac district is a delightful medieval *bastide*. Mirande stands beside the river Baïse, and is surrounded by hills which alternate between gentle slopes and steep drops. The lovely countryside is worth exploring by driving or walking along the winding lanes of the Astarac.

Mirande

A walk in the *bastide*

Start your visit in the heart of the town, the Place d'Astarac, with its arcades, which has an old world charm. From here the streets radiate, intersecting at right angles. Wandering along the **Rue du Président-Wilson** and **Rue de l'Évêché**, you will see superb half-timbered houses before reaching the **Church of Sainte-Marie**. This imposing building is flanked by a porch which straddles the street, a unique structure which also houses a strange bell-tower with turrets and little belfries. Inside there are lovely stained glass windows.

The Musée des Beaux-Arts

Place de l'Église
☎ 05 62 66 68 10.
Open Mon.-Fri., 10am-noon and 3-6pm; Sat., 10am-noon and 3-6pm; open Sun. morning and public holidays July-Aug., 10am-noon.
Admission charge.

This little museum contains many fine works, including a superb collection of Italian primitive paintings as well as those by Flemish, Italian and

French old masters of the 16th, 17th and 18th C. The Mirande museum also has a beautiful collection of antique pottery and porcelain from the former potteries of Auch and Samadet.

American country music in Gascony

Information
☎ 05 62 66 68 10.
Admission charge.

For four days during the second week of July, medieval Mirande rocks to the rhythm of American country music. There are country music and camp western concerts, rodeos and a meet of American car enthusiasts and fans of the Harley Davidson. These events could hardly take place in a more incongruous setting!

Saint-Michel

8 miles (13 km) S of Mirande via the D939

La Ferme des Saules

☎ 05 62 66 58 78.
Open daily, 10am-noon and 2-6pm.

This farm is typical of Gascony, with its flock of geese raised in the open air on a hillside. Claudine and André Serres make wonderful farmhouse products in true family tradition. They won a silver medal, then a gold, at the Concours Général de Paris for their whole foie gras. You can buy foie gras

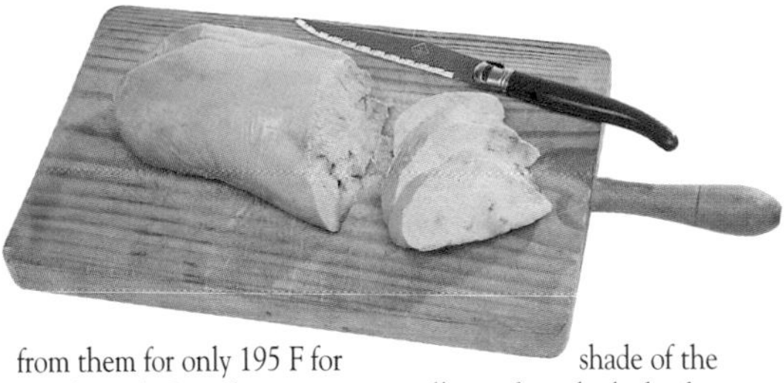

from them for only 195 F for 9 oz (250 g). Spend some time strolling on their land, in the shade of the willows after which the farm is named, sipping a delightful home-made cocktail which you will be offered.

Visit a *Ganaderia*
Jean-Louis Darré, Élevage du Cantau, 32300 Bars, (3 miles (5 km) from Mirande) ☎ 05 62 66 73 73. Open daily by appointment (minimum 20 0people).
Admission charge.
Jean-Louis Darré loves the excitement of bullfights and several years ago he decided to breed fighting bulls. Today, he has more than 100 head of cattle. His animals fight regularly in the bullrings of Aignan. You can visit the outdoor breeding-ground (preferably in a group, by arrangement) and even watch a *corrida*, because before ensuring the line of bulls continues, the future mothers must prove their bravura in the ring. The tour costs 30 F (and lasts about 2 hours) with refreshments. You can also eat the Spanish dish *paella* or a full Gascon meal at the farm (170 to 240 F).

Bassoues

9½ miles (15 km) NW of Mirande via the D137

The castle keep

Bassoues is a picturesque little village, with an unusual wooden market hall which entirely straddles the main street, and old half-timbered houses with decorative angle-irons. The main attraction is the castle keep, a building 143 ft (43 m) high, and a masterpiece of **military medieval architecture**, with machicolations and buttresses of very pure lines. Climb to the top for a view of the village and the Pyrenees and on your way back, see the exhibition about Gascon villages.

Berdoues

2½ miles (4 km) S of Mirande via the D939

Forêt de Berdoues

Hardly anything remains of the old Cistercian abbey, but Berdoues offers a charming escape into the shade of the green trees. The beautiful 1,235 acres (500 ha) *forêt domaniale* (government-owned public forest), crisscrossed with hiking trails and bridle paths covers the slopes of Astarac. They are ideal for hikers and mountain bikers.

Spotcheck
B3

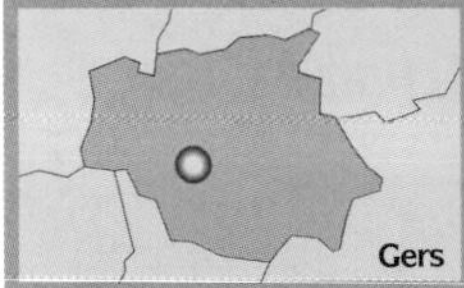

Things to do
- The *Ganaderia* fighting bulls
- Forêt de Berdoues
- Country music festival

Within easy reach

Marciac, p. 115
Auch, p. 118
Tarbes, p. 196

Tourist office
Mirande: ☎ 05 62 66 68 10

La Vallée de la Save
in the land of foie gras ...

The river Save has created a pretty valley between Isle-Jourdain and Samatan. The landscape is dotted with farmhouses, châteaux and chapels built of brick and pebbles, and the rolling hills are covered in fields of maize. The breeding and fattening of geese and ducks, who are fed on maize, is a tradition in Savès. This is the heart of foie gras country.

Samatan

Campan (½ a mile (1 km) from Samatan via the D39)

The Duplan cannery

☎ 05 62 62 31 33.

Open Mon.-Sat., 9am-noon and 2-7pm; Sun., 10am-noon and 5-7pm.

Bernard Duplan breeds geese and owns a small **cannery**. Depending on the time of year, you can witness the birth of goslings, help with feeding and the preparation of many house specialities, including his delicious whole goose foie gras (147 F for 7 oz (200 g), or duck foie gras (137 F for 7 oz (200 g)).

Foie gras markets

Samatan is the Mecca of foie gras! Every Monday at 10am, the biggest foie gras market in France attracts thousands of producers. Total sales can amount to 5 to 6 tons (4.9 to 5.9 tonnes)! On Sundays in winter, go to the *grasse matinée* at Gimont. This is the name of its foie gras market, which has a high reputation in the region. It is held in the old market-hall which straddles the road (retail sales).

Lombez

2 miles (3 km) SW of Samatan

The Sainte-Marie Cathedral

Open daily, 9am-6pm.
Free admission.

This cathedral is built in typical Toulouse style, despite the fact that it is in Gers. It is made of red brick and has buttresses and arches. It houses a masterpiece of the goldsmith's art, and a rather rare lead baptismal font. The octagonal brick belltower dominates a lovely urban landscape of old houses built of brick and plaster with wooden eaves and half-timbering.

L'Isle-Jourdain

12½ miles (20 km) NE of Samatan via the D634

Musée Européen d'Art Campanaire

Place de l'Hôtel-de-Ville
☎ 05 62 07 30 01.

Open daily except Tues., 15 June-15 Sept., 10am-noon and 2.30-6.30pm; out of season, 10am-noon and 2.30-5.30pm.
Admission charge.

This old, restored corn exchange houses an impressive collection of bells, handbells, carillons and rattles. More than 1,000 exhibits have been assembled from all over the world, some of which are more than 5,000 years old. The items include the monumental carillon of the Bastille, miraculously saved in 1789.

Bejouets gascons

Ferme d'En-Bladé
☎ 05 62 07 00 88.
Visits on Tues. by appointment; Wed. and Thurs., 2-5pm.
The *bejouet* is a part of Gascon folk art. It basically consists of a long wooden stick, decoratively carved and hung with bells, which was placed in the centre of the yoke of a horse's harness in order to prevent wear on the reins. Thanks to master craftsman Jacques Bernadet, *bejouets* have emerged from oblivion and he takes commissions for special designs to order (they cost between 500 F and 1,500 F).

Catonvielle

5 miles (8 km) of Isle-Jourdain via the D161

La ferme de l'Héritier

☎ 05 62 65 73 32.
Open every afternoon.
Martine and David Gauthé breed and fatten ducks on their farm, which are then processed into great delicacies: whole foie gras (112 F for 6 oz (180 g)), preserves, duck breast, *rillettes* and various other specialities, especially breast stuffed with foie gras (94 F for 1 lb 2 oz (500 g)). Take advantage of your visit to get advice on cooking and collect a few local recipes.

A CRUNCHY SPECIALITY

Croustad'Oc, Chemin d'Enducasse, Gimont
☎ 05 62 67 82 33.
Open Mon.-Thurs., 8.30am-noon and 1.30-5pm; Fri. until 4pm.
The Gascon *croustade* is deliciously light. It consists of multiple layers of flaky pastry interspersed with fruit and flavoured with Armagnac. To taste this traditional pastry,

arrange a visit to the Croustad'Oc (telephone the day before). They have a large choice of flavours, including apple, prune, bilberry, Morello cherry, and pear with chocolate ... (40 F for a small pie, 55 F for a medium-size one and 70 F for a large one).

Spotcheck
B3-C3

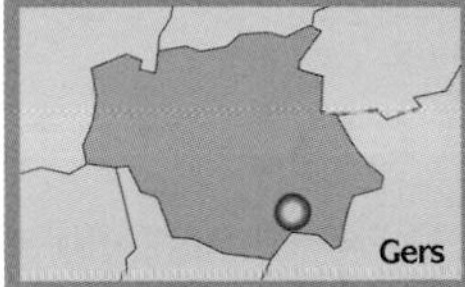

Things to do
- The Duplan cannery
- Gascon *béjouets*
- La Capelle leisure centre

Within easy reach
Toulouse, p. 170
Auch, p. 118

Tourist Office
Samatan: ☎ 05 62 62 55 40

Saramon

9½ miles (15 km) NW of Samatan via the D626

La Capelle leisure centre

☎ 05 62 65 40 19.
Open July-Aug., Mon.-Fri., noon-8pm; Sat., Sun. and public holidays, 11am-9pm.
Admission charge.
There are water chutes, pedalos, canoes and much more around this lake which is surrounded by a huge park. There is a 500 ft (150 m) long sandy beach, perfect for making sand castles or just relaxing in the sun.

From brick-red Albi to the banks of the Tarn

Albi is a town of brick and tiles, a magnificent city which looks as if it ought to be in Tuscany. Its famous cathedral and fortress, both built of brick (the latter containing works by the painter Toulouse-Lautrec) are an impressive display of power and beauty. Its old districts are a pleasure to wander through. Upstream of Albi, the Tarn has cut deep and sinuous meanders into the rugged countryside.

Albi

The city on foot

Visit Albi on foot along the ***sentiers du patrimoine***, four routes containing explanatory panels all of which leave from the Tourist Office (Place Sainte-Cécile, ☎ 05 63 49 48 80. Open daily, July-Aug., Mon.-Sat., 9am-7.30pm, Sun. 10.30am-12.30pm and 3-6pm; out of season, Mon.-Sat., 9am-noon and 2-6pm, Sun. 10.30-noon and 3.30-5.30pm). The Purple Route takes you through the streets of old Albi, the Gold Route crosses the restored parts of the old centre and the Azure and Pastel Routes lead you along the right bank of the river Tarn, through a very picturesque neighbourhood with lovely views over the water.

The Sainte-Cécile Cathedral

☎ 05 63 49 48 80.
Open daily, 15 June-Sept., 8.30am-7pm; out of season, 8.30-11.45am and 2-5.45pm.

The cathedral has been compared to a brick sailing vessel or a threatening dragon. At any event, it is a masterpiece of southern French Gothic art. Among other treasures, there is a remarkable painting of the Last Judgement, the most beautiful rood-screen in France, painted statues and the largest **Italian Renaissance fresco** in Europe. In summer, a 1-hour **son et lumière show** takes the audience back to the height of the Middle Ages (Thurs.-Sat., June-Sept., 10pm. Admission charge).

Toulouse-Lautrec: Le Salon de la Rue des Moulins (detail).

Musée Toulouse-Lautrec

Palais de la Berbie
Place Sainte-Cécile
☎ 05 63 49 48 70.
Open daily, June-Aug., 9am-6pm; Oct.-March, open daily except Tues. and public holidays, 9am-noon and 1-5pm; April-May and Sept.-Oct., open daily 10am-6pm. Audioguides available in 4 languages.
Admission charge.
The largest collection in the world of the works of Henri de Toulouse-Lautrec are housed in this massive brick fortress. The collection contains more than 1,000 paintings, drawings and lithographs, but the museum also has an excellent collection of contemporary art. The gardens offer a splendid view over the Tarn and its bridges.

The ice creations of Michel Thomaso Défos

12 Avenue du Général-de-Gaulle
☎ 05 63 54 15 59.
Open Tues.-Sat., 9am-noon and 2.30-8pm, Sun., 8am-12.30pm, closed Mon.
Thomaso Défos is an artist who creates amazing iced desserts. Among an array of original creations there are two that are particularly special; the **Puy-Saint-Georges**, a chestnut and walnut parfait (120 F for 2 lb 4 oz (1 kg)) and the **Lubéron**, a nougat-ice flavoured with lavender honey (140 F for 2 lb 4 oz (1 kg)).

A trip down the Tarn on a barge

For information
☎ 05 63 49 48 80.
Daily, 13 June-27 Sept.
A 35-minute barge trip down the Tarn to discover the most amazing monuments of Albigensian heritage, the history of the river and its role in industry, which lasted until the 19th C. and the coming of the railways.

Spotcheck

D2

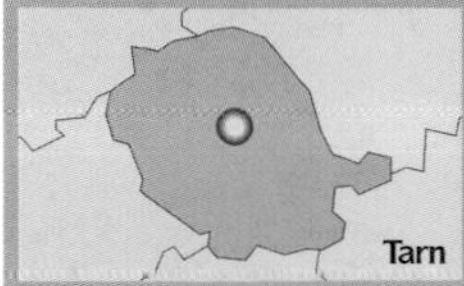

Things to do

- A trip down the Tarn on a barge
- Water sports at Aiguelèze
- A Glassblower's workshop
- Forêt de Sérénac

Within easy reach

Gaillac, p. 142
Cordes, p. 140

Tourist Office

Albi: ☎ 05 63 49 48 80

CHOCOLATE IN ALL ITS GUISES

Michel Belin, 4 Rue Docteur-Camboulives
☎ 05 63 54 18 46.
Open Tues.-Sun., 9am-noon and 2.30-7.15pm.
Michel Belin has been dubbed the greatest chocolate chef in France and he creates original flavours, combining cocoa beans with endive, lime, orange and sweet spices. The *Marco Polo* is a cake of dark chocolate flavoured with ginger and figs (36 F for 3½ oz (100 g)). Another smaller creation he calls *Mélissa,* a chocolate truffle flavoured with liquorice (35 F for 3½ oz (100 g)).

Albi foie gras

29 Rue Mariès
☎ 05 63 38 21 33.
Open daily except Sun. and Mon. morning, 9am-noon and 2-7pm.

The **Maison Lascroux** has been delighting food-lovers for three generations with its impressive catalogue of regional foods. The whole foie gras (400 F for 2 lb 4 oz (1 kg) of semi-cooked foie), cassoulet (105 F for a four-portion jar), *confits*, pâtés and preserves are excellent. Those who are curious can also visit the cannery where these specialities are made (Route de Carmaux. Open Mon.-Fri., 8am-noon and 2-6pm).

Rivières

9½ miles (15 km) W of Albi, between Gaillac and Marsac-sur-Tarn

❀ Water sports

Planète Obade, Aigueléze
☎ 05 63 41 50 50.
Open daily, July-Aug.
Admission charge.

This 96.4 acre (39 ha) leisure centre on the banks of the Tarn has a **swimming pool** (open 10am-8pm), **children's play area** and a **marina** (11am-1pm and 2-7pm). Windsurfing boards (70 F for half a day), kayaks (40 F/h) and pedalos (70 F/h) are available for hire for a trip on the lake. Those who prefer terra firma will be able to rent mountain bikes, or enjoy a round of golf or a game of tennis. Refreshments are also available.

Saint-Juéry

3¾ miles (6 km) E of Albi via the D77

Kayaking down the Tarn

Les Avalats, Chemin de la Plage
☎ 05 63 45 19 49.
Open daily, July-Aug., 9am-6pm; May, June and Sept., weekends only.
Admission charge.

The Lo Capial centre organises **canoeing lessons** (beginners and intermediate). The principle is simple. You can choose between a 6¼ mile (10 km) trip down the Tarn (lasting for half a day) or a one-day 11¼ mile (18 km) excursion (120 F/pers.; 1,000 F/10 pers.). Real enthusiasts can go the whole hog and do the two-day 25 mile (40 km) trip which includes an overnight stop, camping along the route. The cost includes qualified training, supervision and all the equipment needed for the trip.

❀ Le Saut-du-Tarn

Espace Culturel du Saut-du-Tarn

☎ 05 63 45 91 01.
Open daily, May-Oct., 2-7pm; out of season, Mon., Thurs. and Sun., 2-6pm.
Admission charge.

For nearly a century, there have been metalworking factories at this site which were able to harness the power of the water to produce electricity. **The Musée du Saut-du-Tarn** is installed in a former power station built in 1898, which is classified as a historic monument. Animated models explain the history of the place, show the old trades and recreate the major floodings of the Tarn. Opposite,

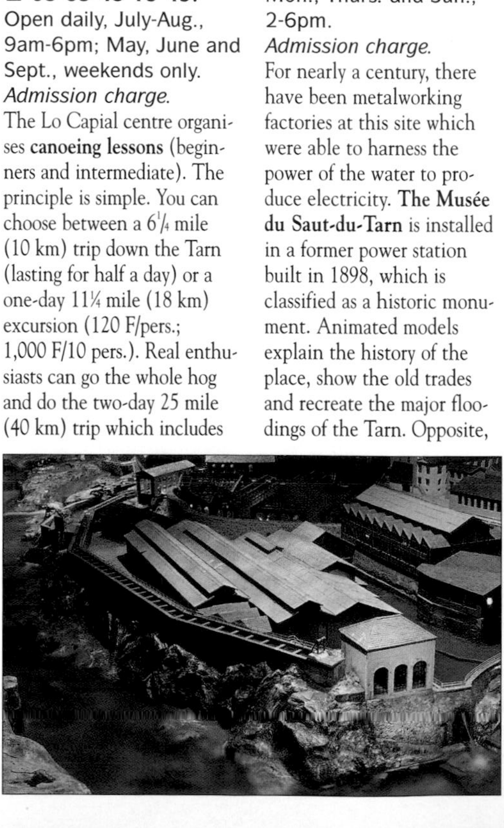

at the site of a waterfall which has been used for industrial purposes since the Middle Ages, **the Saut-du-Sabo power station** is the most recent hydroelectric plant in the region (visits daily, June-Oct., 10am-7pm. Admission charge.)

The magic of glass

Les Avalats
☎ 05 63 45 39 39.
Open daily, 10am-noon and 2-6pm; demonstrations out of season by appointment.
Philippe Merloz uses a stick, a pipe and enamelling to combine glass with stone or metal to make unique creations. He produces jewellery, vases and perfume flasks, which you can see when you visit the display which is open daily. If you want to visit the glassblower's workshop for a demonstration, you are advised to phone in advance.

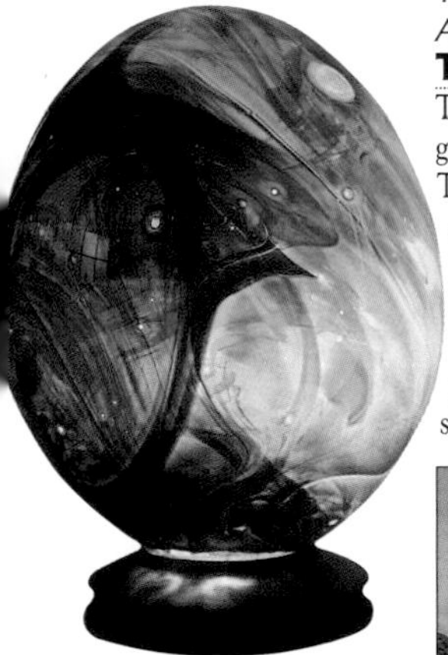

Sérénac

9 miles (15 km) NE of Albi via the D100

Forêt de Sérénac

☎ 05 63 56 43 52.
This lovely 741 acre (300 ha) forest, planted with conifers and oaks, is criss-crossed with signposted footpaths and mountain bike trails. You can also ride through its avenues in a carriage on Thursdays and Sundays (June-Sept., from 2.30pm). A half-hour trip through the woods costs 20 F/adult and 15 F/child.

At the farm next to the forest leisure centre, you can order a home-made picnic to eat under the trees (50 F/pers., including the ride in a carriage).

Ambialet

13¾ miles (22 km) E of Albi via the D77

The Tarn Loop

The Boucle d'Ambialet is a geographical curiosity. The Tarn appears to be turning and biting its own tail! It is the best known and most spectacular meander of this winding river and forms a peninsula linked by a narrow strip of land to the shore.

HONEY AND VINEGAR

Apis Vinaegria,
La Borde, Trébas
(22½ miles (36 km) E of Albi via the D77)
☎ 05 63 55 91 42.
Open daily, July-Aug., 10am-7pm; guided visits by appointment; out of season by appointment. Free admission.
Honey and excellent gingerbread is on sale here, but the Apis Vinaegria also makes an old-style honey vinegar which is aged in oak barrels. It is a very delicately scented vinegar when plain (23 F for 18 fl oz (½ l) and is also sold in eleven flavours, raspberry, wild thyme, marjoram, ginger, etc.; 18 F for 9 fl oz (¼ l). It makes a perfect fat-free salad dressing.

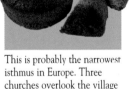

This is probably the narrowest isthmus in Europe. Three churches overlook the village of Ambialet; one has a chapel containing painted wooden carved figures.

Cordes-sur-Ciel

a leap into the blue

Cordes is in a spectacular location, on an isolated hilltop, and seems to be reaching towards the sky. This town of arches has managed to retain its lovely Gothic houses, cobbled streets and picturesque shops. Lingering in this fortified town is a delight. However, it is one that is best sampled out of season.

A medieval walk

Walk up the **Grande-Rue** from the Ville Basse. After the **Porte de l'Horloge** (clock gate) and the **Escalier du Pater Noster** (a staircase with as many steps as the Lord's Prayer in Latin has words), there is a row of sandstone houses. Their frontages are decorated with imaginary creatures, amusing hunting scenes and troubadours. The best are the **Maison Prunet, Maison du Grand Écuyer, Maison du Grand Fauconnier** and the **Maison du Grand Veneur**.

❀ Museums à la carte

The **Musée de l'Art du Sucre** (Place de la Bride, ☎ 05 63 56 02 40. Open daily, 10am-noon and 2.30-6pm; closed Jan., admission charge) is a sugar art museum which displays some amazing creations by confectioners of the Yves Thuriès school. There are horses, carnivorous flowers, birds of prey and pharaohs all made from sugar! Cordes also has a lovely collection of **old musical instruments (L'Art du Luthier,** Rue Saint-Michel, ☎ 05 63 56 13 39. Open daily, July-Aug., 3-6pm; May-June and Sept., weekends and public holidays 3-6pm. Admission charge). The **Musée Charles-Portal** tells the story of Cordes (☎ 05 63 56 00 40. Open daily, July-Aug., 11am-noon and 3-6pm; out of season, Sun. and public holidays, 3-6pm; closed Nov.-March).

❀ Le Jardin des Paradis

Place du Théron
☎ 05 63 56 29 77.
Open daily, 21 June-18 Oct., 10am-7pm.
Admission charge guided tour by appointment).

A mosaic of flowers arranged in terraces, an unusual kitchen garden, a museum of precious objects brought back from the Orient and a lily pond to cool the air – these are some of the elements that make up the Paradis de Cordes. The garden changes every year, depending on the whim of its creators.

Fêtes du Grand Fauconnier

☎ 05 63 56 00 52.
Mid-July.
Admission charge.
For three days, acrobats and knights invade the walled town. There are medieval games, tournaments, a wine and local food fair and a large parade of people dressed in period costume. Free admission if you are dressed as a dashing knight or a fair and gracious lady!

Salles-sur-Cérou

5½ miles (9 km) NE of Cordes via the D91

The Bellevue animal farm

☎ 05 63 76 11 77.
Open daily from 10am.
Admission charge.
If you have never heard of the rabbit-ram or the four-horned sheep, visit the Bellevue farm. It has a stock of 1,500 amazingly rare breeds. You can picnic there or, if you make advance reservations, you will be offered a delicious meal including spit-roast pork (booking only; 150 F a day

with a grilled pork lunch, guided tour and access to the swimming pool). You can also buy duck or quail specialities from the farm (85 F a can for a two-person serving). After watching newborn chicks being hatched, the children can enjoy a swim in the pool.

Vindrac

2 miles (3 km) W from Cordes via the D600

❀ Musée de l'Outil et des Métiers Anciens

☎ 05 63 56 05 77.
Open daily, July-Aug., 10am-7pm; out of season, closed on Wed. and Dec.-Feb.
Admission charge.
Take a step back in time in this museum of old trades and occupations, including the poacher, harness-maker, cooper and laundry-maid. This is a huge collection (more than 5,000 tools!), where you will be able to see what the nail-maker's wheel looked like or the terrifying pincers wielded by the tooth-puller! If you telephone before coming, the owner will prepare a snack for you or feed you with mouthwatering crêpes (from 29 F per person).

Spotcheck
D2

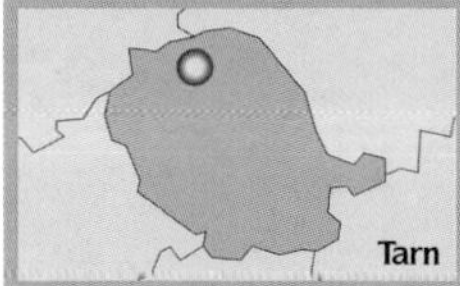

Things to do
- Jardin du Paradis
- Fête du Grand Fauconnier

With children
- Bellevue animal farm

Within easy reach

Albi, p. 136
Gaillac, p. 142
Castelnau-de-Montmiral, p. 150

Tourist Office

Cordes-sur-Ciel:
☎ 05 63 56 00 52
☎ 05 63 56 14 11 (summer)

Marie Costes' Ceramics

Frausseilles (towards Vaillard)
☎ 05 63 56 19 28.
Open daily except Fri. morning, 9am-noon, 2-7pm.
Marie Costes loves rust and autumnal colours as well as cobalt blue. She covers her pottery with thick glazes, smooth washes and grainy textures. Her ceramics are inspired by ancient mouldings and more contemporary lines. There are everyday pots and teapots (from 50 F), as well as superb plant pots decorated with watercolours.

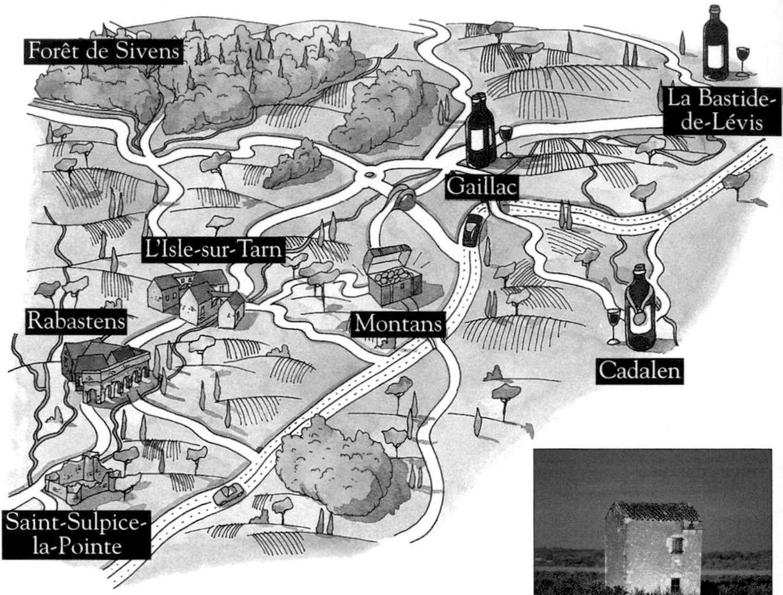

The Gaillac area and its wines

The oldest vineyards in France stretch as far as the eye can see on both sides of the Tarn, on terraces and slopes, interspersed with cypress trees, umbrella pines and cedars. Against this green canvas, the pink roofs of the three local towns, which are Tuscan in appearance, stand out sharply. There is Gaillac, dominated by its powerful abbey, Rabastens behind its city walls and Lisle-sur-Tarn with its curious *pountets*.

Gaillac

A historic market

Signs dotted through the town will show you the history of Gaillac through its ancient buildings. It all began with the foundation of a Benedictine monastery in 819. The **Church of Saint-Michel** was built in the 10th C. and was completely finished by the 13th C. On your way, stop at the **Musée d'Histoire Naturelle**, which has an exceptional collection of fossilised birds and insects (2 Place Philadelphe-Thomas, ☎ 05 63 57 36 31. Open daily except Tues., 15 June-15 Sept., 10am-noon and 2-6pm; out of season, closed Mon.-Thurs.). From the tower

of the **Hôtel Pierre-de-Brens**, an historic mansion, admire the pink roofs of Gaillac as they stand out against the green of the grapevines, then visit the old districts of Portanelle by the riverbank.

Parc de Foucaud

Avenue Dom-Vayssette.
Same opening hours as the Musée d'Histoire Naturelle.
Free admission.
This beautiful park is laid out with terraced formal gardens in the French style, with fountains, pavilions, ornamental pools and ramps

leading down to the Tarn. The Château de Foucaud, built in the 17th C., contains the **Musée des Beaux-Arts,** which is dedicated mainly to French artists of the 19th C., many of whom were local painters.

A model train

Association Train Miniature Gaillacois
3283 Chemin Toulzé, Les Houms
☎ 05 63 41 00 93.
Open daily, July-Aug., 2-6pm; out of season, weekends and public holidays only.
Admission charge.
This is one of the great French model rail and train networks, with more than 3,330 ft (1,000 m) of track and 190 sets of points. The model covers 2,153 sq ft (200 sq m) and can handle the movements of 50 locomotives and 200 wagons, all controlled from an impressive luminous console. For children aged from seven to 77!

The wine route

The Gaillac district has more than 100 vineyards. The **Fédération des Caves Particulières,** which like the Maison du Vin is located in the vaulted rooms of the Saint-Michel Abbey (☎ 05 63 57 53 77 or Tourist Office ☎ 05 63 57 14 65. Open daily, 10am-noon and 2-6pm), offers a wonderful vineyard tour of the Gaillac region.

THE GAILLAC WINE FESTIVAL

☎ 05 63 57 15 40. Free admission. The Gaillac wine festival, held each second weekend in August, is a huge success. Fifteen thousand visitors crowd around the 50 stands of local wine-makers which have been set up in the gardens of the Parc de Foucaud. There are shows and concerts all day long, culminating in a gargantuan feast and a firework display. But the main attraction is always the wine-tasting, sampling the vintages from the wines of Gaillac and elsewhere in the region.

Thirty-one vine-growers will show you their wine cellars. If you buy six bottles, you will be given a pass which will give you the right to **reductions** or **free admission** to some museums, châteaux or other attractions such as barge trips on the Tarn, shows, etc.

Spotcheck
D2

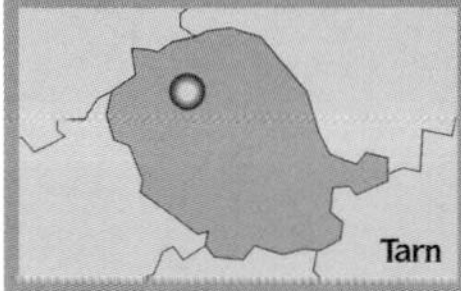

Things to do
- The Gaillac model train
- Tasting the wines of Gaillac

With children
- Forêt de Sivens
- The labyrinth of Castela

Within easy reach
Albi, p. 136
Cordes, p. 140
Lavaur and Lauragais, p. 146

Tourist Office
Gaillac: ☎ 05 63 57 14 65

Forêt de Sivens

7½ miles (12 km) W of Gaillac via the D999
This 1,483 acres (600 ha) of mixed woods has **play areas** for children, **picnic areas** and a network of **signposted footpaths.** So there's something here for young and old alike. For nature-lovers and those who are keen on hiking, the **Maison Forestière de la Jass** (☎ 05 63 33 10 23) organises nature exhibitions and offers guided walks through the forest to discover the local flora and fauna (9.30am-noon. By prior arrangement. 30 F per person).

Montans

2 miles (3 km)
S of Gaillac

❀ Pottery and gold coins

Archéosite de Montans,
Avenue Élie-Rossignol
☎ 05 63 57 59 16.
Open daily, June-Sept., 10am-noon and 2-6pm; weekends, public holidays and school holidays except Christmas, 2-6pm.
Admission charge.

The 40 gold coins exhibited here are copies, but the treasure found at Montans is real. Those with some knowledge of archaeology will appreciate the value of the extremely rare **Gaulish pottery** excavated from this important Gallo-Roman town. There are reconstructions of a Roman street with shops, the interior of a potter's workshop and a delightful villa.

Labastide-de-Lévis

6¼ miles (10 km) E of Gaillac via the RN88

The cooperative cellar

☎ 05 63 53 73 73.
Open daily except Sun., 9am-noon and 2-6pm.
Admission charge.

The guided tour of this cellar (July-Aug., daily except Sat. at 10am and 4pm; from Sept. to June, by arrangement) shows the stages of vinification, from harvesting to bottling. To appreciate the end result, there is nothing better than a little sampling of the Gaillac wines. If you would like to buy a few bottles, among those recommended are a light, fruity Prestige red (19.60 F a bottle) and a Labastidié (35.60 F a bottle).

A very left bank wine-maker

Alain Rotier, Le Petit Nareye, Cadalen (6¼ miles (10 km) SE of Gaillac)
☎ 05 63 41 75 14.
Open daily except Sun., 8am-noon and 2-7pm.
He is the leading light of the New Wave. This wine-maker on the left bank of the Tarn uses humus for his wines rather than fertiliser and ploughs his fields in preference using weed-killer. To reduce yields and concentrate the sugars, he thins out his vines by hand. The result is that his red wines are delicate and powerful and his whites sweet or dry with the scent of vanilla and toast. They win gold medals every year! You can enjoy a visit to Alain Rotier's estate and cellar, and he will be happy to let you taste his wines. If you like the wines, you are free to buy them (42 F for a sweet Gravel, 44 F for a red Renaissance).

Lisle-sur-Tarn

5½ miles (9 km) SW of Gaillac via the RN88

The *bastide* with *pountets*

The central square of this *bastide* (fortified town) is one of the largest arcaded central

Interior of the Château de Saint-Géry in Rabastens

squares in the region. But the true glory of Lisle-sur-Tarn are the strange ***pountets***: bridges lined with dwellings which span the houses above street level. There is one with a single arch which spans the Tarn and offers a lovely view of the terraced gardens of the town's mansions.

Rabastens

5 miles (8 km) SW of Lisle-sur-Tarn via the RN88

The Church of Notre-Dame-du-Bourg

Rabastens is a lovely town of brick-built houses which is enjoyable for its walks, ancient moats and massive city walls which overlook the Tarn. The highlight is the church of Notre-Dame-du-Bourg. It is impossible to miss because of its massive, fortified belltower. Inside, there are beautiful 14th C. paintings illustrating scenes from the Bible and depicting the exploits of the heroes of the Crusades. The priory is also worth visiting.

❀ Musée du Pays Rabastinois

2 Rue Amédée-de-Clausade
☎ 05 63 40 65 65.
Open daily except Sun. morning and Mon., Feb.-15 Dec., 10am-noon and 3-6pm.
Admission charge.

This museum in a 17th C. mansion contains a wonderful collection, including the **magnificently embroidered gowns created by the master embroiderer René Bégué.** You can see models of the wedding dress worn by the former Empress of Iran, Farah Diba, created by Dior in 1959. Other items not to be missed include work by the master carpenter Roger Bellegarde, a magnificent Gallo-Roman mosaic, ceramics by Leonardi, a friend of Picasso, or the wonderful little religious paintings dating from between the 14th and 18th C.

The Rabastens bookshop

Librairie Étant Donné, 4 Rue des Cordeliers
☎ 05 63 33 77 59.
Open Wed.-Sat., 2-7pm.

This attractive house is in fact an antiquarian bookshop. Lovers of ancient, rare or out-of-print books can stock up here, or simply enjoy a fascinating browse amongst the shelves.

Saint-Sulpice

5 miles (8 km) SW of Rabastens via the RN88

The labyrinth of Castela

☎ 05 63 41 89 50.
Open daily, July-Aug., 3-7pm; out of season, daily except Mon., 2-7pm.
Admission charge.

The Château of Castela has remained a ruin since the Wars of Religion, but its 9th C. underground tunnels are well preserved. The maze is 474 ft (142 m) long and is the **largest labyrinth in Tarn.** The four rooms carved into the rock were used as shelters, as well as secret hide outs used by forgers and for making gunpowder.

A visit to Lauragais
the land of plenty

The plain of Lauragais is not in Aquitaine nor is it in Languedoc. It has long lines of rolling hills, dotted with dovecotes and windmills, cedars and cypress trees. In the times of the Renaissance, this corner of the South West experienced incredible prosperity with the cultivation of woad. Today, the land of plenty is still peaceful and enticing, but owes its wealth to wheat and sunflowers, pink garlic and fattened geese.

Lavaur

The Jacquemart in the cathedral

Open daily, 8am-noon and 2-6pm.
Free admission.

The Jacquemart is an automaton who rings in the hours by hitting a bell with an axe. It is said that a prisoner was incarcerated in the tower and forced to sound the hours in order to show he was still there. To make his escape, he made this wooden figure in order to deceive his jailers and ran away with a local beauty. The cathedral of Saint-Alain, a brick fortress in the centre of a formal garden, has two other attractions, the **paintings in the choir** and the **painted organ.**

Giroussens

6¼ miles (10 km) N of Lavaur via the D87

The potters in the square

The pretty village of Giroussens was once an important pottery centre. Several years ago it revived the old tradition. Once again, there is a **potter's workshop** in the main square (Terre et Terres, ☎ 05 63 56 64 97) and on the last weekend in April, there is an **exhibition** of glazed earthenware and a large and well-known pottery market in the main square.

Jardins des Martels

☎ 05 63 41 61 42.
Open from March to the first frost, 10am-7pm.
Admission charge.

This lovely English-style landscaped garden contains no fewer than 2,500 species of flowers. The avenues wind between ornamental ponds edged with irises, rose-bushes, lotuses and water-lilies, and lead you to the

glasshouse full of exotic plants and the little zoo. There are chamois, goats and dwarf pigs to amuse young children.

Saint-Lieux-lès-Lavaur

1¼ miles (2 km) W of Giroussens

The steam trains of the Tarn

Information

☎ 05 61 47 44 52.

Open weekends and Mon., 14 July-Aug., 2.30-6.30pm; out of season, Sun. and public holidays. Closed Nov.-March.

Admission charge.

The steam train which leaves from Saint-Lieux station, will take you on a short 4½ mile (7 km) (50 min.) train ride across the Agout over an impressive viaduct and through a forest, before reaching the Jardin des Martels. Several of the steam locomotives date from World War I and are classified as historic monuments.

Graulhet

17 miles (27 km) NE of Lavaur via the D87, and the D631

La Maison des Métiers du Cuir

33 Rue Saint-Jean

☎ 05 63 42 16 04.

Open daily, July-15 Sept., 10-6.30pm; May, June, and 15 Sept.-15 Oct., 2-6pm.

Admission charge.

Spotcheck

D2-D3

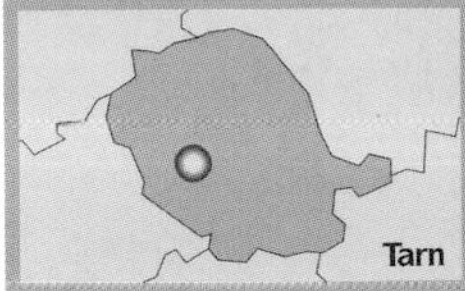

Things to do

- The potters of Giroussens
- Jardins des Martels

With children

- A ride on a steam train
- The Cambournet bird sanctuary

Within easy reach

Toulouse, p. 170
Albi, p. 136

Tourist Office

Graulhet: ☎ 05 63 34 75 09
Lautrec: ☎ 05 63 75 31 40
Revel: ☎ 05 61 83 50 06

THE WIND OF AUTAN

The Lauragais is a windswept area. The wicked wind of Autan, which whips up from the south-east, is harsh and dry and sweeps over the plain in summer. It is unpredictable and fickle. It may be accompanied by menacing clouds or suddenly sweep out of a clear sky. It is said to have the same effect on some people as the full moon – making them go mad!

Graulhet is famous in France for its rugby players, but also for its leather-dressers. Leather factories and skilled leather-workers have made the place famous. The Maison des Métiers du Cuir allows you to learn more about this industry by visiting a workshop, with a live demonstration of some of the techniques involved and a description of the various stages of leather-working. You can also buy a range of leather goods from their shop.

Lombers

12 miles (19 km) E of Graulhet via the D631

The pigeons of Mont-Royal

Les Goutines

☎ **05 63 45 52 33.**

Open daily except Tues., 10am-7pm.

Admission charge.

Pigeon is a dish which is a speciality of the département of Tarn, as is the breeding of grain-fed pigeons for the table. The breeders will take you to see their pigeon-lofts where 2,500 breeding pairs live. You can leave with a range of home-made goodies, including pigeon pâté (25 F for 7 oz (190 g)), potted wings and thighs (90 F for 1 lb 4 oz (540 g)), pigeon stuffed with foie gras (120 F for a 1lb 9oz (700 g) can) and oven-ready pigeon (90 F for 2lb 4oz (1 kg)). Ask for the breeders' special recipes.

Lautrec

9½ miles (15 km) SE of Graulhet via the D83

Moulin de la Salette

☎ **05 63 75 31 40.**

Open daily, July-Aug., 3-7pm; out of season, Sun. and public holidays, 3-6pm.

Admission charge.

Since it is so windy, Lauragais was once covered with windmills. The Salette windmill at Lautrec is still in working order and its sails turn again every year to celebrate the **Fête du Pain** (15 Aug.). During the bread festival, flour is made in the traditional way, and all the locals help with the baking and in

The tiled roofs of the village of Lautrec

the mill. There is a lovely view from the nature trail to the top of the hill and the **village of Lautrec** is delightful. In fact, it is known as one of the prettiest villages in France!

Saint-Paul-Cap-de-Joux

13.1 miles (21 km) S of Graulhet via the D84

Château de Magrin

☎ **05 63 70 63 82.**

Open Sun. and public holidays, Apr.-Nov. 10.30am-noon (every day 10.30-noon, 3-6pm in July-Aug.).

Admission charge.

This museum, in the heart of the land of plenty, retells the story of woad through an exhibition dedicated to the history of the Albi district (daily, July-Aug.). The Château de Magrin also contains a unique woad drier and a genuine woad grinder.

Cambounet-sur-le-Sor

3 miles (5 km) E of Puylaurens via the D126

Bird sanctuary

☎ **05 63 35 65 07.**

Open daily.

Free admission.

This is one of the largest nature reserves in the Midi-Pyrénées. Almost every species of heron that nests in France can be found here, as well as coots, kingfishers, egrets, teal and ducks.

THE PINK GARLIC OF LAUTREC

This mild, pink garlic has been given a red label for its flavour and exceptional keeping qualities. The garlic is grown in 18 districts and the crop of about 4,000 tonnes (3,937 tons) is harvested in early summer. The heads are swollen with moisture and are dried at first then braided into bunches. You will find them in the market at Lautrec, every Friday from July to September. The first Friday in August is dedicated to the garlic festival, with art competitions and other events. The whole village enjoys garlic soup, a relation of the garlicky *tourin gascon*, another garlic-flavoured soup-stew. (Information at the Tourist Office, ☎ 05 63 75 31 40.)

On a walk between the ponds, two wooden hides make it possible to watch the birds without disturbing them.

Revel

8¾ miles (14 km) S of Puylaurens via the D84

A medieval bastide

This ancient *bastide* (walled town) has retained its lovely 14th C. **wooden market hall.** There are medieval houses with façades decorated with carvings. Every Saturday, one of the best markets in the whole district is held in the lovely **central square**.

Elegant furniture

Revel is also the capital of hand-made furniture and many master craftsmen have grouped together in the **Espace Art et Meuble** to be able to display their wares and sell them (Chemin de Beauséjour, ☎ 05 61 83 56 58. Open daily except Sun. and Mon. morning, 10am-noon and 2-6.30pm.). At the **Conservatoire des Métiers du Bois** (13 Rue Jean-Moulin, ☎ 05 61 27 65 50. Open Tues.-Sun. except Fri. morning and Sun. morning, 10am-noon and 2-6pm), you will learn the history of timber, from plantation to its conversion into elegant furniture or paper pulp.

Saint-Félix-de-Lauragais

9½ miles (15 km) W of Revel via the D622

Fête de la Cocagne

Each year at Easter (Sun. and Mon.), St.-Félix revives the golden age of Lauragais. The lovely central square, with its ancient market-hall complete with tower, hosts an old-fashioned fair, with people in period costume, jugglers and traditional games. A maypole is set up and you can win local produce by dislodging one of the famous *cocagnes*, the little balls of woad which made the fortune of the Toulouse region. (Information at the Tourist Office, ☎ 05 62 18 96 99. Open July-Oct., 10am-12.30pm and 2-7pm. Admission charge.)

Durfort

3 miles (5 km) E of Revel via the D44

The copper museum

43 Rue des Martineurs
☎ 05 63 74 22 77.
Open July-Aug., daily except Tues., 3-7pm June-Sept., Mon., Thurs., Fri. and weekends 2-6pm.

Durfort has lived off copper since the 14th C. There is plenty of evidence in the street names, shops, and a thousand and one other details in the village. You can learn all there is to know about copper and its alloys at the **Musée du Cuivre** (copper museum), before visiting **Pierre Vergne coppersmith's** workshop (Le Plo, ☎ 05 63 74 10 52. Free visits daily except weekends, 8am-noon and 2-6pm by arrangement), who has a fine 15th C. *martinet*, a complex mechanism of paddle wheels used for crushing old copper before it is resmelted. In the shop you can buy copper pots (from 80 F), jam-making pans (from 300 F) and many other copper articles which are made on the premises.

The hilltop *bastides* of la Vallée de la Vère

Between the magnificent Forêt de la Grésigne and the vines of the Gaillac district, the *bastides* of the Albi district follow a line along the narrow valley of the Vère, then above the gorge of the Aveyron. Puycelci, Penne, Castelnau-de-Montmiral are all villages built of white limestone.

Puycelci

Forêt de la Grésigne

This is the largest oak forest in southern France, covering 8,896 acres (3,600 ha). The GR46 highway runs beside it which makes it easy to get to for hikers. In the days of Colbert (17th C.), it was surrounded by a wall and its timbers were reserved for Louis XIV's navy and for glassmakers. There are farms and chapels in the forest clearings, which can be reached by mountain bike. These can be hired from Les Aventuriers des Bastides Tarnaises, Puycelsi, ☎ 05 63 33 20 97 (70 F for half a day, 100 F for a full day).

The village of Puycelci

This village overlooks the Vère from a rocky peak. With its ramparts, terraced gardens and waterfalls over the Audoulou, it has much to recommend it. To discover all its attractions follow the signposted **sentier du Patrimoine,** marked in yellow and green, which links Puycelci to the Massif de Montoulieu, in the Forêt de Grésigne. You can choose from six routes lasting between 1 and 5 hours. Try the longest path (7½ miles (12 km)). (Information at the Tourist Office, ☎ 05 63 33 19 25.)

The conservation orchard

☎ **05 63 33 19 41.**
Open Wed.-Sat., 15 June-12 Sept. 10am-noon and 2-4pm. Guided tour from 4pm to 5.30pm.
Free admission.

No fewer than 900 varieties of fruit trees and vines are cultivated here. But the trees are not exhibits. They produce an annual 20 tonnes (19.68 tons) of apples, pears, plums, cherries and apricots. After the guided tour (daily at 4pm), buy fruit in season or apple, pear or grape juice (18 F for 1½ pt (1 l) at the farm attached to the orchard, to taste forgotten flavours.

Castelnau-de-Montmiral

8 miles (13 km) SE of Puycelci via the D664

Stonework and half-timbering

Castelnau has a lovely arcaded central square surrounded by medieval streets in which stone houses alternate with half-timbered buildings. The church contains a beautiful **byzantine**

cross encrusted with 310 precious stones (open daily, July-Aug, 10am-noon and 3-7pm; out of season, 2.30-6pm). On 15 August, there is a **honey and local produce fair** in the square.

Vère-Grésigne watersports centre

1¼ miles (2 km) from Castelnau-de-Montmiral by the D964

☎ **05 63 33 16 00.**

Open, July-Aug., 10.30am-8pm; April-June and Sept.-Oct., Sun. afternoon.

On this 17 acre (7 ha) lake there are all kinds of water sports, including supervised **swimming** (8 to 12 F/pers.), **fishing** and **tennis** (12 F/h per pers.). Equipment hire (2-8pm): **canoe** (35 F/h), **kayak** (25 F/h) and **pedalo** (30 F for half an hour). There are picnic areas and a children's play area (free admission).

VAOUR, CAPITAL OF FRENCH HUMOUR ...

Anyone passing through Vaour in winter would find it hard to believe that this little *bastide* could accommodate some 12,000 visitors in early August, which has been the case for more than 10 years. The success is due to the high calibre of the acts – comedians, clowns, mime artists and puppeteers – who come here every year. Although the International Burlesque Festival (☎ 05 63 56 36 87, *admission charge*) has acquired national renown, the atmosphere still remains warm and friendly.

Penne-du-Tarn

20 miles (19 km) N of Puycelci via the D964

The vertigo citadel

This old village is built on a rocky spur and its château overlooks a sheer drop. It is thus one of the most remarkable sights in the Valley of the Vère. The houses have heavy wooden eaves and massive old doors. To see the **magnificent views over the gorge of the Aveyron**, take the corniche road towards Saint-Antonin-Noble-Val.

Monsieur Sorin's goats

Ferme de Valeyres

☎ **05 63 33 11 87.**

Open daily, 10am-6pm.

Free admission.

Monsieur Sorin loves to show people his herd of cuddly angora goats and explain how mohair is made. You can buy a selection of knitting wool at the farm (from 32 F a skein). Alternatively, there are sweaters, scarves and gloves on sale, as well as blankets and woven shawls (from 120 F), cardigans and knitted gloves

(90 F a pair). You will get a warm welcome and if you let Monsieur Sorin know you are coming, he may let you taste his home-made goat pâté.

Spotcheck

D2

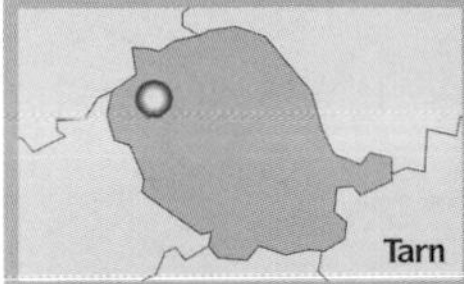

Things to do

- Forêt de la Grésigne
- Conservation orchard of Puycelci
- Vère-Grésigne leisure centre
- The gorge of the Aveyron

Within easy reach

Gaillac 15 miles (24 km) SE, p. 142
Montauban 17 miles (27 km) W, p. 164
Cordes-sur-Ciel 17 miles (27 km) E, p. 140

Tourist Office

Puycelci: ☎ 05 63 33 19 25
Castelnau-de-Montmiral: ☎ 05 63 33 15 11
Penne-du-Tarn: ☎ 05 63 56 36 68

Castelsarrasin

a flower garden amid orchards

The fertile plain of the Garonne is a fruit-lover's paradise. Plums, cherries, nectarines, apples, peaches and grapes ... 80% of the fruit of the Midi-Pyrénées is grown here. Castelsarrasin, which stands amidst these vast orchards, peacefully cultivates its brightly-coloured gardens and wins the annual Concours des Villes Fleuries (competition for the town with the loveliest flowers).

The Church of Saint-Sauveur

Place Saint-Sauveur
☎ 05 63 32 75 00.
Open daily, 8am-6pm (except during services).

The church is an early example of **southern Gothic**, and the interior is a baroque profusion of cherubim, musician angels, sirens, fruit and flowers. All these items comes from the former Abbaye de Belleperche. The most impressive sculpture is a winged genie carved over a massive wooden door. The prize for originality goes to a prie-dieu decorated with a unicorn resting on the lap of a veiled Virgin.

Canal du Midi

At the end of the Rue de la République.

The canal, which runs parallel to the Garonne in this section, is a beautiful place for a walk. Walk along its towpaths or take a bicycle ride down to the **Moissac lock** (2½ miles (4 km)) and visit the **bridge-canal**, an amazing feat of engineering which carries the canal over the river Tarn.

The market

Thurs. morning.

This regular, lively market is an absolute must for sightseers. In summer it is full of all the fruits of the valley of the Garonne. From Nov. to March, a large **foie gras market** brings all the producers together in the market hall in the Place Occitane. This is where all the local news and gossip is exchanged and you can learn the Occitan language (a romantic dialect spoken in southern parts of France). *Ba pla?*

Labastide-du-Temple

7 miles (11 km) NE of Castelsarrasin via the D45

Domaine de Gazania

☎ 05 63 31 63 25.
Open daily, 9am-noon

and 2-7pm (5pm out of season); Sun. by appointment.

Next to this vineyard there is a huge greenhouse, containing flowers, pot-plants, tomato and melon seedlings and salad greens. The main attraction is the **tropical greenhouse** (*admission charge*). A maze of aquatic and exotic plants, above which hang cages full of brightly coloured birds.

THE WINES OF LA VILLE-DIEU

Cave Coopérative de la Ville-Dieu-du-Temple
☎ 05 63 31 60 05.
Open daily 8am-noon and 2-5pm, except Mon. morning, Sat. afternoon, .

This little vineyard just outside Castelsarrasin produces velvety red wines with an agreeable bouquet, which marry happily with *cassoulet*, game stew and *ceps* (dried wild mushrooms). It has had an AOVDQS since 1947 and deserves to be better known outside the locality. Taste the Cuvée des Capitouls, the Domaine du Gazania or the Domaine de Magnac at the cellar of Ville-Dieu-du-Temple (18 to 22 F a bottle for 1995 or 1994 vintage).

Spotcheck
B2

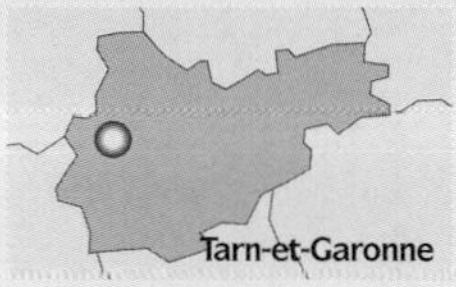

Things to do
- Canal du Midi
- The wines of la Ville-Dieu
- Forest d'Agre
- The Montech water slide

Within easy reach
Moissac, p. 162
Beaumont-de-Lomagne, p. 131
Montauban, p. 164

Tourist Office
Castelsarrasin:
☎ 05 63 32 75 00

Montech

12 miles (19 km) SE of Castelsarasin via the RN113

A walk in the Forêt d'Agre

1¼ miles (2 km) E of Montech

An ocean of greenery and tranquillity. This is the only large forest in Tarn-et-Garonne. It consists of 3,212 acres (1,300 ha) of oak, hornbeam and pine trees, covering the slopes situated between the Garonne and the Tarn. Several **paths** are available for hikers and horse-riders. The Montech Tourist Office (☎ 05 63 64 83 90) also offers orientation courses.

The water slide

This engineering feat is unique in the world and makes it possible to pass through a series of five locks on the canal all at once. A motorised system hauls the barges up to the top of the water slide. The mechanism is still in working order and in summer it is used by pleasure boats on the canal.

Angeville

5 miles (8 km) SW of Castelsarrasin via the D12

La Ferme des Jouberts

☎ 05 63 95 40 58.
Open daily except Sun. from 4pm.

Duck and only duck. André Couderc can sell you whole foie gras in glass jars (100 F for 9 oz (250 g)), *confits*, pâtés, duck with prunes and duck breast stuffed with foie gras (70 F each). You can visit the farm to see where he breeds the ducks and in the evening (from 15 September) you can even help Monsieur Couderc during feeding time.

HOW THE MONTECH WATER SLIDE WORKS

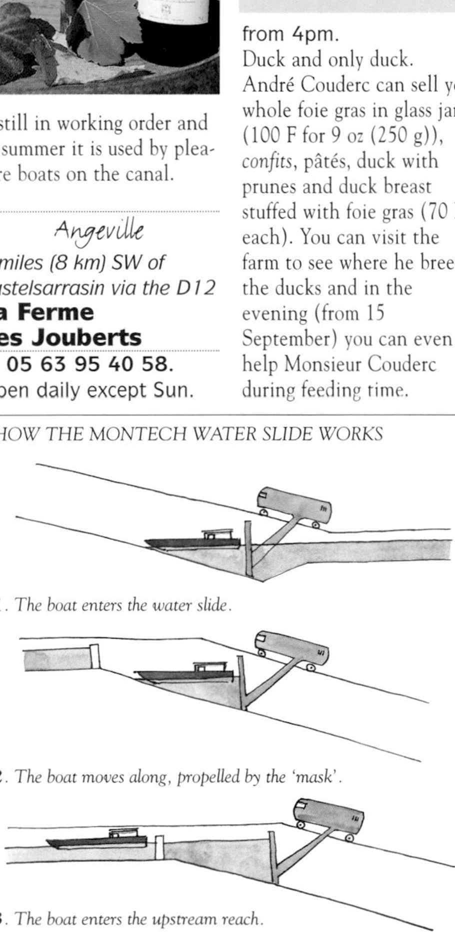

1. The boat enters the water slide.

2. The boat moves along, propelled by the 'mask'.

3. The boat enters the upstream reach.

Frontonnais

The region above Toulouse could be described as the northern South of France. Thanks to its sheltered climate, Frontonnais has been a vine-growing and fruit-growing area since the 12th C. The négrette, a local grape variety, proliferates on stony terraces and hillsides between the forests and the rivers. In the west, there are the châteaux of the Toulouse district, including the country seat of the Comtesse de Ségur, the children's author.

Merville

12½ miles (20 km) NW of Toulouse via the D2

The gardens of the château

Rue Principale

☎ 05 61 85 67 46.

Open weekends only, 2-6.30pm.

Admission charge.

The gardens of this 18th C. privately owned château consist of some 3 miles (5,000 m) of pruned boxwood hedges between grassy avenues and the famous **knot garden**. Wander through its 10 acres (4 ha) and get lost in the **maze** and the **green arbour**. Don't miss the elliptical ballroom. Inside the château, there is a reception room with lovely painted chinoiseries.

Larra

3¾ miles (6 km) SW of Grenade

❀ The château

☎ 05 61 82 62 51.

Open Thurs.-Sun., 15 April-15 Nov., 3-6pm.

Admission charge.

Nothing has changed here since the time of Louis XV. The interior decoration of this handsome 18th C. brick-built château is preserved just as it was. Stucco, a grand staircase with wrought-iron balustrade and a reception room full of paintings. Outside, there is a flower-decked courtyard, **formal gardens** and a **37 acre (15 ha)** park, designed in a French style (and typical of the Toulouse district). The château also has guest rooms for visitors.

Saint-Géniès-Bellevue

5½ miles (9 km) N of Toulouse via the D1

Château de Bellevue

☎ 05 61 74 26 45.

Guided tours daily except Mon., July-Aug., at 2.30pm and 4pm.

Admission charge to the park and château.

This 16th-18th C. brick-built château just outside Toulouse is evidence of the main contribution of the Renaissance to the region. It has a large courtroom, with an imposing fireplace in carved brick and a straight staircase that is typical of Languedoc.

Les Côtes du Frontonnais

4500 Avenue de Grisolles, Fronton
☎ 05 34 27 91 91.
Guided tour, Mon.-Fri., by appointment except Sept. and Oct.
Free admission.
At the Château Bellevue-la-Forêt, Patrick Germain sells wines made from négrette, a grape he knows well. The variety is the main one used in Côtes-du-Frontonnais, the most well known regional wine which has had an AOC since 1983. Visit the wine cellars and taste these dry fruity wines with their aromas of liquorice and violet (Château-Bellevue 1997, 26 F a bottle; Sevin 1996, 31 F a bottle).

The grounds are laid out in a park which is open to visitors and contains 300-year-old cedars and oak trees.

Cox

22 miles (35 km) NW of Toulouse via the D1

The potter's house

☎ 05 62 13 70 31.
Open daily, July-Aug., 2.30-6.30pm; out of season by arrangement.
Admission charge.

The speciality of the Toulouse district (and of Cox since the 16th C.) is glazed pottery. This old pottery was active until 1952. The five exhibition rooms trace four centuries of manufacture of the wonderful local wares, made between the 16th and 20th C. In the later rooms there are a number of kilns and the potter's workshop. At the time of writing, plans are being made to put the workshop back into practice, reviving the potter's art.

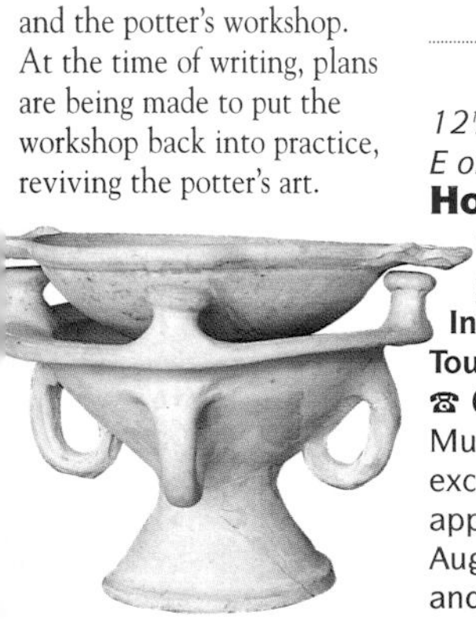

Brignemont

25 miles (40 km) NW of Toulouse via the D1

The windmill

☎ 05 62 65 02 75.
Guided tours, July-Aug., daily, 3-7pm; June and Sept. by appointment.
Admission charge.

This 18th C. mill was still a working business up until 1926. Today, it has been magnificently restored and is classified as a historic working monument, where you can learn how flour was made and see a real mill in action.

Verfeil

12½ miles (20 km) E of Toulouse

Home of the Comtesse de Ségur

Information at the Tourist Office
☎ 05 61 35 88 84.
Museum open daily except Sun. (by appointment) July-Aug., 9am-noon and 2-6.30pm.

Spotcheck
A5

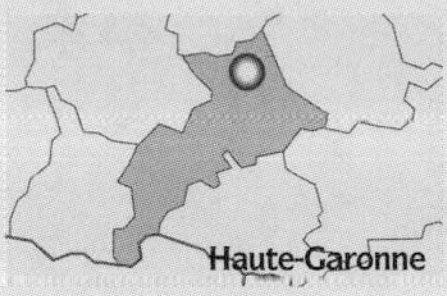

Things to do

- The wines of Frontonnais
- The potter's house at Cox
- The château of the Comtesse de Ségur at Verfeil

Within easy reach

Toulouse, p. 170
Albi, p. 136
Montauban, p. 164
Castelsarrasin, p. 152

Tourist Office

Verfeil:
☎ 05 61 35 88 84
Grenade:
☎ 05 61 82 93 85

The Comtesse de Ségur, one of the most famous French children's writers, created her 'good little girls' here at Verfeil, in the Frontonnais district, her country seat. The remains of the 13th-C. château can be visited, but personal effects, reflecting the story of her life, are in the town hall museum. Both her grand-daughters, Camille and Madeleine, who were the heroines of her stories, are buried in the local cemetery.

Le Val de Garonne

like a little corner of Tuscany

North of Toulouse, between Moissac and Valence-d'Agen, the river Garonne runs through a narrow plain covered in poplar trees and orchards. The south-facing slopes are planted with the vines for making Brulhois wine. The northern valleys are part of the Serres district. The rolling hills and brick and stone houses bathed in a gentle light give these villages a particular charm that is reminiscent of a Tuscan landscape.

Valence-d'Agen

The wash-houses

This former *bastide* (fortified town) was founded by the English king Edward I in 1283 – so it has quite a pedigree! It has three ancient public wash-houses which are considered to be among the best in the Midi-Pyrénées. They were built in the 18th and 19th C., but they are sadly all that remain of the old village.

The poultry market

Valence-d'Agen holds a poultry market in the Halle Dumon every Tuesday. All the farmers in the region sell their birds here. Free-range chickens (which rule the roost) are for sale alongside hens, turkeys, ducks, pigeons, rabbits and guinea-fowl, in a loud cacophony of clucking! However, to buy fresh fruit or home-made jams, you will need to find the town centre where market-gardeners and growers sell their produce. From November to March, there is a foie gras market.

The Golfech Power Station

☎ 05 63 29 39 06 or 05 63 29 47 01.
By appointment.
Free admission.

This is the place to learn all about the mysteries of the atom and nuclear power. The Golfech Power Station lies 2½ miles (4 km) from Valence-d'Agen. No one under the age of ten is admitted and you will have to make a prior arrangement by telephone as far as possible in advance. From the lookout post above the power station you can see the 'salmon-ladder', which is unique in Europe. It allows the migrating fish to swim up the Garonne on their way to the breeding grounds.

Auvillar

5 miles (8 km) S of Valence-d'Agen via the D953

Musée du Vieil-Auvillar

Rue du Château
☎ 05 63 29 05 79.

Open daily except Tues., 2.30-6.30pm (5.30pm out of season).
Admission charge (the ticket can also be used for the Musée de la Batellerie).

The wonderful collection of 18th and 19th C. **Auvillar** ***faïences*** and **country pottery** are the highlights of this museum, which also has on display some touching votive **offerings from the boatmen of the Garonne.** Every October, a **pottery**

Paths through the district

Information at the Tourist Office of Auvillar, ☎ 05 63 39 89 82. The district has a dozen signposted circular trails which are accessible to all and can be traversed on foot, on horseback or by mountain bike. The Valence-d'Agen route follows an old Roman road and climbs the hillsides, from the top of which there is a picturesque view of the Garonne. At Auvillar, two trails lead along the banks of the river and the former port, before separating and climbing to the hilltops.

market is held in the Place de la Halle, thus perpetuating the tradition of tin-glazed earthenware. At this market more than forty craft potters come from all over France to show their work and sell their wares.

Under the arcades of Auvillar

This village overlooking the Garonne is one of the loveliest in Tarn-et-Garonne. Its **market hall** is perfectly circular and its public square is lined with old arcaded houses with cross-bars and brick infill. There is a lovely view of the river and the old port at Auvillar. The clock tower (Tour de l'Horloge) contains a permanent **exhibition about river traffic** (open daily except Tues., 2.30-6.30pm. Admission charge) which recalls the days when the river was busy with trade and commerce.

Angora goats at La Ferme du Cap-du-Pech

☎ 05 63 39 08 34.
Open daily, 2-6pm.
Admission charge.

Marie-Josée Joly breeds small white goats with curly hair at this farm. The goats do not produce milk, but yield a soft, fluffy wool called mohair. In a visit lasting a little over an hour, you will learn all about how the fibre is processed and how angora goats are bred. You can also buy **skeins of knitting wool** (38 to 42 F) or stock up for winter on **gloves, scarves** (from 165 F) or **socks** (65 to 90 F) in every colour. As a bonus, you can taste the **farmhouse goat's cheese**.

Spotcheck

B2-C2

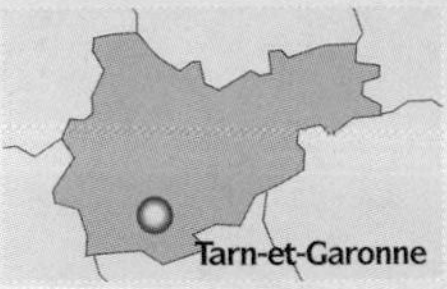

Things to do

- The poultry market at Valence-d'Agen
- An angora goat breeding farm
- Tasting the *vins noirs* of Donzac
- River cruise on the Tarn or the Garonne

Within easy reach

Moissac, p. 162
Saint-Clar, p. 128

Tourist office

Valence-d'Agen:
☎ 05 63 39 52 52
Auvillar:
☎ 05 63 39 89 82

Donzac

5½ miles (9 km) NW of Auvillarvia the D12

The *vins noirs* cellar

Route de Dunes

☎ 05 63 39 91 92.

Open daily except Sun. and Mon. morning, 8am-noon and 2-6pm.

The Val de Garonne produces a very special wine, dark ruby in colour with a bouquet of blackcurrant and redcurrant, which is aged in oak casks. The Côtes-de-Brulhois wines are dubbed *vins noirs* (black wines) due to their colour and have a VDQS appellation d'origine. The Donzac cellar offers **free wine-tastings** of the reds or rosés, a visit to the cellars where the barrels are stored and to the bottling plant. You can take some of the wine home with you. (Cuvée Tradition 1996 20 F a bottle; Château-Grand-Chêne 1995 aged in the wood, 34 F a bottle).

Conservation Centre for Traditional Occupations

☎ 05 63 29 21 96.

Open daily, July-Aug., 9.30am-noon and 2-7pm; out of season, 2-6pm. Closed in Jan.

Admission charge.

This museum has collections of more than 10,000 items from the cultural and craft heritage of the region, in reconstructed scenes from the period. You can also visit the **Museum of the Vine and of Wine**, containing a huge 17th C. wine press with massive wheels – the only one in France.

Dunes

2¾ miles (4½ km) SW of Donzac via the D30

Queen Margot's village

Despite its name, Dunes is actually a tiny *bastide* (walled town) a long way from the sea, but it has attractions all of its own. Wander around the arcaded central square which is surrounded by extraordinary houses, where Queen Margot stayed. The church of Sainte-Madeleine has a magnificent altar screen and one of the loveliest Gothic naves in the region.

The potter's studio

Rue Basse

☎ 05 63 39 97 76.

Open daily, 9am-6pm.

Nicole et Alain Morellini are craft potters who have been working in Dunes since 1981. They specialise in **glazed earthenware** and **unglazed pottery**. You can watch live demonstrations of the potter's craft, as their expert hands transform crude clay into works of art. You can buy bowls (from 35 F), pitchers (from 110 F) and dishes (from 150 to 500 F).

Saint-Vincent-Lespinasse

2½ miles (4 km) NE of Valence-d'Agen via the D74

Pottery cats

☎ 05 63 04 93 42.
Open by appointment.
Christian Pradier is mad about cats. He surrounds himself with real moggies as well as beautiful ceramic renditions of felines. His workshop also

contains sculptures and garden fountains. There are some very expensive original items as well as affordable short runs (from 150 F to 3,000 F or more). Call before visiting, as this famous artist may well be exhibiting abroad, something he does quite often.

Castelsagrat

9¼ miles (15 km) N of Valence-d'Agen via the D953 then the D46

A bestiary in the church

This is a typical medieval ***bastide*** with its large central square surrounded by covered arcades. Walking through its narrow streets you will discover picturesque stone-built or half-timbered houses with carved eaves. The church contains a wonderful wooden altar screen which is gilded

The square at Castelsagrat

and painted. Squirrels and birds play at the tops of the columns decorated with vine tendrils.

Montjoi

1¾ miles (3 km) of Castelsagrat via the D46

A listed village

This is a delightful little listed village. Its arched gateway leads to the half-timbered houses with corbels, beside the path that runs alongside the walls. There is an old well, picturesque squares and narrow lanes. From its hilltop position, Montjoi has a strategic view of the valley of the river Séoune.

A RIVER CRUISE FOR BIRD-LOVERS

Lou Malaousenc, Quai Blanc, Malause
☎ 05 63 39 55 78.
Sun., Apr.-Sept., 3-5pm.
Admission charge.
Take a family river cruise on the *Lou Malaousenc* for a trip lasting an hour and a half (40 F for adults, 20 F for children aged from 5 to 15). There are several different routes, either along the Tarn or the Garonne, and you will discover the Canal du Midi and its locks. You will cross the huge lake of Saint-Nicolas-de-la-Grave, as far as the Île aux Oiseaux (Bird Island), which has a large colony of mallards, redshanks, gulls and coots.

The Canal du Midi
a royal waterway

This astonishing feat of engineering, initiated by Pierre-Paul Riquet and built in the reign of Louis XIV, brought prosperity to the whole of the Upper Garonne valley. The canal is 150 miles (240 km) long and linked the Atlantic Ocean with the Mediterranean sea, meaning that French ships could avoid the dangerous Straits of Gibraltar. Until 1970, it was still used for carrying cargo, especially wheat from Lauragais. It is now a UNESCO World Heritage Site and a favourite with tourists for its canal cruises.

The Bassin Saint-Féréol

15½ miles (25 km) from Toulouse via the D2 then the D622

This basin collects waters from the Montagne Noire and is the cornerstone of the Canal du Midi. It is 222 acres (90 ha) in size and is surrounded by shady avenues so it is a lovely place **for a walk.** It is also a good place for an excursion on foot or mountain bike and an ideal place to laze about or **rent a boat.** (Le Bivouac sailing centre, ☎ 05 61 27 53 94.)

Biking along the canal banks

Nearly **25 miles (40 km) of cycle paths** make it possible to ride beside the Canal du Midi from Toulouse to Port-Lauragais, on the south bank. Access to this 10 ft (3 m) wide, two-way cycle path is completely free. You are bound to meet other cyclists (10,000 of them use it every year) who are also using the towpath once reserved for the horses who pulled the barges. (Bike hire at Temps Libre Location, ☎ 05 61 53 51 83.)

In a barge

Loisirs-accueil de Haute-Garonne
14 Rue Bayard, Toulouse
☎ 05 61 99 44 00 (booking only).

Whether you spend a few hours or a few days on the Canal du Midi you can do so without a permit. Between March and November, take the tiller of a small barge (book in advance) and discover the wonders of this waterway while travelling at the speed limit of 3¾ mph (6 kph). The locks (the exciting moments) are only open

from 8am to 7pm in the summer, but there are lots of moorings if you arrive too late. (Estimate on spending 1,500 F a week for two people.)

The Négra lock

1¼ miles (2 km) E of Montesquieu-Lauragais, 18¾ miles (30 km) SE of Toulouse

Its quayside paved with cobblestones was a well-worn route for passengers in the

Spotcheck
C3-D3

Things to do
- Boat hire on the Bassin Saint-Féréol
- River trip on a barge
- Festival d'Ecluse en Garonne

Within easy reach
Toulouse, p. 170
Lauragais, p. 146
Volvestre, p. 168

Tourist Office
Revel: ☎ 05 61 83 50 06
Villefranche-de-Lauragais: ☎ 05 61 27 20 94

17th C. who were travelling to Toulouse or Agde via the Canal du Midi. Stop here for a bite to eat and visit the inn, the chapel, the lock-keeper's house and the grain store, which was used to house the horses who towed the riverboats. Five minutes downstream, the Laval lock-keeper's house remains intact.

A *cassoulet* pitstop
From the little port of Gardouch (3¾ miles (6 km) after the Négra lock) drive to **Villefranche-de-Lauragais** (only 1¾ miles (3 km) away), a famous place for *cassoulet*. In this 13th C. *bastide*, Friday morning is the day on which the **traditional market** is held. All kinds of food and produce is sold including white Tarbes beans, garlic, onions, thyme, bay leaves, pork crackling, and more. The **Hôtel de France** (106 Rue de la République, ☎ 05 61 81 62 17.) does a wonderful *cassoulet* with *confit* (menus from 70 F).

D'Ecluse en Garonne
Information ☎ 05 62 19 06 06.
This is the name of an itinerant festival on a barge called *Le Chèvrefeuille*. In July, it runs up and down the Canal des Deux-Mers (the section of the Canal between Toulouse and Castets). From Toulouse to Bordeaux via Montech, Castelsarrasin, Moissac and Agen, there are 12 evening events, including concerts and dances.

The revival of the canal
There has been an increase of more than 60% in river tourism on the Canal du Midi since 1992! One century after its decline, pleasure boats have taken over from commercial barges, which are too big to negotiate this masterpiece of civil engineering. The new boating fraternity is 30% French, 25% German and 15% British. The banks are lined with tens of thousands of umbrella pines, cypress and plane trees, which were planted from the 17th C. onwards.

Moissac

fine art along the water

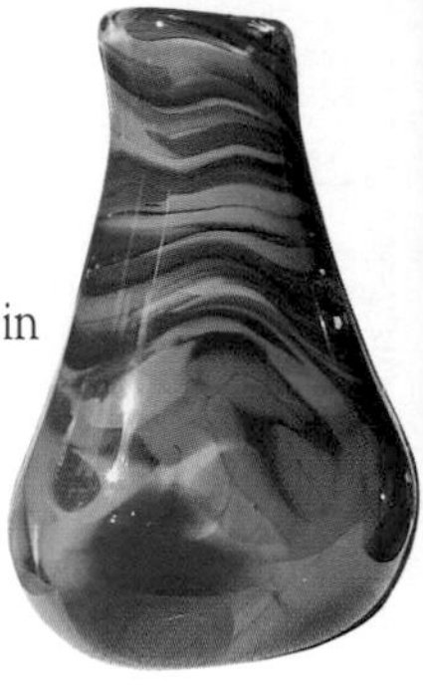

Whether you prefer nature or culture, you will fall in love with Moissac. Art is everywhere here, from the sculptures in the Romanesque cloister to the craft workshops in Rue Moura and the many summer concerts. To escape to the countryside, just follow the canal banks, the meanders of the Garonne or the banks of the Tarn. The lush vegetation is home to colonies of herons, gulls and mallard ducks.

The cloister of Saint-Pierre abbey

Place Delthil
☎ 05 63 04 01 85.
Open daily, July-Aug., 9am-7pm; 15 March-June and Sept.-15 Oct., 9am-noon and 2-6pm; 15 Oct.-15 March, 9am-noon and 2-5pm. Closed 25 Dec. and 1 Jan. *Admission charge.*

This is the oldest, the largest and **the most beautiful of the Romanesque cloisters.** It is also beautifully preserved, including the ornate sculptures on the capitals. The **great portal** of the abbey church with its finely carved tympanum, is famous throughout the world. Because of its renowned beauty, the abbey can become quite busy with visitors. So arrive there early and have some time to enjoy it in peace.

Craft workshops

Rue Moura
Workshops open daily except Mon.

A dozen craftsmen along this street open the doors of their **workshops** to visitors. You'll find glassblowing, lacemaking, pottery, stonecarving, painting and china restoration. Go as a group to visit the various craftspeople and see them in action, preferably on Saturday. During summer evenings, you can enjoy a free **concert** in the cloister square.

Magnificent views

Climb up behind the old Carmelite convent to the **Virgin outlook** where there is a good view of the Tarn and the canal. On the way down, you will pass through a pine wood which contains the largest colony of black-backed herons in France. Moissac seems always to want to be biggest and best! For the best view of the **Garonne**, drive 2½ miles (4 km) out of Moissac in the direction of Valence-d'Agen. The Boudou outlook offers one of the loveliest views of the confluence of the Tarn and the Garonne.

The bridge-canal over the Tarn

This amazing bridge is 1,190 ft (356 m) long and enables the canal, running alongside the Garonne, to cross the Tarn. It is also an

attractive place for a walk with one of the prettiest, flower-decked locks in France. You can walk there from the Uvarium (see box below).

Ciboulette

Rte de Toulouse
☎ 05 63 32 23 09.
Open daily except Sun afternoon, 9am-12.30pm and 3-7pm.

This shop, whose name means 'chive', is like a garden. Surrounded by flowers and fragrant herbs. It sells a cornucopia of fresh fruit and vegetables, wines, cheese and home-made jams (15 F for 12 oz (330 g)), goose *confit* (100 F), semi-cooked duck foie gras (120 F for 6½ oz (180 g)), honey (15 to 35 F for 9 oz (250 g)), free-range eggs and ham. The growers distribute their produce through the shop, so it goes straight from basket to table.

Vibrations of the Voice

Information
☎ 05 63 04 32 69.
Early July.

Moissac pays homage to the singing voice with its festival combining gospel, French *chansons* and humour. The performances take place on the banks of the Tarn, in the abbey church of Saint-Pierre or its cloister. Every evening, as a fringe event, jazz bands play in the cafés and restaurants.

Saint-Nicolas-de-la-Grave

5 miles (8 km) SW of Moissac via N113

Boating at the leisure centre

Base de Loisir de Saint-Nicolas-de-la-Grave
☎ 05 63 95 50 00.
Open daily, Apr.-Sept., 8am-noon and 2-5.30pm
Free admission.

This 988 acre (400 ha) lake is ideal for those who love water sports. You can hire **windsurfing boards** (50 F for half a day) or a **catamaran** (165 F for half a day), **pedalos** (50 F/h), as well as **motor-boats** (without a permit), **dinghies** and **canoes**. On the hottest days, you can go for a dip in the pool or rent bicycles for gentle cycling in the shade. The lake is also home to a large colony of migratory birds.

Spotcheck
C2

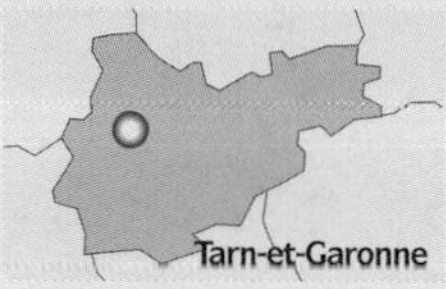

Things to do

- The craft workshops of Moissac
- The bridge-canal over the Tarn
- Boating on the Lac de Saint-Nicolas-de-la-Grave

Within easy reach

Castelsarrasin, p. 152
Valence-d'Agen, p. 156
Lomagne, p. 128

Tourist Office

Moissac: ☎ 05 63 04 01 85

GRAPE JUICE FOR A PEACHES AND CREAM COMPLEXION

In the 1930s, Moissac was a well-known health resort where society women came to take the grape juice cure. The kiosk bar at the Uvarium (☎ 05 63 04 53 16) has revived this tradition. On a superb terrace overlooking the Tarn, from May to Sept., you can taste fresh fruit juices (18 F a glass) and, of course, the juice of the Chasselas grape. The façade has retained its lovely frescoes and elegant art nouveau decor from the *belle epoque*.

Montauban
the Florence of the South West

Montauban is another pink, brick-built town. It is a lively, joyful and dynamic place, full of architectural curiosities and bucolic views. Explore the town on foot at sunset when the house façades turn to gold. Montauban is also the home town of the artist Ingres and the sculptor Bourdelle. It is a city of great monuments and lovely gardens.

❀ The Ingres Museum

Rue de l'Hôtel-de-Ville, near Pont-Vieux
☎ 05 63 22 12 91.
Open daily except public holidays, July-August, 9.30am-noon and 1.30-6pm; out of season, 10am-noon and 2-6pm. Closed Mon., Sept.-June; Sunday morning, 15 Oct.-Easter.
Admission charge.
The whole of the first floor is devoted to the work of Ingres, who was born in Montauban in 1780. The paintings include *Jesus Among the Sages*, 4,000 drawings and a collection of portraits including the *Portrait of Gilibert* and the *Portrait of Mme Gonse*. The museum also contains paintings by David and Delacroix, some excellent primitives, 40 sculptures by Bourdelle and some medieval works.

Portrait of Mme Marcotte by Ingres (1826)

A trip down the Tarn

For information
☎ 05 63 63 60 60.
This is a lovely way of seeing the pink city from the river, discovering the Pont-Vieux (bridge) and the quays and taking a look at the black-backed herons on the Île de la Pissote. There are daily trips (15 June-15 Sept., 10am-7pm) leaving from the car park behind the Musée Ingres and the Pont-Vieux (3 to 5 seater boats, 70 F for half an hour).

Place Nationale

This central square dates from the original building of the walled city in 1144. The wooden roofs over the arcades were destroyed by fire and rebuilt in brick. The houses decorated with pilasters and double galleries, the warm tones of the brick and elegant porticos, make this one of the prettiest squares in the region.

The handsome brick façade of the Ingres Museum

Every Saturday, a **farmer's market** and an **antiques fair** are held here.

The Pont-Vieux

This is a wonderful feat of engineering built between 1304 and 1335 as protection against the terrible floods of the Tarn. It is exceptionally long (683 ft (205 m)) for that period and has a flat span instead of the typical hump-back popular at the time. The seven ogival arches, with massive stone piers, were perforated with openings to enable water to flow out when the level of the river rose.

A tour of the elegant mansions

The old town has retained the grid pattern of the original *bastide* and some of its elegant mansions. Take your time strolling in the **Rue Cambon**, **Rue de la Comédie** and the **Rue de la République** (at no. 43, there is a lovely portico with a spiral decoration). The Tourist Office (☎ 05 63 63 60 60) organises **guided tours** (several options, lasting 1 to 4 hours; 15 F to 30 F per tour) and publishes a free brochure about the most interesting buildings.

Spotcheck

C2

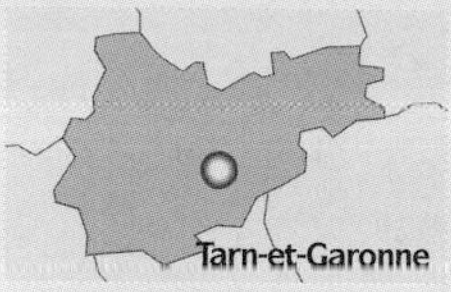

Things to do

- The Ingres Museum
- Bird collection at the natural history museum
- Cheese-tastings
- The Gorge of the Aveyron

Within easy reach

Castelsarrasin 13¾ miles (22 km) W, *p. 152*
Frontonnais 15½ miles (25 km) S, *p. 154*
Vallée de la Vère 17½ miles (28 km) E, *p. 150*

Tourist Office

Montauban:
☎ 05 63 63 60 60

The gardens of Montauban

The parks and gardens surrounding the centre are one of the charms of Montauban. You can linger in the magnificent **Bishop's Garden**, rest in the shade of tulip-trees from Virginia and Chinese ginkgos in the **Jardin des Plantes**, or walk down the **Cours Foucault**, an

COBBLESTONES AND BULLETS

To commerorate Montauriol Hill on which the present town is built, the confectioners of Montauban created the montauriol, a delicious chocolate filled with local cherries and Armagnac. You can find them at **Pâtisserie Marty** (70 Rue Léon-Cladel, ☎ 05 63 03 46 52). You might also like to try the famous ***boulets de Montauban,*** toasted hazelnuts coated with rich, dark chocolate and sugar. You will find them at the **Confiserie Pécou** (11 Rue de la République, ☎ 05 63 63 06 38). These 'bullets' cost 25 F for 6½ oz (180 g).

A TOWN FULL OF SCULPTURES

Montauban has many sculptures by Antoine Bourdelle, another native son. His works are useful landmarks for visitors. The *Centaur* lies in front of the Ingres Museum, *Penelope* still awaits Ulysses in front of the former Jesuit college near the Pont-Vieux, the *Monument to the Dead* commemorates the Franco-Prussian War of 1870 and, in the Cours Foucault, the *Goddess of Wisdom* seems to be scanning the horizon, symbolising France watching over her dead.

esplanade planted with a thousand elms which overlooks the Tarn and offers a lovely view of the old town. In May and June, when the flowers are in bloom, visit the pretty **rose-garden of the Espace François-Mitterrand**, which has a collection of 16,000 plants and 960 varieties of rose-bush.

Notre-Dame Cathedral

Place Franklin-Roosevelt
☎ 05 63 63 10 23.
Open daily, 8am-noon and 2-7pm (Sun., 10am-noon).
Free admission.

This is one of the few cathedrals in the region which is built of white stone rather than brick. It symbolises the triumph of Roman Catholicism over this Protestant city after the revocation of the Edict of Nantes. A painting by Ingres, *The Wish of Louis XIII*, can be seen on the left wall of the transept.

The natural history museum

Pl. Antoine-Bourdelle
☎ 05 63 22 13 85.
Open daily except Sun. morning, Mon. and public holidays, 10am-noon and 2-6pm.
Admission charge (free on Wed.).

This is a **remarkable ornithological collection** of nearly 400 birds, some of which are very rare. The museum also exhibits **fossils from Quercy** which are unique to the region, as well as and fragments of the meteorite which fell near here in 1864. The **Musée du Terroir** (☎ 05 63 66 46 34), in the same building, displays implements and everyday objects illustrating daily life as it was once lived in the lower Quercy region.

Cheese from La Ferme du Ramier

After Montauban, on the Rte de Saint-Antonin-Noble-Val
☎ 05 63 03 14 49.
Open daily, 9am-7pm.
La Tomme du Ramier is an unpasteurised farmhouse cheese, only produced in the Montauban region. It is used in fondues, melted on toast or in a salad (134 F for a 4 lb 8 oz (2 kg) cheese). It is a speciality of La Ferme du Ramier, which offers **free tastings** and a **guided tour** of the cheese-making facility, including the milking parlour, a copper cauldron that holds 196 gallons (900 l) of milk, the cellar in which 4,000 cheeses ripen and the herd of 120 cows.

La Fête du Goût et des Saveurs

Ferme du Ramier, ☎ 05 63 03 14 49.
The Sunday following 15 August.
Free admission.

For a real Sunday in the country, this is the place to be to sample fine flavours and the best quality. Local growers and producers display their wares and there are many events taking place under the plane trees, including the inevitable barrel-rolling contest. There are picnics and various tastings, and of course you can buy whatever is on sale, all of it to introduce you to the flavours of the Toulouse district.

Albias

3¾ miles (6 km) NE via the RN20

❀ Domaine de Montels

☎ 05 63 31 02 82.
Open daily, 9am-7pm.
Red, rosés and white vins de pays are produced by this little vineyard on the terraces of Montauban. They regularly win regional and national prizes. You can choose between a red Prestige 1998 (21 F a bottle), which won a gold medal in Paris, a Rosé Tradition 1998 (19 F a bottle), another prizewinner, or a fruity, rounded dry white from 1998 (19 F a bottle).

Monclar-de-Quercy

11¼ miles (18 km) E via the D8

The three lake leisure centre

Base de loisirs
☎ 05 63 30 31 72.
Open daily, 15 June-15 Sept., 8am-7pm.
Admission charge (free for children under five).
This leisure centre boasts 136 acres (55 ha) of landscape and three lakes with **water sports facilities**, including **flumes** and **paddling pools** for children, as well as rowing-boats (10 F/pers. per day), sailing dinghies and wind-surfing boards (20 F for the day). A **scenic railway**, a miniature reproduction of the Orient Express 1900, circles the lakes in 40 minutes. (☎ 05 63 30 34 37. Daily at 5pm in July-Aug.; out of season, Sun. and public holidays at 4pm).

Montricoux

16¼ miles (26 km) E via the D115

The Gorge of the Aveyron

Upstream of the village of **Montricoux**, the Aveyron has cut a deep gorge into the local limestone. Old châteaux and picturesque villages line the route to **Saint-Antonin-Noble-Val**, a lovely spot which is also the starting point for a dozen or so walks and hiking trails (information at the Tourist Office of Saint-Antonin, ☎ 05 63 30 63 47).

Muret and the Volvestre

between Toulouse and the foothills

This is a valley of green pastures through which the Garonne has cut a deep ravine. On one side there are cliffs and on the other wide terraces. Volvestre is the point at which the plains of the Garonne meet the mountains of Ariège. It was once the scene of the battles against the Cathars, but it is now a peaceful land of museums and leisure pursuits.

Cap Al Campestre Musée

Muret

10 miles (16 km) SW of Toulouse via the RN20

The Musée Clément-Ader

Town Hall
27 Rue Castelvielh
☎ 05 61 51 95 95.

Open daily except weekends, 9am-noon and 2-5pm. *Free admission.*

Clément Ader, a pioneer of aviation, was born in Muret in 1841. He was a prolific inventor who in addition to inventing the first aeroplane, which took the form of a large bird, also invented a caterpillar-tracked vehicle, the dynamo, rubber tyres and even sort of telephone. Learn about the little-known work of this high-flyer (even though his first flight went no further than 170 ft (50 m)!).

Aquarium of the Garonne and Pyrenees

13 Rue Cugnot
☎ 05 61 51 50 59.

Open Wed., Sat. and Sun., 10am-noon and 2-7pm; the other days, 2-7pm (morning by appointment)
Admission charge.

Fish and other aquatic life which are native to the region can be found in this elegant 18th C. home. They swim in huge purpose-built aquariums within the large rooms of the house (the biggest is 40 ft (12 m) long!). Outside, a **shady park** contains a **'teaching pond'** filled with free-swimming fish. Perfect for children.

Lherm

5 miles (8 km) SW of Muret via the D43b

Musée Cap Al Campestre

Rte de l'Aérodrome,
☎ 05 61 51 14 56.

Open daily, 9.30-noon, 2.30-7pm; out of season, 5.30pm.
Admission charge.

Delve into life in the region at the beginning of the 20th C. This huge museum contains tools from old trades, early agricultural machinery and modes of transport which were in everyday use just over 100 years ago. Fifteen buildings

THE LAST FERRY

Le Fauga
(5 miles (8 km) S of Muret) Departure below the village. March-Oct., daily except Sun. and public holidays, 8am-12.30pm and 1.30-6.30pm; Nov.-Feb., daily except Wed. afternoon, Sat. afternoon and Sun., 8.30am-12.30pm and 1.30-5.30pm.
Cross the Garonne on the last public ferry, which operates out of Fauga, on the left bank of the river. (The local children still use it to go to school.) Take a pleasant stroll along the towpath which lies near the lovely Romanesque chapel of Laouach.

Spotcheck

C3

Things to do

- Muret Aquarium
- Ferry across the Garonne
- Insectarium du Volvestre

Within easy reach

Toulouse 10 miles (16 km) NE, p. 170
Le Pays du Mas-d'Azil 15 miles (24 km) SE, p. 210

Tourist Office

Muret:
☎ 05 62 23 05 03
Rieux-Volvestre:
☎ 05 61 87 63 33

provide an insight into the changes in the Toulouse district over the centuries. Don't miss the flour mill (you can take some bread home with you) and Chappe's fascinating telegraph.

Rieux-Volvestre

17½ miles (28 km) SW of Muret via the RN117

The pearl of Volvestre

This ancient bishopric, which lies on a bend of the river Arize, has preserved its ancient beauty. Admire the **half-timbered medieval houses** (Rue de l'Évêché, Rue du Moulin, Rue du Sac), the two **bridges** and the **fortress cathedral** which contains a number of liturgical ornaments and a very beautiful reliquary bust of Saint Cizy. The Toulouse-style, octagonal belltower (143 ft (43 m) high) is one of the loveliest in the Midi.

Fête du Papogay

For information
☎ 05 61 87 63 33.
First weekend in May.
Free admission.

The papogay is a carved wooden parrot fixed on a 150 ft (45 m) pole. Whoever manages to knock the parrot of its perch becomes king of Rieux for a year! The contest takes place on a Sunday, in the midst of general frivolity. On the day before, archers in period costume parade through the village and there is an archery contest, like something out of Robin Hood!

Bax

5½ miles (9 km) SE of Rieux-Volvestre via the D25

❀ Tropical insect house

Volvestre Entomologie
Centre Cétonia
☎ 05 61 87 17 02.

Open daily, May-Sept., 11am-6.30pm; out of season, weekends only.
Admission charge.

You can guarantee to have any number of frights among the **regional and tropical insects** in this insectarium, which is designed so that you walk through a series of caves. There is also a **tropical greenhouse**, inhabited by butterflies who peacefully fly in and out of the huge plants from Guyana. Watch out, some of the plants are carnivorous!

Toulouse, the pink city

Toulouse, the rose-brick city, has never looked quite so fine. It looks to the future as the European capital of aeronautics, and is the fifth largest city in France. This lively university town is full of students, scientists – and charm! The capital of Gascony, it has played a vital role in the history and development of the South-west. Toulouse is as strong as its rugby team and as sweet as a bunch of its famous violets.

The Capitol

Place du Capitole
☎ 05 61 22 29 22.
Galleries open daily except Sat. afternoon and Sun., 8.30am-noon, 2-5pm; public holidays, 11am-6pm.

Free admission.
This building is the symbol of Toulouse. It is here that the *capitouls* (members of the town council) ruled the city until 1789. Enter through the Renaissance portico, climb the grand staircase to the ornate **salle des illustres** (207 ft (62 m) long!) dedicated to the glories of Toulouse, the wedding room and the **salle Henri-Martin**, a local painter. The handsome 18th-C. classical brick-and-stone façade gives the building an air of authority.

Les Jardins de l'Opéra

1 Place du Capitole
☎ 05 61 23 07 76.
Open daily except Sun. and Mon. noon. Closed for three weeks in Aug.
Elegant cuisine is on the menu at this restaurant set in magnificent surroundings. The gardens are splendid and the food is among the best in the region. The prices are high (dinner menus from 295 to 540 F; for lunch, menu at 200 F, wine not included), but the chef's talents are worth the extravagance. Dishes include foie gras ravioli, knuckle of mutton, *cassoulet* with broad beans, duckling, stewed Lauragais pigeon, red mullet fillet and baked figs.

The basilica of Saint-Sernin

Place Saint-Sernin
Church open daily except on Sun. morning, 8am-noon and 2-6pm. Crypt open daily except Sun. morning, 10am-6pm; out of season, 10-11.30am and 2.30-5pm.
Admission charge to the crypt.
The church's proportions are sheer perfection. The basilica was begun in the 11th C. and completed in the 13th C. The nave is 180 ft (54 m) long, 90 ft (27 m) high beneath the cross of the transepts, and there are two exquisite transepts of 107 ft (32 m) each. This **masterpiece of Romanesque art** is dedicated to Saint Saturnin, the martyred bishop of the city, who was killed by being tied to a bull by pagans, in the year 250.

Musée Saint-Raymond

Place Saint-Sernin
☎ 05 61 22 21 85.
Open daily, 10am-6pm; out of season, by appointment.
Admission charge.
Upon leaving the basilica of Saint-Sernin, go into the museum. It was recently renovated and occupies a 16th C. building which was once a

school for poor children. It contains some amazing artefacts which have survived from the first millennium. The display starts in prehistoric times with **Bronze Age weapons** and includes **jewels from the Middle Ages, Greek statuary** and **Roman coins.** You'll find this 'bazaar of antiquities' in a charming setting.

Aerospatiale

3¾ miles (6 km) W of Toulouse town centre
Avenue Jean-Monnet
☎ 05 61 15 44 00.
Guided tour daily except on Sun. and public holidays, by appointment.
ID compulsory.
Admission charge.
It is impossible to ignore the impressive sight of the

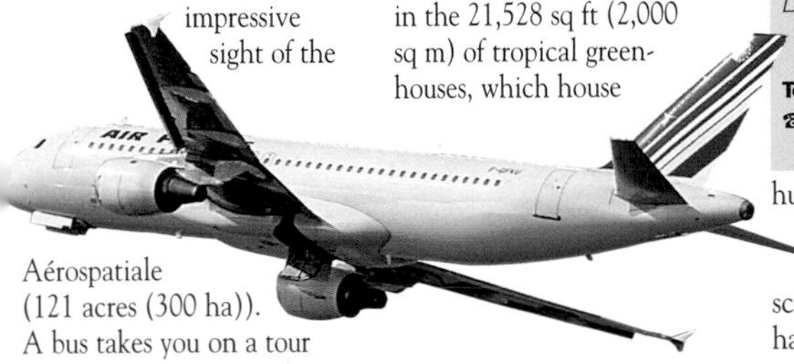

Aérospatiale (121 acres (300 ha)). A bus takes you on a tour of the vast site to see where the Airbus A340 is made. The final stop is at a lookout post above a gigantic assembly hall, so large that everyone passes through it by bike!

Behind the scenes at the airport

Blagnac
☎ 05 61 71 62 11.
Guided tour Mon.-Fri. by appointment.
Admission charge.
Learn how a big airport is run by going behind the scenes at Toulouse-Blagnac airport. Discover how sniffer dogs work tracking down suitcases containing suspicious substances and see the baggage-handling machines at work. Watch the technicians who regulate (to the nearest millimetre) all the stages of take-off and landing, and experience what it is like to pilot a plane by taking the controls of a real Boeing. Please note that you must book at least two weeks in advance, because the airport will have to do a security check on you!

The orchid world

Beyond the airport of Blagnac
Exofleurs
Chemin de Faudouas
Cornebarrieu
☎ 05 61 85 27 25.
Open daily except Mon., 9am-12.30pm and 2-6.30pm; Sun., 10am-noon and 3-6pm.
Travel to the heart of an equatorial forest in the midst of the city! Discover the mysteries of the world of orchids, in the 21,528 sq ft (2,000 sq m) of tropical greenhouses, which house hundreds of varieties of this queen of flowers in such delightful colours and scents. This orchid collection has attained worldwide fame.

Spotcheck

C3

Things to do

- Visit to Aérospatiale
- Behind the scenes at the airport
- A cruise down the Garonne
- Visit the Cité de l'Espace
- Markets and antiques
- Visit the Dépêche du Midi
- A trip on the Canal du Midi
- Try the violet scents and sweets
- African Safari

Within easy reach

Muret, p. 168
Le Lauragais, p. 146
Le Frontonnais, p. 154

Tourist Office

Toulouse:
☎ 05 61 11 02 22

The convent of the Jacobins

Parvis des Jacobins (entrance from the Rue Lakanal)
☎ 05 61 22 39 52.
Open daily, 10am-7pm.
Admission charge.
Massive on the outside, light and airy on the inside, the contrast in this 14th C. local Gothic masterpiece is striking. Inside the church you will discover the famous '**palm tree**' formations, the point at which the ribs and cross-pieces of the vaulted arches converge. Then go to the **cloister**, a haven of peace in the bustling heart of the city. The former refectory of the monks in the Rue Pargaminières is sometimes used for important **exhibitions** (☎ 05 61 21 22 92).

Musée des Augustins

21 Rue de Metz
☎ 05 61 22 21 82.
Open daily except Tues., 10am-6pm; at night until 9pm on Wed.
Admission charge.
In this former Augustinian convent, you will find one of the best **collections devoted to the history of art**, from Roman art to the art of the 19th C. In this ideal setting Romano-gothic sculptures and religious paintings, from Rubens to Manet, are on display. The Festival Quatre Etoiles is held here.

❀ Hôtel d'Assézat and the Bemberg Foundation

Place d'Assézat
☎ 05 61 12 06 89.
Open daily except Mon., 10am-6pm (Thurs. until 9pm). *Admission charge.*
This is the loveliest mansion in Toulouse (16th C.), which

❀ On the Garonne

Les Bateaux Toulousains,
Quai de Tounis
☎ 05 61 32 84 84 or 06 07 43 48 28.
July-Aug., daily at 2.30, 4 and 5.30pm (40 F/pers.; 20 F for children under 12); lunch on Sun. (booking 48 hours in advance; 130 F/pers.; 65 F for children under 12). Out of season, open Sun. afternoon.
The splendid buildings of Toulouse gain a new perspective when seen from the river. To see the pink city at its most intimate, take a trip on the barge *Baladine*, which sails, both night and day, beneath the bridges of the Garonne, revealing magic effects of the light. The best time to take the trip is at the moment that the sun goes down, when the city turns a dusky mauve.

Hôtel d'Assézat

was never completed, but is nevertheless lived in. Two square central blocks of the house, three stories high, now contain the art collection of the Bemberg Foundation. It includes Renaissance paintings, the works of Derain, Matisse, Gauguin, Bonnard (30 canvases), Toulouse-Lautrec, Rouault, and many others. All of these works are complemented by the remarkable decor and furnishings in this mansion, where the exterior is as wonderful as the interior.

Parc de la Reynerie

Impasse de l'Abbé-Salvat
☎ 05 61 40 46 76.
Open daily, dawn till dusk.
Free admission.

It was Louis XV who donated this garden to the husband of his favourite mistress, Madame Dubarry, as a sort of compensation for the 'loan' of his wife! Monsieur Dubarry was an explorer and brought back many exotic plants from his long voyages. They have been harmoniously incorporated into this 15 acre (6 ha) garden which contains all kinds of delights, including groves and arbours.

Cité de l'Espace

Avenue Jean-Gonnord (périphérique E, exit 17)
☎ 05 62 71 48 71.
Open daily except Mon., 9.30am-6pm (July-Aug. until 7.30pm, June and Sept. until 7pm).
Admission charge.

Take your first steps on the moon – this is just one of the amazing experiences offered in this 8½ acres (3½ ha) location devoted entirely to the great Toulouse

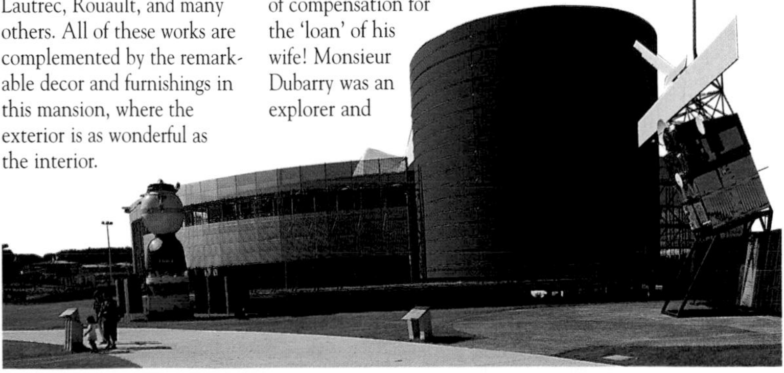

space adventure. In this interactive museum you can feel what it is like to be sent up in a rocket or what it is like to see the Earth from the space capsule, as well as many other fascinating exhibits. An out of this world adventure which ends at the foot of the rocket Ariane 5, which is stationed on the site.

Le Caillé du Sud-Ouest

Laiterie Trois A
183 Ave des Etats-Unis
☎ 05 61 58 87 35.

This is 'clabbered' milk, not to be confused with yoghurt, although they look very much alike! *Le caillé du Sud-Ouest* has a much closer texture and a smoother taste. This delicious regional speciality is made from ewe's milk and cow's milk. The curds are pressed, like cheese, as soon as the cow or ewe is milked. Whether plain or flavoured with vanilla, caramel, lemon, coffee or chocolate, *caillé* can be found in any grocer's as well as in all the big supermarkets.

The Cathedral of Saint-Étienne

Place Saint-Étienne

This cathedral is like an extraordinary Gothic puzzle in various disparate parts.

The Markets of Toulouse

If you want to take the trouble to make a genuine Toulouse *cassoulet*, get the best ingredients from the market held at the Place des Salins on Wednesday or Friday mornings. There are also excellent locally-produced foie gras and lovely bouquets of wild flowers. The organic market is held on Tuesdays and Saturdays in the Place du Capitole. Slightly out of town, the picturesque Saint-Aubin market is held in the square of the same name. The market still resembles a large country fair, with its cages stuffed with straw containing cackling chickens, all in the middle of an incredible mixture of languages and dialects.

In chronological order, the original façade dates from the 11th C., there is an initial nave (early 13th C.), then a second, offset nave (late 13th C.), stained glass windows (14th C.), the porch (15th C.), and a bell-tower-keep (16th C.). It houses a splendid organ in a loft 60 ft (18 m) above ground, an instrument whose console dates from the 17th C.!

Musée Paul-Dupuy

13 Rue de la Pleau
☎ 05 61 14 65 50.
Open daily except Tues. and public holidays, June-Oct., 10am-6pm; out of season, 10am-5pm. *Admission charge.*
This museum is dedicated to **medieval applied art**. Exhibited within the lovely 17th C. Hôtel Besson, there are a thousand and one objects and some amazing works of art. There are display cabinets

containing artefacts, applied art and measuring instruments. Do not miss the exceptional collection of clocks.

Jardin des Plantes

Allée Jules-Guesde
☎ 05 61 11 02 22.
Open daily, in summer, 8am-9pm.
The indestructible tree grows here, the *ginkgo biloba*, a Japanese tree which even grew again at Hiroshima after the devastation of the atom bomb. Discover its history and that of its 200 neighbours, including some true rarities. There is the yellow wooded vigil tree and the Siberian elm of the garden and in the centre, a wonderful pink and white magnolia which flowers in April. Stroll through the 17 acres (7 ha) which includes a hillock and a pond.

La Dépêche du Midi

Avenue Jean-Baylet
☎ 05 61 18 06 01.
Guided tour Mon.-Fri. (by appointment) at 10am, 2pm and 9.45pm.
Admission charge.
This is the Midi's newspaper, which you can visit at night when the rotary presses are turning. During the tour you will learn about the principal stages of manufacture of a large newspaper, from journalists' interviews and newsgathering in the region, to writing the articles, computer input, etc. This newspaper is the flagship of the local press and you will be able to read it as it comes off the press, as hot as a croissant from a bakery!

❀ Galerie Municipale du Château d'Eau

Place Laganne
☎ 05 61 77 09 40.
Open daily except Tues., 1-7pm.
Admission charge.
This is a trend-setting museum. It is housed in the brick tower of the former municipal pumping station and is where some of the **great photographers** meet. Bizzarely, the building is exactly the same age as photography itself, which was first invented in 1823. The gallery houses temporary exhibitions, which are displayed against the warm brickwork of this former working building.

L'Espace d'Art Moderne et Contemporain

76 Allée Charles-de-Fitte
☎ 05 61 59 38 67.
Open daily, June-Sept., 10am-6pm; out of season, 10am-noon and 2-6pm.
Admission charge.
The contemporary art museum, which is fairly new, is housed in the great hall of the former abattoirs of the city. Contemporary artists have allowed their creativity to flow (and there is plenty of room for them to do so). The theme of the museum's collections is 'international developments in post-war abstract art and Expressionism'. The avant-garde French artists such as Tàpies, Burri and Mathieu are all represented here.

The brickmaker of Toulouse

Maison Giscard
25 Avenue de la Colonne
☎ 05 61 48 87 03.
The pink city owes its hue to the light and its bricks, the predominant material used throughout the Toulouse district. Joseph Giscard is the only remaining brickmaker in the city, and he continues to make ornamental bricks. In his workshop-museum, you will find round windows, rose windows, balustrades and many decorative designs. Between the moulding and firing, ask him to tell you about the days, not so long ago, when his father made religious statues because, as he says, 'even then, bricks were not selling well'. Telephone first.

❀ African Safari

41 Rue des Landes
Plaisance-du-Touch
☎ 05 61 86 45 03.
Open daily, Apr. 1 Oct., 9.30am-8pm; out of season, 10am-6pm.
Admission charge.

ON THE CANAL DU MIDI

Société Dune, Port Saint-Sauveur ☎ 06 11 63 37 81. Open daily, 11am-7pm. Escape on to the Canal du Midi by renting a small family-size motor-boat, for an hour or a day, from the port of Saint-Sauveur, at the end of the Allée Paul-Sabatier in the east end of town. You don't need a permit to take to the waters on this wonderful water course, which is a UNESCO World Heritage Site. (440 F for half a day for 5 pers.; 650 F/day for 7 pers.).

The famous violet sweets of Toulouse

At this safari park the wild animals of Africa roam free while you can watch them from the safety of your car. This vast 37 acre (15 ha) plain is full of lions, zebras, rhinoceros and dromedaries. There is also a 12 acre (5 ha) zoo, where you can observe big cats at close quarters pacing up and down behind the barriers

The violet liqueur

Don't leave Toulouse without trying a taste of the liqueur that symbolises the capital of the South-west. The violet is a winter flower that begins blooming in October, and reaches its maturity in March. It is celebrated every 28 February in the garden of the Capitole, where you can pick the flowers from a restored greenhouse and make them into pretty bunches. For the rest of the year, the liqueur made from these sweet flowers is drunk in the much same way as *pastis* is drunk in Provence (or almost). At **Busquet** (10 Rue Rémusat, ☎ 05 61 21 22 16), you will find violet-scented sweets (79 F for a 3½ oz (100 g) box), the violet liqueur (95 F for a 12 fl oz (35 cl) bottle), as well as violet-scented teas (28 F for 1¾ oz (50 g)) and jellies (45 F for a 4¼ oz (120 g) jar).

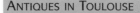

Something for the rugby fan

Fair Play (4 Allée Paul-Feuga, ☎ 05 62 26 56 57). This is a watering hole dedicated to the Toulouse rugby team. This pub-brasserie is owned by the Carbonneau brothers, former centres of the legendary Toulouse team. The accent is on sport with the decor to match. Immerse yourself in the sporting atmosphere then pay a visit to the **official stadium shop** (46 Rue d'Alsace-Lorraine, ☎ 05 62 27 06 37), for a thousand and one items printed with team's insignia, from the official shirt (499 F adult) to a perfume (120 F for a 3½ fl oz (100 ml) bottle).

Antiques in Toulouse

The antique market marks the beginning of the month in Toulouse. To discover a rare find, to rummage or go bargain-hunting, meet on the first Fridays, Saturdays and Sundays of the month in the Allées Jules-Guesde. Every Sunday, there is a flea-market in front of the Saint-Sernin basilica.

The perfume factory

Éts Berdoues
131 Route de Toulouse, Cugnaux
☎ 05 61 07 58 58.
Shop open Mon.Fri., 8.15am-noon and 1-4.30pm. Closed in Aug.
Within these fragrant workshops the scent of the Toulouse violet is turned into exotic perfume and other beauty products. Violets are such a valuable resource to the region because so many products

Rugby, king of the Toulouse sportswear shops

have been created from this humble flower, and the 'nose' of this establishment is constantly inspired to create

new products (violet scented soap, 26 F; violet water, 140 F for 7 fl oz (200 ml)).

Violet *cachous*

Lajaunie is a little violet-scented breath-freshening lozenge, which was created in Toulouse in 1880 by Léon Lajaunie, a local pharmacist. The *cachous* were sent all over the world. They were once flavoured with liquorice and packed in a little round tin, the exact size of a fob-watch. They have now diversified and become a breath-freshener for smokers and, allegedly, a cure for sea-sickness. The creator's pharmacy is still going at 2 bis Rue d'Alsace-Lorraine, ☎ 05 61 52 09 11, even though the decor has changed considerably since the creation of the *cachous'* famous little yellow box, which now remains a relic of the past.

A bunch of violets

Éts Jean Colombié
206 Route de Launaguet
☎ 05 61 47 82 62.
Open Mon.-Fri., 8am-noon and 2-6pm; Sat., 8am-noon and 2-6pm.

Jean Colombié, a Toulouse horticulturalist, loves his violets, these 'fragile little sisters' which he cultivates under glass. He will welcome you to his shop and tell you about the traditional crop which he is trying to revive. He is determined to improve the fragile strain of this local flower, the emblem of the city, which was for so many years in decline (see p. 60). He cultivates the traditional species as well as new strains, which he hopes will boost the local industry. You can buy violet seeds and bunches of violets, which are sold by weight (1 to 2 F per flower) or take some home in a pot (45 F a pot 4½ in (12 cm) in diameter). This way, you will always have a souvenir of Toulouse in your garden.

THE GARONNE FESTIVAL

Information
☎ 05 61 88 32 00.
First two weeks in July.
Admission charge.
Every summer, this festival marries the Garonne with the great rivers of the world and invites performers who live along the banks of the Garonne to come to the pink city. Music, exhibitions, and theatre – there is a lot going on during this lively festival.

Bagnères-de-Bigorre

This Pyrenean city was a favourite with the French writers Michel de Montaigne and George Sand. The natural hot springs and cold snow offer a a stark contrast, while just outside the town the vertiginous heights of the Pic du Midi are matched by the depths of the Médous cave.

The Observatory of the Pic du Midi

In the old town

First visit the old town. The 16th C. church of St. Vincent has an extraordinary bell-wall 25 ft (40 m) high, on three storeys. The 15th C. Jacobin tower is in a flamboyant Gothic style and there are the ruins of the cloister of Saint-Jean.

The museums of Bagnères

At the **Musée du Vieux-Moulin** (5 Rue Hount-Blanque, ☎ 05 62 91 07 33. Open Tues.-Fri. except public holidays, 10am-noon and 2-6pm. Admission charge), dedicated to popular art and traditions, the local cuisine is

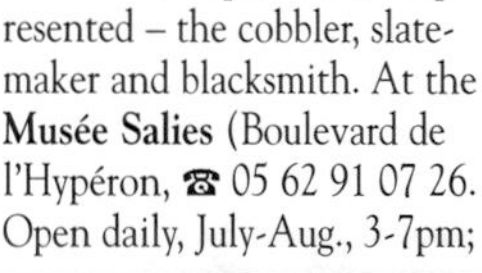

still going strong and all the old local occupations are represented – the cobbler, slate-maker and blacksmith. At the **Musée Salies** (Boulevard de l'Hypéron, ☎ 05 62 91 07 26. Open daily, July-Aug., 3-7pm; daily except Mon., May-Nov., 3-6pm. Closed Dec.-Apr. Admission charge), there is an overview of the great artistic movements from the 15th to the 20th C. The museum has Chinese and French pottery and porcelain, paintings of the Italian and Flemish schools and more.

Pic du Midi

Access by cable-car from La Mongie or by car via the D918 towards the Col du Tourmalet, then toll motorway on the right (+ 40 min. walk).

The peak is so-called because it reveals the Midi, and thus the south for the whole of the valley of the Adour. It has lovely views over the Pyrenees, including the mountain ranges of Maladeta and Néouvieille, the summits which overlook the Cirque de Gavarnie and the Vignemale. The foundation stone of the Observatory of the Pic du Midi, at an altitude of 9,550 ft (2,865 m), was first laid in 1878. The observatory is currently being renovated, and at the time of writing it was not yet reopened.

Musée du Vieux-Moulin, dedicated to local traditions

The caves of the Médous

Route des Cols, Asté (1¼ miles (2 km) S of Bagnères)

☎ 05 62 91 78 46.

Open daily, July-Aug., 9am-noon and 2-6pm; Apr.-15 Oct., 8.30-11.30am and 2-5.30pm. Closed 15 Oct.-March.

Admission charge.

These caves are like cathedrals. In the upper galleries there are the extraordinary accretions which decorate

Spotcheck

A4

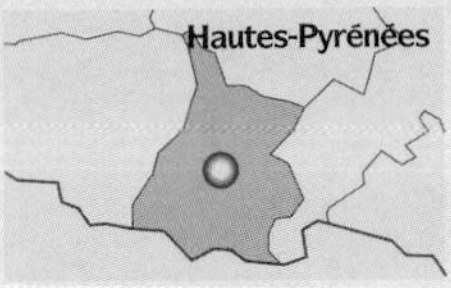

Things to do

- Pic du Midi
- The caves of Médous
- Relax at the Bagnères hot baths

Within easy reach

Tarbes, p. 196
Les Baronnies, p. 182
Lourdes, p. 190

Tourist Office

Bagnères-de-Bigorre:
☎ 05 62 95 50 71

A HEALTHY WORKOUT

Place des Thermes, Bagnères
☎ 05 62 95 00 23.
Bagnères-de-Bigorre is an old-fashioned health resort which also even looks after the casual visitor. Visit the Grands Thermes daily from 5-7.30pm to enjoy the benefits of the hot springs in winter after skiing or in summer after hiking. You can purchase a *ticket forme* (78 F) to visit year round. There is a swimming pool, jacuzzi, exercise machines, Turkish bath, sauna, aquagym (Tues. and Thurs.). The choice is yours.

the huge chambers, one set of which looks like organ pipes, another like the folds of curtains and the next a wonderful limestone cascade. You can take a trip on a rowing-boat in the lower part, along the subterranean course of the river Adour which goes underground here. An incredible experience!

A family pottery

Éts Cazalas, Vallon de la Gailleste, Pouzac (1¼ miles (2 km) N of Bagnères)
☎ 05 62 91 08 26.
Guided tour in July-Aug., Thurs. 8am-12.30pm and 1.30-7.30pm; other days by appointment.
Free admission.

The Cazalas family discovered they had deposits of china clay in their garden, so they began making ceramics. The family's skills have been passed down through the generations for 75 years. Their designs are hand-painted on an unfired glaze. You can see them for yourself by visiting the workshop and shop (Route de Tarbes, Bagnères. Open daily except Sun., 10am-12.30pm and 3-7pm). A decorated flask typical of Bigorre costs 99 F.

La Fromagerie des Palomières

Quartier des Palomières, Route de Hauban, Bagnères
☎ 05 62 95 20 05.
Open daily except Sun. afternoon, 8am-noon and 2-8pm. Guided tour by appointment.
Free admission.

This is where the famous Palomières cheese is made in its three varieties – pure cow's milk, pure ewe's milk or a combination of the two. Visit the premises and watch the cheese being made. The flavour is said to reflect the excellent quality of the grazing in the pastures overlooking the Adour. Taste them for yourself to see if it is true.

Les Baronnies
a trip through forgotten lands

Les Baronnies, between Bagnères-de-Bigorre and Capvern-les-Bains, is an area that time seems to have forgotten. In this beautifully preserved spot, little villages and hamlets sprinkle the hilltops and deep valleys of this green landscape, once ruled by four powerful barons. The cheese from the pastures continues to be made and the tradition of pig-rearing remains very much alive.

Mauvezin

3 miles (5 km) SW of Capvern-les-Bains via the D938

An impregnable fortress

20 Rue du Château
☎ 05 62 39 10 27.
Open daily, May-15 Oct., 10am-7pm; out of season, 1.30-5.30pm.
Admission charge.

This handsome 12th–14th-C. castle keep (123 ft (37 m) high), built on a strategic site, has been turned into a museum. It was used in the Middle Ages for protecting the Baronnies and its vicinity.

The war machines in the courtyard are evidence of this, and inside, you will find a magnificent golden book covered with prestigious dedications. There is a lovely view.

Bonnemazon

4 miles (7 km) SW of Capvern-les-Bains via the D938

The Cistercian abbey of the Escaladieu

Quartier du Couvent
☎ 05 62 39 16 97.

The Abbey of Escaladieu at Bonnemazon

Open daily, May-Sept., 10am-1pm and 2-7pm; out of season, daily except Tues., 10am-noon and 2-5pm.
Guided tour.
Admission charge.

The ruins here are evidence of the presence of Cistercian monks who came in the 12th C. to reclaim the Baronnies. The cloister, now gone, was surrounded by the remaining monastery buildings. The chapter house has an ogival ceiling and the abbey-church has an 18th C. belltower. Concerts are held here in the summer.

Esparros

8 miles (13 km) SW of Lannemezan via the D929

The Gouffre d'Esparros

☎ 05 62 39 11 80.
Open by appointment, 10am-noon and 2-6pm. Tour every 30 min. For opening days, call first as

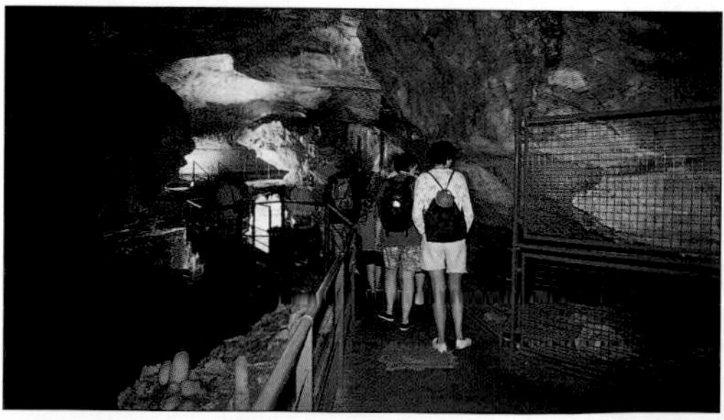

The little fruits of the Pyrenees

Ets Guillaume et Lesgards, Quartier Pierrefitte Lies, Route de Banios (20½ miles (33 km) SW of Lannemezan)
☎ 05 62 95 49 50.
Open Mon.-Fri., 9am-7pm; Sat., 9am-noon.
On the road to Bagnères-de-Bigorre, after the Col des Palomières, a magnificent garden containing a thousand and one fruits opens up before you. There are redcurrants, mulberries, raspberries, blackcurrants, strawberries, bilberries, all of which are made into the most wonderful jam (17 F for 11¼ oz (320 g)) or delicious liqueurs. After visiting the factory, taste the Pyrenean speciality, Liqueur de Génépi (63 F for 12 fl oz (35 cl)), made from an alpine mugwort.

this is a protected site and access is restricted.
Admission charge.
This subterranean jewel lies more than 370 ft (110 m) underground, with a profusion of breathtaking stalactites and stalagmites. In this deep grotto, a *son et lumière* show brings the stone lacework to life. You can also attend the mass celebrated around a statue of the Virgin which was placed down here more than 50 years ago.

Trie-sur-Baïse

18¾ miles (30 km) N of Lannemezan via the D17

The pig festival

2nd Sun. of August
☎ 05 62 35 50 05.
The houses in this pretty *bastide* are made of sandstone and golden limestone. It is a centre for pork cookery and the sale of piglets. Every year, a festival (known as La Pourcailhade) is held, which is dedicated to the pig. There are championships for mimicking pig grunts and squeals, piglet races and a contest to see who can eat the most black pudding. It all ends in a huge banquet – of pork dishes of course (60 F/pers.). Trie is also famous for its ***foires au broutard*** (sheep born that year which are old enough to graze) and its **poultry market** (held in January).

Spotcheck

A3-A4

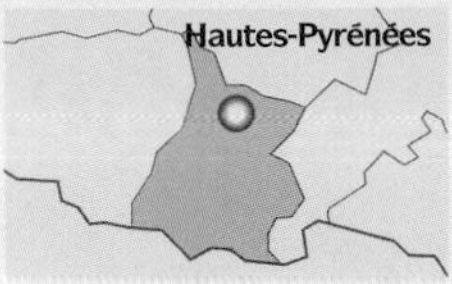

Things to do

- The gouffre d'Esparros
- Fruits of the Pyrenees
- The pig festival at Trie-sur-Baïse
- Cheese of the Baronnies

Within easy reach

Bagnères-de-Bigorre, p. 180
Saint-Bertrand-de-Comminges, p. 204
Tarbes, p. 196

Tourist Office

Lannemezan:
☎ 05 62 98 08 31
Trie-sur-Baïse:
☎ 05 62 35 64 37

Lombrès

12½ miles (20 km) SE of Lannemezan via the N117

The best cheeses

☎ 05 62 99 02 19.
Guided tour daily except during Whit Sunday weekend.
Free admission.
At this dairy, the milk from cows fed on the lush pastures of the Pyrenees is turned into Lou Lombrès cheese, a local speciality. You can watch the cows as they are milked twice a day, then visit the dairy and storeroom where the cheese is matured for at least three months. Each cheese weighs 3 lb 5 oz (1½ kg) and cost 65 F to 70 F per 2 lb 4 oz (1 kg), dependant on vintage.

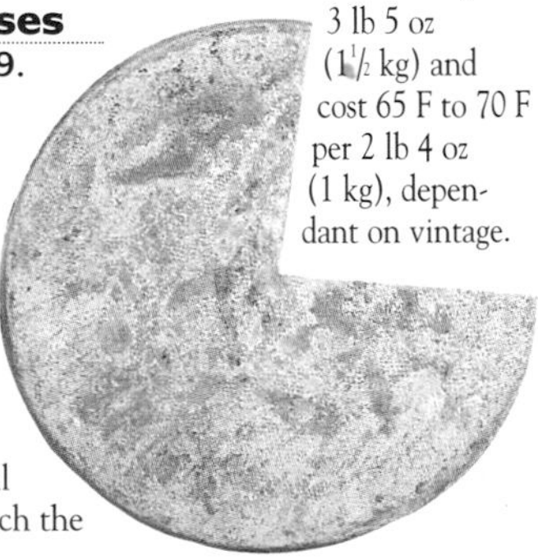

Gavarnie and the Pyrenean *cirques*

'Gavarnie: a miracle, a dream ...'. This is how Victor Hugo described these incredible rock formations in 1843. It is an astonishing sight. There are sheer cliffs, deep waterfalls, sloping, snow-covered ledges all surrounding the *cirque*, a semi-circular rock formation 2,666 ft (800 m) in diameter, widening at the top, the summits of which are more than 10,000 ft (3,000 m) high. The rock formations are soon to be registered as UNESCO World Heritage Sites.

The Cirque de Gavarnie

Access from the village of Gavarnie.
12½ miles (20 km) S of Luz-Saint-Sauveur via the D921

From the village, take the route to the Hôtel du Cirque. It is a 45 minute walk to get a close-up view of the **snow bridge** and the **great cascade** which is 1,470 ft (440 m) high and which freezes every winter. Be sure to wear sturdy footwear for walking on the permanent snow! Come back along the superb Pailha footpath which is rich in Pyrenean flora and has outstanding views.

Cirque de Troumousse

Access from the village of Gèdre.
13¾ miles (22 km) S of Luz-Saint-Sauveur via the D921, then D922

South of Gèdre, take the fork leading to Notre-Dame-d'Héas. Above the chapel, a toll road will lead you to paradise: 6¼ miles (10 km) of peaks surrounding a *cirque* nearly 3,330 ft (1,000 m) deep. From there, you can take a number of easy walks, to the statue of the Virgin with its unforgettable view, the **Lac des Aires**, or into Spain via the **Port de la Canaou**, which was once used by smugglers (this route is lightly more difficult).

45 GAVARNIE et le Cirque. - Hotel du Cirque. - LL.

The Cirque d'Estaubé

Access from the village of Gèdre.
13 miles (21 km) S of Luz-Saint-Sauveur via the D921

Go towards Héas, but take the turning on the right to the Gloriettes dam, a major Pyrenean hydroelectric station. From there, it will take two hours to get to the bottom of the *cirque* which is right inside the **Pyrenees National Park**. It is a wonderful walk with a unique view of **Mont Perdu** and the **Tuquerouye Gap**, which opens into Spain.

The Cirque de Barroude

Access from Aragnouet.
6¼ miles (10 km) SW of Saint-Lary via the D929

Allow a whole day. Above Aragnouet, after the turn-off for Piau, take the mountain footpath which turns off on

THE *PATOU BLANC* OF THE PYRENEES

This is the real name of the Pyrenean mountain dog. You may meet one guarding a flock of sheep. This huge sheepdog is an excellent shepherd, but don't get too close. He may look like a friendly pet, but he is unpredictable and may become aggressive. This is due to the fact that he is descended from the Tibetan mastiff, which accompanied its master in war (during the Middle Ages) and it will attack a wolf or a bear without hesitation. So be careful!

the right just after the first hairpin bend. The three-hour walk is along a **signposted footpath** which runs beside the **Neste d'Aure** of the **Géla**. This will bring you to the **Lac de Barroude** (8,446 ft (2,534 m)), which is surrounded by a wall of mountains. The *cirque* and the route are superb.

Luz-Saint-Sauveur

Pyrenean woollens

Éts Lafonds
☎ 05 62 92 81 95.
Free tour Mon.-Fri.
by appointment.
Closed Nov.
Free admission.

The traditional Pyrenean wool has been woven for five generations. It is warm and hairy and is used to make mountain blankets. The fleeces are washed and dried

in the sun, then dyed and woven in front of you. Then the wool is carded, the fibres combed and fluffed. The shop has woollens available in 15 colours.

Gèdre

7½ miles (12 km) S of Luz-Saint-Sauveur via the D921

Pragnères Power Station

Hameau de Pragnères
☎ 05 62 92 46 66.
Guided tour all year round, Mon.-Sat., 2-6pm (Sept.-June, by appointment). *Free admission.*

As well as the mountain stream, three lakes feed the biggest power station in the Pyrenees. The guided tour includes the turbine room and control room from which the water is forced down channels straight from the mountains. The output from this is 300 million kW/h annually, at 220,000 v!

Spotcheck
A4-A5

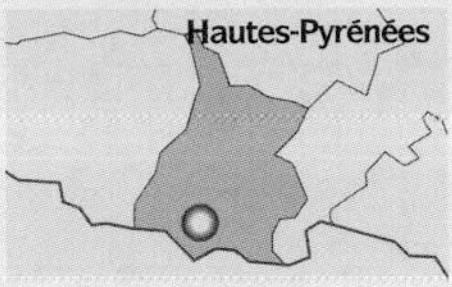

Things to do
- The Pyrenean cirques
- Pragnères Power Station
- The Gavarnie mountain Festival

Within easy reach
Bagnères-de-Bigorre 27 miles (43 km) NE, p. 180
Vallée d'Aure 26¼ miles (42 km), p. 198

Tourist Office
Gavarnie: ☎ 05 62 92 49 10
Luz-Saint-Sauveur:
☎ 05 62 92 81 60

Gavarnie

(8 km) S of Gèdre via the D921

A festival in the mountains

Information at the Tourist Office,
☎ 05 62 92 49 10.
Second fortnight in July.
Admission charge.

Every year, a huge theatrical and musical performance, created especially for the Cirque de Gavarnie, is held at an altitude of 4,830 ft (1,450 m). The setting is quite magical! Even though it is July, you will still need to bring warm clothing and sturdy footwear as it is a 20 minute walk to the festival site.

Le Lavedan and the mountain valleys

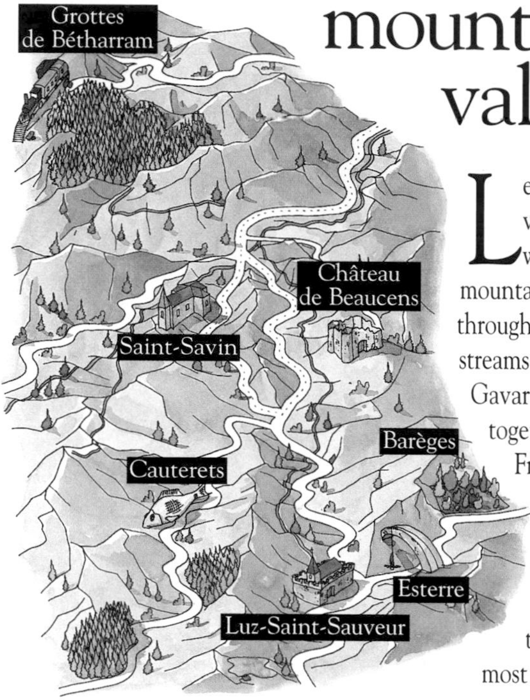

Le Lavedan covers the valleys of the streams which flow down the mountain, join up and run through Lourdes. The mountain streams of Arrens, Labat, Bun, Gavarnie and Cauterets flow together to become the Pau. From mountain landscapes to the plain of Lourdes, this part of the Hautes-Pyrenees is the most popular with tourists. It is also the most varied.

Saint-Pé-de-Bigorre

8¾ miles (14 km) W of Lourdes via the D937

The Bétharram Caves

☎ **05 62 41 80 04.**
Open daily, Apr.-Oct., 9am-noon and 1.30-5.30pm; Jan.-March, Mon.-Fri., guided tour at 2.30pm.
Admission charge.

The trip through these magnificent caves takes you partly by boat and then by a small train. These modes of transport will take you to waterfalls made from huge rock formations and the chandelier room – incredible limestone deposits five storeys high! Try to come in the morning and bring a sweater as it can get chilly in the caves.

Beaucens

5 miles (8 km) SE of Argelès-Gazost via the D100

❀ Falconry at the castle keep

☎ **05 62 97 19 59.**
Open daily, Apr.-Sept. The release of birds at 3.30pm and 5pm (at 3pm, 4.30pm and 6pm in August).
Admission charge.

In the ruins of a medieval castle which overlooks the village of Beaucens, falconers practise their traditional skills. You can witness the flight of these birds of prey, which come from all over the world. The display includes the condor of the Andes with its 10 ft (3 m) wing span and the kestrel which dives at 202 mph (324 kph).

La Biscuiterie des Pyrénées Latapie

ZA du Saillet
☎ 05 62 97 50 51.
Guided tour Mon.-Fri., 8.30am-noon.
Free admission.

You will melt when offered the 'snow of the Pyrenees' which covers this typical *croustade*. Latapie has been making cakes and biscuits since 1919, including this local speciality, based on traditional recipes. The *croustade* is filled with candied fruit and sprinkled with candied sugar. Among other treats, try the galette of the Pyrenees.

Saint-Savin

2 miles (3 km) S of Argelès-Gazost via the D921

The abbey-church

Said to be the loveliest church in the region, this monumental 12th C. abbey-church is in Romanesque style. It has a superb nave and famous font of the Cagots. Its altar screens represent the life of Saint Savin. The church has two unusual features. One is a splendid organ (1557) which has three grimacing heads on the console which roll their eyes and stick their tongues out whenever the organ is played! Next to the organ, the large Christ on the cross seems to be alive on one side and dead on the other!

Luz-Saint-Sauveur

12 miles (19 km) SE of Argelès-Gazost via the D921

The Church of Saint-André

God can feel quite safe inside this church, surrounded as it is by crenellated ramparts. The church dates from the 12th C. but was not fortified until the 14th C. – like no other church before. Enter through a narrow doorway protected by machicolation (the pulpit and staircase are 17th C.). Outside, there is a porch with a tympanum representing Christ in majesty, including the symbols of the authors of the four gospels.

Spotcheck

A4

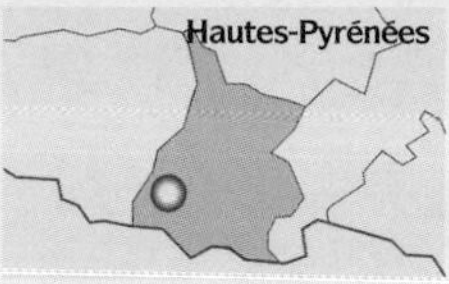

Things to do

- Bétharram Caves
- The falconers of Beaucens
- Bungee-jumping at Luz-Saint-Sauveur
- Rafting and canoeing on the gave de Pau
- The botanical garden of Tourmalet

Within easy reach

Lourdes 8 miles (13 km) N, p. 190
Bagnères-de-Bigorre 17 miles (27 km) W, p. 180

Tourist Office

Argelès-Gazost:
☎ 05 62 97 00 25
Cauterets:
☎ 05 62 92 50 27

The Church of Saint-André in Luz-Saint-Sauveur

❀ Thermal hot springs

Établissement Thermal,
Avenue Impératrice-Eugénie
☎ 05 62 92 81 58.
Open daily except Sun., May-15 Oct., 7.30-9.30am, 5-7.30pm; out of season, 4-8pm.
Admission charge.

Take advantage of the hot sulphurous waters of the Pyrenees, which spring from the ground in this mountain setting at 90°F (32°C). They are said to cure ailments caused by pollution and the stress of urban life. Come late in the day, after skiing in winter or hiking in summer (there are special evening rates for work-outs or relaxation), and bring your swimsuit (85 to 140 F).

Bungee Jumping

Elastic Pacific,
Esterre Bookings on
☎ 05 62 92 33 47.
Open all year round.

The Napoleon Bridge at Luz-Saint-Sauveur is one of the most well known sites in France for bungee jumping enthusiasts. Master your courage during the summer months and throw yourself from the top of this impressive engineering feat (400 F/pers.). Don't worry – the bridge spans a ravine which is only 300 ft (90 m) deep! You will be able to talk about it afterwards for a long time to come. On the Cauterets cable-car, only the bravest try a jump of 500 ft (150 m) (500 F/pers.).

Whitewater rafting

Pierre Maystre,
Chemin de Hountalade
Bookings on
☎ 05 62 92 86 45
or 06 81 63 18 18.

At the gates of the valley Luz, discover the sensation of whitewater rafting down one of the loveliest mountain streams of the the Pyrenees, the Gave de Pau. If you only have one day, you could do the section between Pierrefitte and Lourdes (6¼ miles (10 km)), or go as far as Betharram (15½ miles (25 km)). Although the experience is certainly exhilarating, it is all quite safe and suitable for a family outing (150 F/pers.).

CAUTERETS HUMBUGS

La Reine Margot
2 Avenue du Mamelon-Vert, Cauterets
☎ 05 62 92 58 67.
Open daily, from 9.30am (until 12am in July-Aug.). Closed Wed. out of season.
Discover the humbug known as the *berlingot de Cauterets*. It is native to the city and was invented during the reign of Napoleon III, when it was a simple throat pastille full of honey from the Pyrenees moistened with spa water and only for those taking the cure. It is still made from the original ingredients in small factories, but it has diversified. There are now 30 flavours to choose from (90 F for 2 lb 4 oz (1 kg)). If you fancy one late at night, La Reine Margot is open until 11pm.

Barèges

7½ miles (12 km) NE of Luz-Saint-Sauveur via the D918

The botanical garden of Tourmalet
5 Route du Tourmalet
☎ 05 62 92 18 06.
Open daily, May-Sept., 9am-6pm.
Admission charge.
The garden covers five acres (2 ha) of rocks, lawns, heath and forest, full of the infinite diversity of Pyrenean flora. Each plant is labelled with its name and characteristics, grouped by environment and altitude. Don't pick the flowers – you'll be able to buy some specimens in the gift shop at the exit.

Cauterets

10½ miles (17 km) S of Argelès-Gazost via the D920

La Pisciculture Domaniale
☎ 05 62 92 53 73.
Free or guided tour, Mon.-Fri., by appointment. *Free admission.*
This publicly-owned establishment has only one mission, that of repopulating the lakes and rivers of the Hautes-Pyrénées with fish of the salmon family: trout, salmon, char, etc. It produces 13 millions eggs a year, the result of the 'encouraged' egg-laying of some 19 tons (20 tonnes) of fish. The trout does not breed like a rabbit, so see what incentives are offered to the fish to improve their fertility!

Le pavillon des Abeilles
23 bis Avenue du Mamelon-Vert
☎ 05 62 92 50 66.
Open daily except Sun. morning, 10.30am-12.30pm and 3-7pm; out of season, Wed.-Sat., 3-7pm. Closed Nov.
Guided tour by appointment. Admission charge.
This is the kingdom of organic honey. Here the hives are full of mountain bees who will never know the flavour of chemical fertiliser! They gather pollen from heather, fir trees and rhododendrons, and use it to make pure Pyrenean nectar. Visit the bees, sample the honey, then you can purchase beauty products, honey (approx. 40 F), royal jelly, spiced bread (approximately 25 F depending on size), beeswax candles, and other products.

Lourdes the holy

This is one of the most famous pilgrimage sites in the Christian world. Sneak in amongst the five million annual visitors (of whom one million are pilgrims) who invade the village of Bernadette Soubirous. It is impossible to ignore the religious influence in what is now a prosperous town nestling at the foot of the Pyrenees.

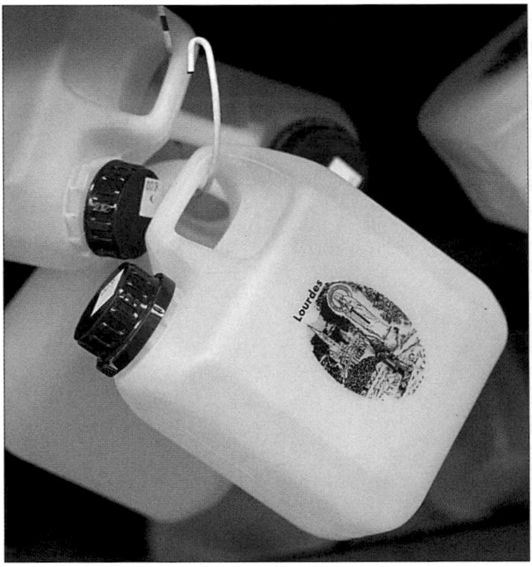

The sanctuary

Enter via the Esplanade des Processions, which can accommodate 40,000 people at a time, then visit the Rosary Basilica (1889). Above, the Upper Basilica of the Immaculate Conception was erected in 1876. Beneath the esplanade, the St. Pius X underground basilica was consecrated in 1958 and can hold 20,000 people. Fervour, traffic jams and silence surround the famous grotto where visions of the Virgin Mary were seen.

La Grotte de Massabielle

Beneath the upper basilica.

This is where the famous spring welled up at the time of the ninth vision (on 25 February 1858). Enter this tiny grotto (barely 30 ft (9 m) deep) dominated by a statue of the Virgin. It is supposedly based on the description given by Bernadette, yet when she saw it, she did not recognise 'her' Virgin in it. The spring continues to flow to the left of the altar.

Musée de Lourdes

Parking de l'Égalité
☎ 05 62 94 28 00.

Open daily, Apr.-Oct., 9-11.45am and 1.30-6.45pm (Sun. from 10am).

Admission charge.

Go back 150 years to the time when the little village of Lourdes had not yet seen any miracles. Discover the occupations traditionally followed by the villagers in Bernadette's day, such as the miller and the farrier, the little shops, the costumes and the site of the grotto as they existed before the visions. The life-size reconstructions have light and sound.

Sacred music festival at Lourdes

From Good Friday to the Sunday after Easter.
For information ☎ 05 62 42 77 40.
Admission charge.
This important annual event takes place in the Rosary Basilica at Lourdes, as well as in the Romanesque Saint-Savin Abbey and in the Cathedral of Notre-Dame-de-la-Sède at Tarbes. Every year, there are ten or so concerts performing the great musical classics, as well as little known or rarely heard works.

The castle and the Musée Pyrénéen

Rue du Bourg
☎ 05 62 42 37 37.
Open daily, Apr.-Sept., 9am-noon and 1.30-6.30pm; out of season, daily except Tues. and public holidays, 9am-noon and 2-6pm (Fri. 5pm).
Admission charge.
This 11th C. fortress dominates the town from its rocky spur. It contains a splendid museum dedicated to regional arts and traditions. The ancient residence of the Comtes de Bigorre was in the 15th C. castle keep. Inside, don't miss the Béarnaise kitchen and the Pyrenean room, the paleontology gallery, the costumes and ceramics.

Musée Grévin

87 Rue de la Grotte
☎ 05 62 94 33 74.
Open daily, Apr.-Oct., 9-11.30am and 1.30-6pm (at night July-Aug., 8.30-10pm).
Admission charge.
For the whole story of Bernadette Soubirous and life of Christ, wander through the five levels of this temple in which the 18 most important episodes of these two exceptional lives are recorded in wax with some hundred life-size figures. There is a large tableau of the Last Supper based on the painting by Leonardo da Vinci.

The Pic du Ger

Funicular at 59 Avenue Francis-Lagardère
☎ 05 62 94 00 41.
Open daily, Easter-Oct., 9.30am-noon, 1.30-6.15pm.
Admission charge.
Go up to the huge cross above Lourdes, which is illuminated every evening at nightfall, by taking the funicular. At the top (3,166 ft (950 m)), walk for 10 minutes to see the panorama over the plains of Tarbes and Pau. Wander back to the town on foot, by leaving the paved road from the observatory at the first turning and following the signposted path on the right.

Spotcheck

A4

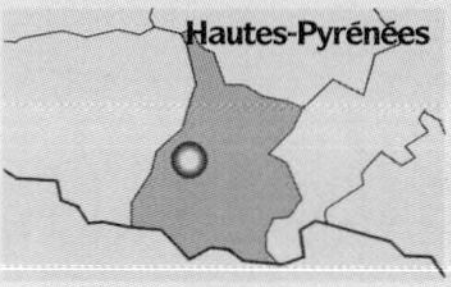

Things to do

- Sacred music festival during Easter
- Musée Grévin (waxworks)
- The Pic du Ger funicular

Within easy reach

Tarbes, p. 196
Bagnères-de-Bigorre, p. 180

Tourist Office

Lourdes: ☎ 05 62 42 77 40

Bernadette's birthplace

Moulin de Boly, Rue Bernadette-Soubirous
☎ 05 62 42 78 78.
Open daily, Apr.-Oct., 9am-noon and 2-6.30pm; out of season, 3-5pm. *Free admission.*
Open the door of the mill where she was born, and experience the home life of St. Bernadette. The machinery of the mill has not been moved and the original furniture has been preserved in the bedroom and kitchen. Right next door is the home of her parents (☎ 05 62 94 22 51), who kept their daughter's room intact with even a few photographs.

The Pyrenees National Park

a very natural detour

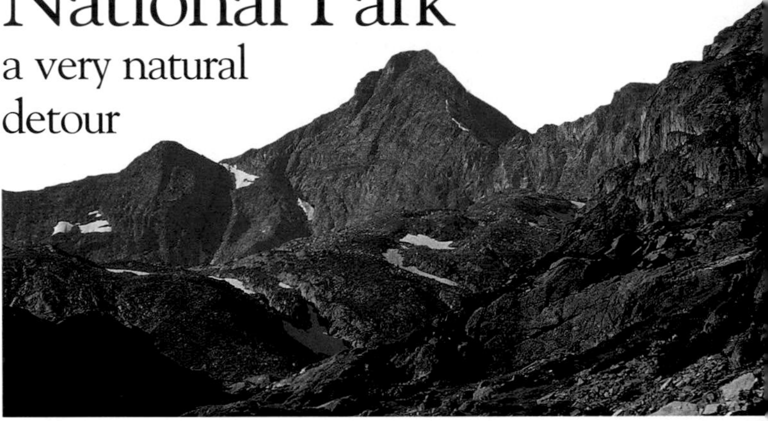

There are 113,700 acres (46,000 ha) of park which stretch for about 62 miles (100 km) along the Spanish frontier. In the Hautes-Pyrénées, access to the western Pyrenees National Park is via four valleys, the Val d'Azun, the Vallée de Cauterets, the Vallée de Luz-Gavarnie and the Vallée d'Aure. The park is a wonderful place full of wild flowers and unusual animals, and the mountain scenery is captivating.

Le Pont d'Espagne

From Cauterets to the Puntas car park via the D920, then by ski-lift.
This is one of the finest sights in the park. Even before arriving, all along the valley as far as Puntas, you can see a succession of splendid waterfalls giving you a taster of what awaits you higher up. The ski-lift will take you 5 miles (8 km) further, to where the Pont d'Espagne spans a 4,986 ft (1,496 m) ravine in a breathtaking landscape. There are lots of hiking trails in the vicinity.

Lac de Gaube

From the Pont d'Espagne by chairlift.
When you dismount the chair-lift (5,773 ft (1,732 m)), a path will lead you to the shores of the lake in less than 15 minutes. The emerald green waters are fed by the glaciers of Vignemale (10,990 ft (3,298 m)), the highest point of the French Pyrenees, whose north face you will be able to see. For a complete tour of the lake and a wonderful hike, follow the GR10.

The peaks of the Lys

From Cauterets by cable-car.
This is the loveliest view in the Pyrenees National Park. At Cauterets, the **Lys cable-car** (open all year round) will take you directly from 3,000 to 6,133 ft (900 m to 1,840 m). Once you reach Lys, the panorama over the glacier and the *cirque* is tremendous. Then travel to the peaks of the Grand-Barbat at 7,666 ft (2,300 m) using the **Grum chair-lift**. A signpost will show you all the major peaks in the range.

Hiking with a guide

Bureau des Guides et des Accompagnateurs,
2 Place George-Clemenceau, Cauterets
☎ 05 62 92 62 02 or
☎ 05 62 92 62 78.
Open daily, 10am-noon and 4.30-7.30pm; out of season by appointment.
For an *à la carte* look at the park, call in the experts. Local mountain guides and instructors organise many

THE HOUSES IN THE PARK

Cauterets
☎ 05 62 92 52 56.
Open daily, 9.30am-noon and 3-7pm; out of season, until 6.30pm.

Saint-Lary
☎ 05 62 39 40 91.
Open daily, 9am-noon and 2-6.30pm; out of season, closed on Wed. and Sun.

Luz-Saint-Sauveur
☎ 05 62 92 83 61.
Open daily except Sat. and Sun. morning, 9am-noon and 2-7pm.

Gavarnie
☎ 05 62 92 49 10.
Open daily in summer, 9am-noon and 1.30-6.30pm.

These are information and education centres where you can learn about what the area has to offer. In addition to publications produced by the park, they offer exhibitions and slide-shows. It is here that you will learn about hiking trails (219 miles (350 km) of signposted footpaths) and the best places for rock-climbing or fishing. They can tell you all you need to know about exploring the mountains. Never ignore their good advice!

guided tours. They know the park inside out and they will teach you about its flora and fauna, explain its traditions, and the history and economy of the valleys. (One-day group excursion, 360 to 400 F/pers. in high mountains; 90 to 190 F/pers. middle mountains. Private guide for 1 to 8 people, 1,350 F for the day.)

In the land of rare animals

The park contains many of the larger mammals that have now become rare in Europe, including the brown bear, the very symbol of the Pyrenees (you are unlikely to see one), or the lynx (also very shy). Fortunately, marmots and isards have been saved from extinction. You may be lucky enough to see some of the rare birds. There are 50 breeding pairs of griffon vultures and bearded vultures. Even rarer are the Egyptian vultures who fly into the park in March in order to build their nests.

Spotcheck
A4-A5

Things to do
- Pont d'Espagne
- Lac de Gaube
- The peaks of the Lys
- Hiking with a guide

Within easy reach
Le Lavedan 11¼ miles (18 km) N, p. 186
Vallée d'Aure 9 miles (15 km) E, p. 198

Tourist Office
Park office at Tarbes:
☎ 05 62 44 36 60

Don't pick the daisies!

The Pyrenean flora consists of 400 species of flowers, and it is particularly well represented and protected in the park. Of particular importance and interest are the saxifrage, the blue cardoon, the ramonda and the fritillary. Try not to miss the only flower that is native to the area, the famous Pyrenean lily. Of course, you must never pick any of these wild flowers, but enjoy their beauty in a natural setting.

The mountain passes of the Tour de France

The mountain passes on the route of the Tour de France are linked to each other by a road called the 'four passes stretch'. This is claimed to be the place where the Tour de France is lost or won. It will take a day to cover the 75 miles (120 km) of mountain roads on foot, but you can also do it by car.

Col de l'Aubisque

27 miles (43 km) SW of Lourdes.
Altitude: 5,696 ft (1,709 m).
The Tour de France competitors know it for its magnificent all-round view. The whole of Béarn is at your feet and to the south there is the magnificent Cirque de Gourette. But further on another surprise is in store for you on the way down to Soulor. In summer, the tunnel often hides a group of cows who are enjoying the cool shade. Immediately after the tunnel, the route twists and turns into a dizzying corniche road.

Col du Soulor

6¼ miles (10 km) E of the Col de l'Aubisque by D918.
Altitude: 4,913 ft (1,474 m).
The pastoral landscape is mainly inhabited by cattle. The cowbells of the brown cows can be heard everywhere. The Mérens horse, a Pyrenean breed with a prehistoric look, also lives here. At the top, buy some cheese at the **Saloir** (open daily, 10am-7pm. Cow's milk cheese, 45 F for 2 lb 4 oz (1 kg); mixed 65 F for 2 lb 4 oz (1 kg); ewe's milk 85 F for 2 lb 4 oz (1 kg)).

Col du Tourmalet

11¼ miles (18 km) NE of Luz-Saint-Sauveur.
Altitude: 7,050 ft (2,115 m).
The name means 'dirty trick', but the view over the high Pyrenean peaks is unforgettable,

THE SAOUSSAS MILL

Georgette Martin, Lieu-dit Saoussas, Loudenvielle (3 miles (5 km) W of the Col de Peyresourde) ☎ 05 62 99 90 50 or 05 62 99 64 17. Open daily, July-Aug., 10.30am-noon and 3-7pm; out of season, by appointment. ***Admission charge.*** **This mill contains some well-preserved old millstones which were recently put back into service. You can witness a live demonstration of the working mill turning grain into flour (which is unfortunately not for sale). There is also an exhibition displaying the tools of the old mountain occupations of the 18th and 19th C. – the carpenter, roof-tiler, clog-maker and of course, the shepherd.**

and especially of the highest of them, the Pic du Midi. The pass is open to cars around Whitsun (Pentecost), once the last snows have disappeared. This is the part of the route where many of the competitors in the Tour de France throw in the towel, by abandoning the race or falling off their bikes. So spare a thought for them as you press your foot down on the accelerator!

Col d'Aspin

18¾ miles (30 km) E of the Col du Tourmalet. Altitude: 4,960 ft (1,489 m).

This classified site is completely untouched and has preserved an exceptional natural look. Just before the summit, the road passes through magnificent fir tree plantations, which have a wonderful fragrance. At the top, the view of the summits of the Vallée d'Aure is incredible. To simply imagine the effort of those scalling the peak on two wheels, come here directly after the Col du Tourmalet: 18¾ miles (30 km) to descend 7,050 ft (2,115 m) and then climb some 4,966 ft (1,490 m)!

Spotcheck

A4-B4

Things to do

- Pyrenean cheeses at the Col du Soulor
- Visiting an old mill

Tourist Office

Argelès-Gazost:
☎ 05 62 97 00 25
Luz-Saint-Sauveur:
☎ 05 62 92 81 60

Col de Peyresourde

18¾ miles (30 km) SE of the Col d'Aspin. Altitude: 5,230 ft (1,569 m).

This is the ultimate obstacle for the Tour de France competitors before they reach the Luchon stage (10 km (16 km) further on). The cyclists throw their last ounce of strength into it, as the route sorts out the men from the boys. This exciting stage is make or break time; there are sure to be some drama-filled scenes! Take some of the hairpin bends on the western side before the summit. This road is incredibly steep – even by car – which makes the achievement of these cyclists even more amazing.

Col de Couraduque

12½ miles (20km) W of Argelès-Gazost. Altitude: 4,500 ft (1,350 m).

This little pass, lost in the mountains, is the departure point in winter of many cross-country skiing runs, which wind through the forests of fir trees to the Soulor pass. In the summer, the 27 miles (43 km) of ski trails become beautiful paths for hikers.

Tarbes, home of the white bean

Tarbes is a very quiet place. It is the capital of the Bigorre district and is above all a garrison town (the home base of the hussar paratroopers) and a place of patriotism. This is the home town of Marshal Foch, hero of World War I. But they also know how to enjoy themselves here, and in the shadow of the Pyrenees, they grow the famous Tarbes bean. It is sweet, delicate, melting and sublime.

The Musée Massey

Rue Massey
☎ 05 62 36 31 49.
Open daily, 10-11.30am and 2-6.30pm; out of season, closed Mon. and Tues.
Admission charge.

The neo-Moorish style building that is home to this fine art museum is not lacking in its own charm. It offers a complete overview of European painting, from the Renaissance to modern times. Look for *Tarbes Cathedral* by Utrillo and *Christ in Chains* by Pontormo. The museum is in the midst of planning a section devoted to local traditions.

Cathedral of Notre-Dame-de-la-Sède

The cathedral began life as a Romanesque building, but was rebuilt many times, starting in the 12th C. The exterior is rather severe, but you'll find the interior much more ornate. Along the nave, the galleries above the pews were added in the 18th C., made from carved walnut. The splendid 18th-C. altar-tomb is topped with a magnificent canopy supported on six columns, which is reminiscent of one in St. Peter's in Rome.

Birthplace of Marshal Foch

2 Rue de la Victoire
☎ 05 62 93 19 02.
Open daily, May-Sept., 9am-noon and 2-6.30pm; out of season, daily except Tues. and Wed., 9am-noon and 2-5pm.
Admission charge.

THE KING OF BEANS

Coopérative Haricot Tarbais,
Z.A. Bastillac-Sud
☎ 05 62 34 76 76.
Open Mon.-Fri.,
10am-noon and 2-6pm.
The Tarbes is the king of white beans: delicate, melting and very slightly sweet. Taste this regional gastronomic delight, which owes its fame to its cultivation in the shade of corncobs and the sworn absence of any chemical fertiliser. Buy fresh or dried beans in packets weighing 17½ oz (500 g) (for 32 F) or 2 lb 4 oz (1 kg) (for 60 F) and enjoy them in a genuine Tarbes-style *cassoulet.*

In this house, typical of the district, Marshal, or rather little Ferdinand Foch, was born in 1851. The museum is full of portraits of the famous soldier and evocations of the 'revenge' for the Franco-Prussian defeat of 1870, which he launched in 1914-18. His office and campaign room are here. There are numerous items, including period furniture, uniforms, swords and statues of the Marshal who was also a member of the Académie Française.

The national stud

Chemin du Mauhourat (visitors entrance)
☎ 05 62 56 30 80.
Open daily, 10am-noon and 2-5pm. Guided tour every 30 min.
Admission charge.
This national stud-farm breeds Anglo-Arab stallions under the protection of the state. The stud-farm stands in a century-old, 20 acre (8 ha) park. You can watch the horses resting in their stables or working in the riding school. You can also visit the high-tech laboratory where the most modern techniques are applied to improve and continue the line. In the **Maison du Cheval**, you can learn about shoeing, saddlery and diet, and see some carriages.

Markets and carriage rides

The **biggest market in the region** is held every Thursday in the Place Marcadieu, in the market hall. All the local produce is on sale: garlic from Gers, carrots from Asté, geese and ducks, cheese and mountain honey. On the first Saturday of the month, an **antiques market** is held in the same market hall. In summer, don't miss the romantic **carriage rides** in the town centre (information at the Tourist Office, ☎ 05 62 51 30 31).

Spotcheck

A3

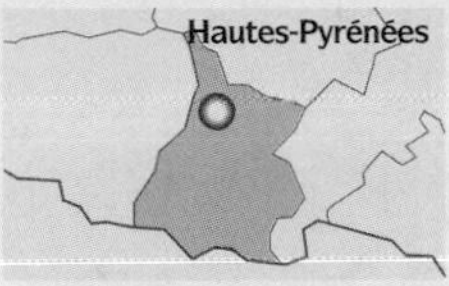

Things to do

- The national stud
- The markets of Tarbes
- Le Jardin Massey

Within easy reach

Lourdes, p. 190
Baronnies, p. 182
Val d'Adour, p. 112

Tourist Office

Tarbes:
☎ 05 62 51 30 31

Le Jardin Massey

Rue Massey/
Place Henri Bordes
(N of the town centre).
Open daily, until 9pm in summer.
There are huge Lebanese cedars, large lawns and shady avenues around two lakes in this 32 acre (13 ha) garden. Tarbes has the most English of public gardens. At each step, there is another surprise waiting, such as

camelias, azaleas, sequoias, flowerbeds, statues, a 15th C. cloister, deer, moufflons, swans and peacocks (among others). This landscaped park is full of all sorts of attractions.

The valleys of the Aure and Louron

the gateway to Spain

South of Lannemezan, the valleys of Aure and Louron are completely Pyrenean. They are dominated by the peaks of Tramezaïgues, protected from rain by Néouvielle and the peaks of the Midi, so the spring weather is amazingly mild. Skiers frequent the district in winter and in summer the area is popular for all sorts of activities – sporting, artistic, ecological and cultural.

The painted churches of Louron

Information and tours at the Tourist Office of the Vallée d'Aure
☎ 05 62 98 63 15.

These are the most interesting features of the region. The churches were painted by shepherds in the 16th C., when neighbouring Spain allowed them to profit from its prosperity. At Vielle-Louron, the ceiling of the Church of **Saint-Mercurial** is covered by a Tree of Jesse. At Estarvielle, the Church of **Saint-Blaise** is painted and the Church of **Saint-Barthélémy** in Mont has a façade that is completely decorated, in addition to the frescoes on the ceiling.

Val-Louron

10½ miles (17 km) S of Arreau

Family skiing

Information at the Tourist Office of the Vallée du Louron,
☎ 05 62 99 92 00.

This family resort at an altitude of 4,830 ft (1,450 m) and 7,170 ft (2,150 m) has 13¾ miles (22 km) of skiing pistes to suit every level (7 blue, 5 green, 6 red and 1 black). It overlooks the magnificent Valley of Louron, and has eight ski-lifts and two chair-lifts. Nursery slopes are laid out for beginners, away from the downhill course. For cross-country skiing, visit **Peyragudes-Balestas** on the other side of the valley (9 miles (15 km) of pistes, ☎ 05 62 99 69 99).

Saint-Lary-Soulan

Les flocons pyrénéens

14 Rue Principale
☎ 05 62 40 09 61.

Open daily, July-Aug. and 15 Dec.-Easter, 9.30am-12.30pm and 3-7pm; out of season, closed on Sun. afternoon and Mon.

NÉOUVIELLE NATURE RESERVE

12½ miles (20 km) from Saint-Lary via the D118, then the D929.

Néouvielle means 'old snow', like the snow on this range, which remains even in the height of summer. This high mountain reserve has been protected since 1968. You can study the flora and fauna while on a hike of at least 3 to 4 hours, very often at above 6,670 ft (2,000 m). Information and details about the trails are available at the Maison du Parc National des Pyrénées at Saint-Lary-Soulan (☎ 05 62 39 40 91. Open daily, June-Sept., 9am-noon and 2-6.30pm; out of season, closed on public holidays, Wed. and Sun.).

These delicious sweets, called Pyrenean snowflakes, melt in the mouth like snow melts in the sun. They are made from a praline mixture of almonds and hazelnuts with dark chocolate, covered in a soft meringue coating. They cost 28 F for 3½ oz (100 g). You can also visit the chocolate factory at Barthe-de-Neste (☎ 05 62 98 82 26. By appointment).

Water sports

La Maison du Canyon, For booking ☎ 05 62 40 76 76.

If you are a thrill-seeker, try your hand at **canyoning**, a sport that combines rock-climbing, abseiling, swimming in white water and walking in the gushing waters of the Pyrenees. Never try this alone. The sport is exhilarating but very active. If you prefer water sports in a group, opt for whitewater **rafting** (École Pyrénéenne des Sports de Montagne, Saint-Lary-Soulan, ☎ 05 62 39 48 49).

Vielle-Aure

1¼ miles (2 km) N of Saint-Lary

Hang-gliding

École de la Vallée d'Aure, Hameau du Soleil, For registration ☎ 05 62 39 58 75.

In the Valley of the Aure, with drops of 1,670 to 4,000 ft (500 to 1,200 m), you can experience total intoxication. You will first learn to fly on a two-person glider (with a qualified instructor), then learn to fly solo, drifting above the Pyrenees. Before landing (in an authorised area), watch the windsock on the ground, it will show you which way the wind is blowing. Half-day introduction (180 F), then first flight (350 F).

Spotcheck

A4-B4

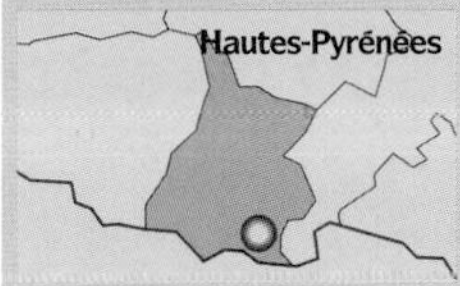

Things to do

- Skiing at Val-Louron
- Hiking in the Néouvieille nature reserve
- Rafting and canyoning
- Hang-gliding at Saint-Lary

Within easy reach

Bagnères-de-Luchon 9 miles (15 km) E, p. 200
Les Baronnies 18¾ miles (30 km) N, p. 182
Bagnères-de-Bigorre 18 miles (29 km) NW, p. 180

Tourist Office

Vieille-Aure:
☎ 05 62 39 50 00
Saint-Lary:
☎ 05 62 39 50 81
Vallées d'Aure et du Louron: ☎ 05 62 98 63 15
☎ 05 62 98 64 12
☎ 05 62 99 92 00

Bagnères-de-Luchon
from lakes to torrents

This district of lakes, mountains and fast-flowing mountain streams in the southern Haute-Garonne has peaks reaching 12,000 ft (3,000 m) into the Pyrenean skies. Bagnères-de-Luchon (also known simply as Luchon) is famous for winter sports, pure air and water, hot springs and natural steam baths. There are lovely Romanesque churches and old marble quarries in the surrounding valleys.

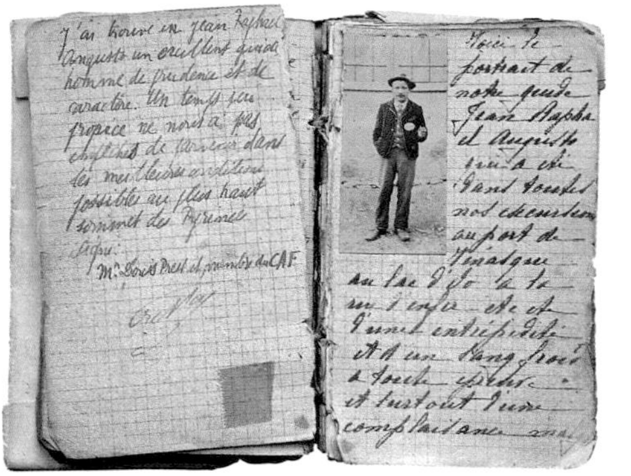

A Pyrenean guide's notebook from the Musée du Pays de Luchon

❀ Musée du Pays de Luchon

18 Allée d'Étigny
☎ 05 61 79 29 87.
Open daily, 9am-noon and 2-6pm; Nov., open only Wed., Fri. and Sat.
Admission charge.

All the secrets of Luchon, are revealed in this museum. There are the mountains (a magnificent relief map), the waters (hot and cold), local traditions, winter sports (see the first skis used in the Pyrenees), native wildlife, traditional occupations and churches. There is also an amusing portrait gallery of celebrities who have popularised Luchon, from Flaubert to James Bond!

The thermal baths

Établissement Thermal
3 Cours des Quinconces
☎ 05 61 94 52 52.

In Luchon's large baths complex, hot water wells up in a continuous stream at 113°F (45°C), inside a huge grotto. There are medicinal cures, of course, but the **Complexe Vitaline** is open to the overstressed who want to use their holiday in order to pamper themselves. Enjoy a natural steam bath in this 'saunatorium', which is unique in Europe. The mists of Luchon are excellent for the mucous membranes, and the hot baths are also highly recommended for complete relaxation. (Vitaline, ☎ 05 61 79 22 97. Open daily, July-Aug., 4-8pm; Apr.-June and Sept.-Oct., daily except Sun., 4-7pm. Head-to-toe water treatment costs about 110 F).

Luchon's local dishes

If you like tripe, then you will enjoy Luchon's local dishes. In this area of good grazing land, ask for a taste of *pélérum*, a typical dish based on mutton tripe (cleverly spiced) and potatoes simmered gently for a long time in white wine. Or try *pistaches* – a combination of white Tarbe beans and duck *confit*. However, don't try both dishes at once – their richness may be too much of a strain on the digestion! If at all possible, go and try them at the Hôtel d'Étigny, which faces the baths. (☎ 05 61 79 01 42. Open Apr.-24 Oct.). When Monsieur Organ, the owner of the Hôtel d'Étigny, begins to describe how he finally bastes the meat in Armagnac, or enthuses over the Tarbes bean, you'll feel as if you'll die of hunger! The welcome is warm and service is excellent at this hotel (*pétéram* or *pistachio*: 145 F per person).

Water, water everywhere

Sté des Eaux Minérales de Luchon
22 Avenue de Toulouse
☎ 05 61 79 85 98.

This is the most precious of Luchon's assets. After enjoying the therapeutic hot baths, put this unique

mineral water on your dinner table. It's so pure it has been classified since 1990! It has a low mineral content and is balanced and refreshing. You can watch as it is poured into the 30 million bottles that emerge from this factory every year.

The arboretum of Joueou

5 miles (8 km) S of Bagnères-de-Luchon
☎ 05 61 79 05 83.
Open daily, Apr.-Oct., from dawn till dusk.
Admission charge.

This enchanting arboretum is

at an altitude of more than 3,330 ft (1,000 m). Try to distinguish between the hundreds of species in this **magnificent collection of trees**. They have all been planted here to test their ability to adapt to the mountain climate. Fortunately, the experiment has been a success. Nearly 250 species have adapted. Enjoy a peaceful stroll through the 12 acres (5 ha) in which thorny trees predominate.

Spotcheck

B4

Things to do

- Treatments at the Luchon hot baths
- Visit to the arboretum of Joueou
- Skiing at Superbagnères

Within easy reach

Saint-Bertrand-de-Comminges 19 miles (31 km) N, p. 204
Vallée d'Aure 9 miles (15 km) W, p. 198
Vic-Fézensac 9 miles (15 km) NE, p. 117

Tourist Office

Bagnères-de-Luchon:
☎ 05 61 79 59 59
☎ 05 61 79 21 21

Skiing at Superbagnères

In winter, thanks to the cable-car which links Luchon directly to Superbagnères at an altitude of 6,000 ft (1,800 m), you will find yourself on the ski slopes within minutes. This famous Pyrenean mountain resort has 23 pistes and 16¾ miles (27 km) of routes for cross-country skiers, 23 of them through forests. In summer, hikers have splendid views of the whole mountain range.

Comminges
between plain and mountain

Around Saint-Gaudens, the historic capital, this former province of Gascony is dotted with châteaux, abbeys and cathedrals. Its roots go right back to the Gallo-Roman era and beyond into prehistory. At Aurignac, traces of the first human life in the area have been discovered, dating from 30,000 BC. Nearby, the craft potters show themselves to be talented descendants.

Montmaurin

12½ miles (20 km) N of Saint-Gaudens via the D9

A trip into Gallo-Roman territory

Villa Gallo-romaine de Montmaurin
☎ 05 61 88 74 73.
Open daily, 9.30am-noon and 2-6pm (closes 5pm out of season); closed Tues. Sept.-May.
Admission charge.

Visit the largest Gallo-Roman villa excavated in France, which has 200 rooms covering 10 acres (4 ha). This was the 4th-C. version of modern convenience. Central heating was installed in all the main rooms, the inner courtyard was a real garden and the marble apartments had balconies. This huge residence was abandoned for 15 centuries after it burned down, but the even the remains of a last meal of oysters was found here.

Aurignac

13¾ miles (22 km) NE of Saint-Gaudens via the D8

A journey back in time

In this medieval village nestling at the foot of its fortress-château, the remains have been discovered of the people who lived here nearly 300 centuries ago! Their history is detailed in the lovely **Musée de la Préhistoire** (Rue Fernand-Lacorre, ☎ 05 61 98 90 08. Open daily, July-Aug., 9.30am-12.30pm and 2-6pm; out of season, Mon.-Fri. Admission charge). All around lie the remains of the 13th-C. town, including fortifications, the city gate, church and château. From the top of the round castle keep, the view of the Pyrenees is unbeatable.

Valentine

1¼ miles (2 km) SW of Saint-Gaudens via the D8

The Palace de Nymphius

☎ 05 61 89 05 91.
Free admission (open site).

Nymphius, the Roman governor of the province of Aquitaine, lived here in the 4th C. The remains of the palace are well worth a detour. There is a forecourt,

THE HOT BATHS OF SALIES-DU-SALAT

15 miles (24 km) E of Saint-Gaudens
☎ 05 61 90 56 41. Open Apr.-Nov.
Sun, salt and water. The very sunny and windless microclimate of this spa reinforces the beneficial effects of its heavily salted water – 11 oz/1¾ pt (322 g/l)!. The Romans patronised the place heavily in ancient times. Follow their example and take a dual salt and sun bath, thus proving the town motto: *In sale salus* (health through salt). It is recommended for rheumatism, gynaecological and pediatric disorders. There are no one-day treatments, but you can book in for a longer stay (of at least a week; Mon.-Fri., 2-5pm, by appointment only).

Spotcheck
B4

Things to do
- The Gallo-Roman villa at Montmaurin
- The Matet Pottery at Martres-Tolosane
- The Cardeilhac arboretum

Within easy reach
Saint-Bertrand-de-Comminges 8¾ miles (14 km) W, p. 204
Le Volvestre 18¾ miles (30 km) NE, p. 168
Saint-Girons 28¾ miles (46 km) SE, p. 218

Tourist Office
Saint-Gaudens:
☎ 05 61 94 77 61
Martres-Tolosane:
☎ 05 61 98 68 26

a swimming pool (once lined with marble) topped by three columns, a reception room and apartments. Just 170 ft (50 m) away are the remains of the pagan temple where the governor worshipped and the church which later replaced it.

Martres-Tolosane

15 miles (24 km) NE via the N117

The Matet Pottery

15 Rue du Matet
☎ 05 61 98 81 30.
Guided tour, Mon.-Fri., 9am-noon and 2-6pm. Shop open daily: Mon.-Fri., 9am-noon and 2-6pm; Sat., 10am-noon and 2-6pm; Sun., 3-6pm. *Admission charge.*
In Carlo Rocca's workshop, you can watch pottery being made. The clay is kneaded, shaped, fired, enamelled and decorated by hand (using a brush made from the hairs from the ears of a cow). The patterns are original with names such as Ibis, Rose de Samadet, Vieux Martres (from 110 F for a plate and from 780 F for a soup tureen).

Cardeilhac

10½ miles (17 km) NW of Saint-Gaudens via the D9 and the D69

The arboretum

☎ 05 61 88 90 69.
Free admission all year round, 2-7pm (Sun. and public holidays, noon-7pm). Paid guided tour in July-Aug.
The 33 acre (13 ha) arboretum was created in 1913 in order to study the behaviour of certain trees and is now open to the public for walks. There are **signposted paths, interpretation paths, running tracks and bridle-ways** through the Japanese spruce, American oak, sequoias and pine trees. There are two adventure trails for children and adults.

Saint-Bertrand-de-Comminges

queen of the Pyrenees

Perched on top of a promontory, Saint-Bertrand-de-Comminges is the St. Michael's Mount or 'Petit Mont-Saint-Michel' of the Pyrenees. On this strategic site overlooking the river Garonne, the Romans built a town in the first century of the common era. As a focal point of the Pyrenees, Saint-Bertrand contains traces of the last 2000 years of local history.

The Cathedral of Sainte-Marie

Open daily, July-Sept., 9am-7pm (Sun. 9-10.30am and 2-7pm); Apr.-June, 9am-noon and 2-7pm (Sun. 9-10.30am and 2-7pm); Nov.-Feb., 10am-noon and 2-5pm (closed Sun. morning).
Admission charge for the entire guided tour.
The cathedral's huge Romanesque belltower, 110 ft (33 m) high, looks like a castle keep.

The interior shows the development of the building. It was Romanesque at first (12th C. portal), but the decor soon changed to Gothic (14th C. apses). There are magnificent 16th-C. choir stalls and just in front an exceptional 15th-C. Renaissance organ, known as 'the marvel of Gascony', which is played on Sunday mornings. Next to the cathedral there is a magnificent **cloister** opening on to the adjacent ravine. The opening hours of the cloister are the same as those of the cathedral.

The Roman town

Information from ☎ 05 61 95 44 44.
Free and permanent admission (admission charge for the guided tour).
At the foot of the hill of Saint-Bertrand, a large part of the old Roman town (1st C. AD) has been unearthed. Walk through the hot baths in the north, the temple, the theatre, the market place and the Christian basilica, all quite well preserved. At the foot of the cathedral, in the Olivetins building, there is a room in which archaeological finds from the site are displayed.

The Festival of Saint-Bertrand-de-Comminges

July-Aug. Booking at least 15 days in advance for major events.
Information from ☎ 05 61 88 32 00 or 05 61 98 45 35.
Admission charge.
Lovers of organ music and other church music should

BAROUSSE CHEESE

This strong-tasting local cheese is made from cow's and ewe's milk, and needs to mature in order to develop its full flavour. It can be found in the markets of Comminges (approx. 70 F for 2 lb 4 oz (1 kg)). A cheese fair is held in its honour at Loures-Barousse on the first weekend in August. (Information from ☎ 05 62 99 21 30.)

spend the summer in Saint-Bertrand. In the cathedral setting, the sounds of its magnificent organ are combined with those of the greatest chamber music orchestras and soloists of international renown. The churches of Valcabrère, Montréjeau and Saint-Gaudens also hold concerts as part of the festival.

Valcabrère

1¼ miles (2 km) NE of Saint-Bertrand

The Church of Saint-Just

☎ 05 61 95 49 06.
Open July-Sept., 9am-7pm; Jan.-Feb., 2-5pm; March, 2-6pm; Apr., 10am-noon and 2-6pm; May, 10am-noon and 2-7pm; June, 9am-noon and 2-7pm.
Free admission.
The village itself seems to be overshadowed by the splendour of this 12th C. Romanesque church, which stands out in the fields. The interior is restrained, and of Gallo-Roman inspiration. From outside, there is a wonderful view of Saint-Bertrand.

The Lugdunum

☎ 05 61 94 52 05.
Open daily from 12.15pm and from 7.30pm; out of season, closed Tues., Mon. and Sun. evening. Book in advance for the evening.
Caesar himself could have been a guest! This restaurant is like no other, since it specialises in the **cuisine of ancient Rome**. All the recipes are authentic and are taken from Apicius, under the supervision of the National Centre for Scientific Research (CNRS). Something different from the constant roast wild boar of the Gauls. Good views of Saint-Bertrand. (Menu at 180 F without drinks.)

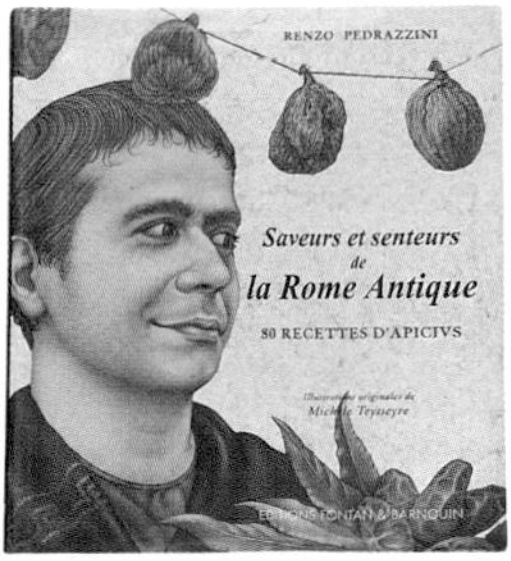

Spotcheck

B4

Things to do

- Barousse cheese
- The sacred music festival
- The Caves of Gargas
- Discover Roman cuisine at Lugdunum

Within easy reach

Saint-Gaudens 8¾ miles (14 km) E, p. 202
Les Baronnies 10½ miles (17 km) NW, p. 182
Bagnères-de-Luchon 19 miles (31 km) S, p. 200

Tourist Office

Saint-Bertrand-de-Comminges:
☎ 05 61 88 37 07

Aventignan

The Caves of Gargas

3¾ miles (6 km) NW of Saint-Bertrand via the D26

☎ 05 62 39 72 39.
Open daily, 2-6pm (also 10-11.30am, July-Aug.). Guided tour every 45 min.
Admission charge.
What is the meaning of the 231 prehistoric handprints on the walls of these two caves? Painted mostly in red, yellow, black or white, the hands appear to be mutilated, as some have fingers missing. Theories abound, but the mystery remains. There are also some lovely engravings of animals.

The green valleys of Couserans

In Couserans, the valleys are wide, green and wooded. There are eighteen of them, and for a long time they managed to escape the pressure of modern life and retain the traces of their rich Gascon past. This region was attached to the Comté de Foix in 1790 to form the district of Ariège. It is wonderful country for hiking, walking and other leisure activities, and it produces some unusual crafts.

Sentein

7 miles (11 km) SW of Castillon-en-Couserans via the D704

A lovely village

Sentein lies in the pretty valley of Biros, on the banks of the Lez. It lies on a hilltop and has a 15th-16th C. church flanked by a square tower and an octagonal bell-tower, and is surrounded by a fortification wall of which three towers remain. Antras, 1¼ miles (2 km) away has a huge Romanesque church and a view of Sentein which is magnificent.

Aulus-les-Bains

22½ miles (36 km) SE of Castillon-en-Couserans via the D17, then D32

The thermal baths

☎ 05 61 96 01 46.
Open daily, Apr.-Oct., 3-7pm (registration). Pool open daily in Aug., 2-8.30pm. Treatments in the morning, 9am-noon (book the day before; 50 to 400 F depending on the treatment).

Four springs, rich in sulphates and magnesium, are said to help the fight against cholesterol and diabetes. In a wonderful mountain setting, drink the water, take showers and enjoy the Turkish bath or aerobath (with bubbles), or exercise on the 'Bear' tracks around the hot baths. These tracks have signs which will tell you how many calories you are burning!

Moulis

3 miles (5 km) SW of Saint-Girons via the D618

The underground laboratory

☎ 05 61 66 31 26.
Guided tour Tues. and Thurs. by appointment (time: approx. 1 hour).
Free admission.

In this laboratory scientists from the French National Centre for Scientific Research (CNRS) research the life-forms unique to this underground cave. These creatures can be found nowhere else in the world – an unforgettable experience.

Andressein

7½ miles (12 km) SW of Saint-Girons via the D618

Jusot, the clogmaker

Rue Principale
☎ 05 61 96 74 39.
Free or guided tour daily, by appointment.
Free admission.

Fifty years of experience and more than 1,000 pairs of clogs a year: this workshop specialises in the Ariège clog. You can see clogs of every size being made or the carving of a pair of *bethmalais* clogs completely by hand. These extraordinary local creations made from twisted wood (from 220 F for small sizes and up to 3,000 F for large feet), rise up to an extravagant point and are decorated with nails in the shape of a heart (see p. 65).

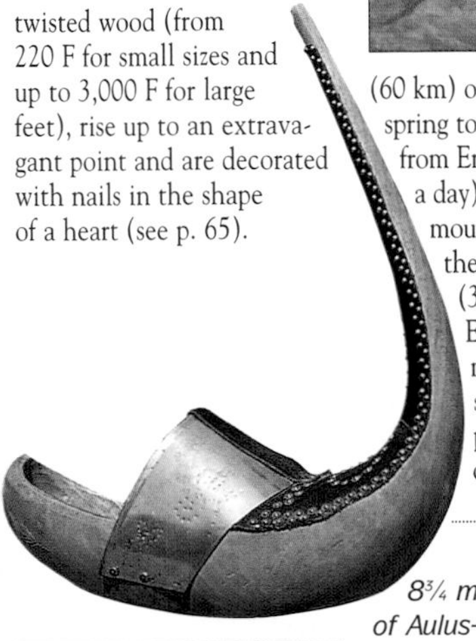

Ercé

5½ miles (9 km) NW of Aulus-les-Bains via the D32

Water sports and mountain biking

L'Escalusse

☎ 05 61 66 88 90.

In upper Couserans, travel is easiest by water. You can go **kayaking, rafting, hydrospeeding, minirafting, canoeing**, and travel over 37½ miles (60 km) of streams, from spring to autumn (leaving from Ercé: 150 F for half a day). If you prefer mountain-biking, from the village of Cominac (3 miles (5 km) N of Ercé) there are 93¾ miles (150 km) of signposted cycle paths (15 magnificent routes).

Seix

8¾ miles (14 km) NW of Aulus-les-Nains via the D32

Local cheese-making

Fromagerie Coumes, La Tuilerie

☎ 05 61 96 54 06.

Guided tour daily except Fri. and Sun., by arrangement. *Free admission.*

Rogallais is a local cheese with a fruity and delicate flavour, named after the Rogalle mountain where the milk comes from. It is made at at the Coumes cheesemakers. Cow's milk is heated to 86°F (30°C) and mixed with rennet. The 'clabbered' milk is then shaped into a ball and pressed, then salted and aged for eight weeks in very damp cellars at 57°F (14°C). The mild-tasting cheese, can be sampled at the factory after watching the traditional process. (64 F for 2 lb 4 oz (1 kg) for a piece of a large cheese and 62 F for a little Rogallais).

Spotcheck

C4

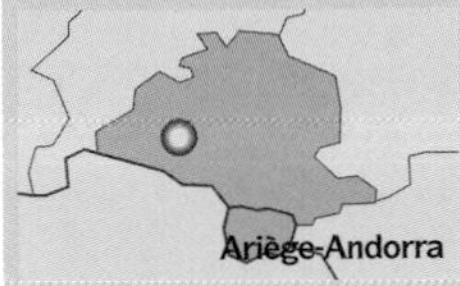

Things to do

- The Moulis underground laboratory
- The Audressein clog-maker
- Water sports at Ercé
- Making Rogallais cheese

Within easy reach

Saint-Girons, p. 218
Saint-Gaudens, p. 202
Le Volvestre, p. 168

Tourist Office

Aulus-les-Bains:
☎ 05 61 96 01 79
Saint-Girons:
☎ 05 61 96 26 60

MILLAS

A society at Saint-Girons updated a dessert called *millas*, which was once very popular in the farmhouses of Couserans. This nourishing dish is made by combining cornmeal with boiling milk and stirring with a stick from a young fir tree (this part is most important). Sugar is added, then the batter is poured out before flaming it with alcohol. There is also a savoury version, in which salt is substituted for sugar. It is traditionally eaten on the day a pig is slaughtered.

Once upon a time in the town of Foix ...

The magnificent château, perched on a rock, can be seen from far away. It looks like something straight out of a fairytale. Foix is the capital of Ariège, a city in which the flavour of the Middle Ages has not quite been dispelled. The strong character of this Cathar city, which once stood firm against the King of France and the Church of Rome, has left its mark.

The château of the counts of Foix

☎ 05 61 65 56 05.
Open daily, July-Aug., 9.30am-6.30pm; June and Sept., 9.45am-noon and 2-6.30pm; out of season, 10.30am-noon and 2-5.30pm.
Admission charge.
Although it looks like a fairytale castle, it is above all an impregnable fortress (only accessible on foot and there's a lot of climbing). The residence of the powerful counts of Foix (one of whom was the famous Gaston III, known as Phoebus) was built around the year 1000 on a rocky outcrop. Its history is preserved in a museum and the graffiti of the last inhabitants (prisoners) can be seen in its round tower. There is a wonderful view over the medieval city from the top.

The Church of Saint-Volusien

Place Saint-Volusien.
This church, which was rebuilt in the 17th C., was once the place where all the important ceremonies in the county were held. It has an impressive vaulted ceiling, a 12th C. Romanesque portal and 17th C. choir stalls from Saint-Sernin Abbey in Toulouse. The street plan surrounding the church is based on the medieval layout. Do not miss the **Rue des Grands-Ducs**, where the houses are linked by strange *pontils*. The door of no. 37, **Rue du Rival**, is magnificent.

The foie gras seller

Annie Barbie, Le Plantié, Vernajoul, (1¼ miles (2 km) N of Foix)
☎ 05 61 65 41 96 or 05 61 65 32 58.
There's an old French song that tells of a woman selling foie gras in Foix, because it

rhymes. Well, here she is, or almost, because her shop is just outside the town! Her farmhouse produce includes specialities (foie gras, *confit*, etc.) and local foods cooked in the tradition of Ariège cuisine. There's a big choice of appetisers and ready-made dishes to take away. This won't be the last time (*fois*) that you buy your *foie* so close to the city of Foix! (foie gras, 195 F for 10½ oz (300 g); *cassoulet*, 60 F a 1 lb 12 oz (800 g) jar). The farm is also an inn, with menus ranging from 95 F to 300 F. A pleasant way of tasting before you buy.

Vernajoul

3¾ miles (6 km) NW of Foix via the Vernajoul, then the D1

The underground river

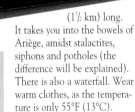

Avenue Labouiche
☎ **05 61 65 04 11.**
Open daily, July-Aug., 9.30am-5pm; Apr., 2-5pm; May-June and Sept.-Oct., 10-11.15am; Nov.-March, Sun. only, 10-11.15am and 2-5pm.
Admission charge.
Row down the longest navigable underground river in Europe. Discovered in 1905, the river is 200 ft (60 m) underground and is 1 mile (1½ km) long. It takes you into the bowels of Ariège, amidst stalactites, siphons and potholes (the difference will be explained). There is also a waterfall. Wear warm clothes, as the temperature is only 55°F (13°C).

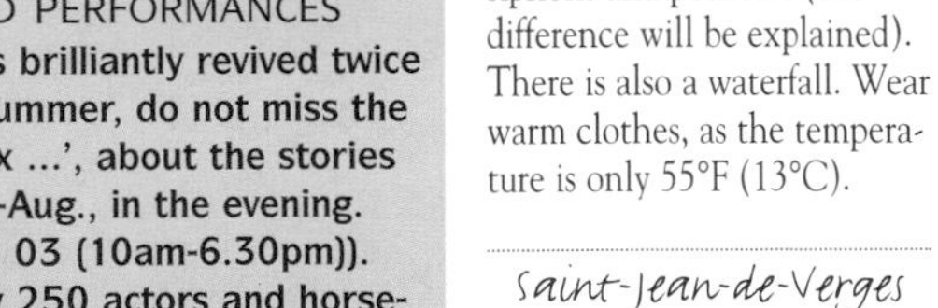

Spotcheck

D4

Things to do

- Foie gras tastings
- Medieval festivals and shows in Foix
- The underground river of Labouiche

Within easy reach

Saint-Girons, p. 218
Tarascons-sur-Ariège, p. 220
Pamiers, p. 216

Tourist Office

Foix: ☎ 05 61 65 12 12

MEDIEVAL FESTIVALS AND PERFORMANCES

The medieval past of Foix is brilliantly revived twice a year. If you come in the summer, do not miss the show called 'Il était une Foix ...', about the stories and legends of Ariège (July-Aug., in the evening. Booking on ☎ 05 61 65 03 03 (10am-6.30pm)). This pageant, performed by 250 actors and horsemen at the foot of the château, retraces the memorable events in local history. It is performed in the second week of July and the week of 15 August. Other events on the Medieval Days include a traditional market, jousting and fireworks.

Saint-Jean-de-Verges

3 miles (5 km) N of Foix via the N20

A Romanesque jewel

This well-restored, 12th-C. church at Saint-Jean-de-Verges is well-proportioned. It was the setting for the declaration of allegiance by the Comte de Foix Roger to the King of France (Louis IX) and the Church of Rome in 1229.

The cavemen of Mas-d'Azil

This area has been inhabited for no less than 35,000 years! All the proof is in the main attraction of the region, the Cave of Mas-d'Azil. There are traces of giant bears, and of the cultures known as Solutrean (18,000 BC), Magdalanian and Azilian, the latter being the last inhabitants of the cave, 10,000 years ago. The local inhabitants, like their distant ancestors, farm honey and drink asses' milk.

Le Mas-d'Azil

A medieval *bastide*

This medieval *bastide* (walled town) in the green countryside has some lovely timber-framed houses. Its ancient fortifications were destroyed in the 17th C. on the orders of Richelieu, but it still has an attractive market-hall, in which a **farmer's market** is held on Saturday mornings. A wander through the town will acquaint you with the slow pace of local life and the excellent food of the region!

The Cave of Mas-d'Azil

☎ 05 61 69 97 71 or 05 61 69 97 22 (museum).
Open daily, Apr.-Sept., 10am-noon and 2-6pm; Oct.-Nov., Sun. and public holidays, 2-6pm.
Admission charge (ticket includes the cave and museum).
A river runs through this ancient cave which was decorated by prehistoric man some 10,000 years ago with **painted murals**. The Musée de la Préhistoire contains tools left behind by the cave's last inhabitants (including a wonderful spear made from a reindeer antler).

Rimont

10½ miles (17 km) S of Mas-d'Azil via the D119, then the D18

Combelongue Abbey

☎ 05 61 96 37 33.
Open weekends in July, daily in Aug., 3-6pm.
Admission charge.
This abbey is one of the great mysteries of the Ariège. It was built of brick, although the local building material is stone. Furthermore, it is typically

Romanesque, although it was built in the early 12th C. See it for its strange anachronisms, as much as for its charm.

Castelnau-Durban

3¾ miles (6 km) E of Rimont via the D117

The donkey farm

Asinerie de Feillet
☎ 05 61 96 38 93
Open daily except Sun.
At Feillet, Charlotte and Olivier Campardou produce Ariège's best kept beauty secret – asses' milk – throughout the year.

Visit this unusual place and buy soap made of pure asses' milk, based on an old traditional recipe. There are five fragrances, suitable for all skin types (20 F). If you visit the farm at milking times (2pm, 4pm and 6pm in the afternoon, but there are also three in the morning), you can try some of the fresh milk, which is said to prevent your complexion from losing the bloom of youth.

Esplas-de-Sérou

7½ miles (12 km) SW of La Bastide-de-Sérou via the D15

The Sérou beehive

☎ 05 61 64 57 06.
Open daily by arrangement.
The wooded hills are visited daily by the bees kept by Liliane Martin. They feast on pollen from the acacias and horse chestnuts, at up to 5,000 ft (1,500 m). They even reach the highest wild mountain passes visiting the rhododendrons, heather and wild thyme. The result of their wanderings is a honey with a flavour special to Ariège (mixed flower 25 F for 1 lb 2 oz (500 g); mountain honey, 27 F for 1 lb 2 oz (500 g); high mountain honey 30 F for 1 lb 2 oz (500 g)). There is a one-hour tour of the workshops including honey tastings.

Spotcheck
C4

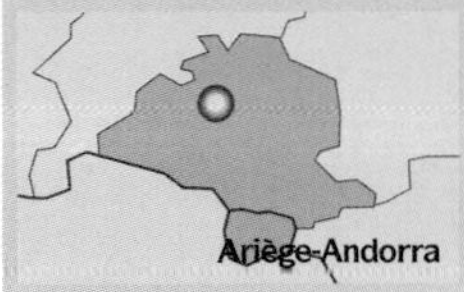

Things to do
- The Cave of Mas-d'Azil
- The Feilhet donkey farm à Castelnau-Durban
- The hives at Esplas-de-Sérou

Within easy reach
Saint-Girons, p. 218
Foix, p. 208
Le Volvestre, p. 168

Tourist Office
Mas-d'Azil:
☎ 05 61 69 99 90

The Dolmen of the Cap-del-Pouech

1¼ miles (2 km) W of Mas-d'Azil
Take a walk around a prehistoric cemetery. This little metalled road leads to a dolmen, a standing stone erected before 2,000 BC, which is very well preserved. This is a rare example of Neolithic funerary architecture. The barrow was emptied of its contents in the 19th C., although the burial site itself remains in excellent condition.

Medieval Mirepoix

Mirepoix lies in the heart of Cathar country and its 12th-C. *bastides* (fortified towns) have been well-preserved. The city looks as though it has hardly been touched since the Middle Ages, but it comes alive on market days (Thursdays and Saturdays) and at its picturesque cattle market, held on the second and fourth Mondays of the month. From the central square, you can take any of the numerous routes through the countryside.

The central square

Place du Général-Leclerc.

This is one of the loveliest central squares in France. The façades of the **half-timbered houses** date from the 13th to the 15th C. They have been built up over wooden arcades, held up by **carved wooden pillars** (see the Consuls' house, where the tops of the pillars have been carved with the heads of people or monsters). In the evening, when the pace of life is more relaxed, wander along under these galleries which conceal cafés and old shops.

The Cathedral of Saint-Maurice

Open daily, 9am-noon and 2-6pm.

The magnificent belltower of this 14th-C. cathedral dominates the largest nave in France. Try to follow the building sequence of this Gothic structure, which was not actually completed until 1866, when the vaulted ceiling was installed. The porch dates from 1506, and, in the early 17th C., the local bishop changed the layout of the chapels – before the French Revolution led to the disappearance of the bells. A cathedral that has had an eventful life!

The Ariège duck

Domaine de Sié

☎ 05 61 68 85 28.

Simone Verdier breeds ducks at her farm for their fat and in order to make other delicacies. There are foie gras, preserved duck portions (*confit*), dried breast of duck and duck legs. Simone Verdier will also give you a cookery book which contains recipes for many local dishes, a great addition to the kitchen.

Mirepoix karting

Kart'Are,

La Planon, Aigues-Vives

☎ 05 61 01 31 89.

This karting track, 2½ miles (4 km) from Mirepoix, is 3,330 ft (1,000 m) long. The circuit is a favourite with karting enthusiasts, beginners and advanced, who will find plenty of fast thrills here (from eight years of age. 60 F for 10 min. over four laps; 120 F for 10 min. over two laps).

THE MIREPOIX PUPPET FESTIVAL

First weekend in Aug. (Thurs.-Sun.). Information from ☎ 05 61 68 20 72. ***Admission charge to the shows* (30 to 70 F – ask for details).**
This lovely event spills into all the streets of the old town surrounding the main square. A major event in the world of puppets and marionettes, puppeteers from all over the world come here and give performances in the local assembly halls (for which you have to pay) and there are many free street events. About 20 companies are invited each year, giving an average of 30 performances. A delight for young and old alike.

Lagarde

5 miles (8 km) SE of Mirepoix via the D625, then the D7

Languedoc's little Versailles

This imposing ruin symbolises the end of the Cathar saga in the region. The powerful Lévis family settled here in the 13th C. to quell the Cathar heretics. The château was destroyed during the French Revolution, but its grandiose remains still dwarf the village below. It can be admired, but there is nothing to visit.

Camon

3¾ miles (6 km) S of Lagarde via the D7

The fortified village

This village has retained the traces of its **ramparts** and is dominated by the abbey which protected it. Visit the **abbey-church** (open daily, 10.30am-12.30pm and 3-7pm. Admission charge) which has a number of preserved religious arte-

facts. The monastery buildings include a 16th C. oratory, the ruins of the cloister and the living quarters of Philippe de Lévis, a bishop of Mirepoix.

Léran

8¾ miles (14 km) S of Mirepoix via the D625

Lac de Montbel

Visit this haven of peace with its turquoise waters. For the pleasures of **fishing**, **swimming** or **water sports**, there is free access to the lake – which is as big as an ocean – throughout the year. It is surrounded by forests, valleys and beaches. It is also frequented by migrating birds. As you arrive, you will pass the **feudal Château de Léran**, still occupied and currently the residence of the Duke of Lévis-Mirepoix.

Spotcheck

D4

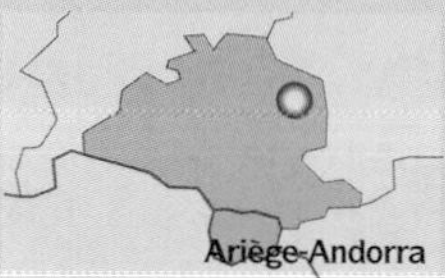

Things to do

- Tasting duck foie gras
- Karting at Mirepoix
- Fishing and water sports on the Lac de Montbel

With children

- The Mirepoix Puppet Festival

Within easy reach

Pamiers, p. 216
Le Pays d'Olmes, p. 214

Tourist Office

Mirepoix: ☎ 05 61 68 83 76

Le Pays d'Olmes
venturing into Cathar country

This is where the finest symbol of Catharism is to be found – the ruins of Montségur. The colourful and eventful history of this region is said to have 'inspired' the rocky and hilly landscape! Nearby Lavelanet, the French capital of carded fabric, jealously guards its local traditions of textiles and combing.

Lavelanet

The Textile Museum

65 Rue Jean-Jaurès
☎ 05 61 03 01 34.
Open daily, 2-7pm.
Admission charge.
This museum is housed in a former textile mill. It contains an extraordinary collection of weaving looms which were used in the area for three hundred years. They range from an 18th-C. hand-loom to the modern automated machine. The exhibits reveal the gruelling work which the craft entailed, involving children who were forced to work in the mill from an early age.

Château de Montségur

6¼ miles (10 km) S of Lavelanet via the D109
Free admission, Nov.-Apr. Paid admission, May-Aug. (9.30am-7.30pm) and Sept.-Oct. (11.30am-5.30pm). Apart from these opening hours, the site is accessible all year round. Guided tour (information on ☎ 05 61 03 03 03).
This massive ruin, to which the only access is via a steep, narrow pathway, is perched on a ***pog*** (rock) at an altitude of 670 ft (200 m). The Château de Montségur was the backdrop for one of the last heroic acts of Catharism, which took place in 1244. More than 200 heretics were burned at the stake by the Inquisition. According to legend, the Holy Grail is still hidden here.

Fougax-et-Barrineuf

4 miles (7 km) E of Montségur via the D9

Wool from the Cathar goatherds

Route de Montségur
☎ 05 61 01 64 42.
Guided tour by appointment only.
Maurice and Véronique Birebent live like the old Cathar goatherds among their flocks. They make delicious

traditional cheeses from the milk and shear the goats for their mohair wool. You can buy balls of mohair yarn and knitted woollen garments from them, as well as honey from their bees.

Roquefixade

5½ miles (9 km) W of Lavelan and via the D17

The castle

Free admission.
The ruins of this castle, razed to the ground in 1632, stand on a rocky spur. As you approach, you will see how

the walls follow the lines of the rocks on which it stands, and there is a wonderful view of the surrounding mountains. This is the same landscape that King Philippe le Hardi (the Brave), who lived here in the 13th C., would have seen. These hilltop châteaux were able to communicate by sending each other smoke signals at times of crisis.

Leychert

6¼ miles (10 km) W of Lavelan and via the D117

The Cathar trail

Time: 3 hours round trip 4 miles (7 km).

Hike to one of the great Cathar strongholds, following the route which they took, over the old cobblestone path. Take the road leading off from the left of the church at Leychert (which has a lovely 17th C. altar screen), then follow the signposted path which starts further on the right. The trail winds up and down, but when you arrive at the site of the castle ruins, you will find yourself at a dizzying height.

Lesparrou

5½ miles (9 km) NE of Lavelanet via the D117

Making combs out of horn

Camp Redon
☎ 05 61 01 11 09.
Open Mon.-Thurs., 8-noon and 2-5.30pm, Fri. until 4pm. Guided tour by appointment daily, except at weekends.

Cow and antelope horn are carved in this workshop, using traditional methods which have been handed down from generation to generation. You can watch the Azéma family performing the 16 separate stages which are required in order to process animal horns and antlers into unique combs (they make 2,000 a day). They include cutting, marking, polishing, a mud bath (essential at the end) and more (see also p. 65).

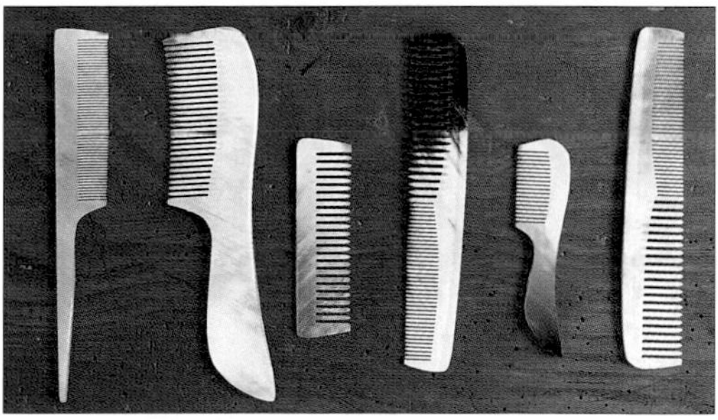

Spotcheck

D4

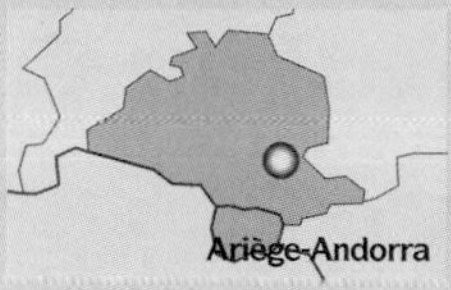

Things to do

- The Cathar trail from Leychert to Roquefixade
- Making combs out of horn at Lesparrou
- The cobbled road from Lavelanet to Montségur

Within easy reach

Foix, p. 208
Mirepoix, p. 212

Tourist Office

Lavelanet:
☎ 05 61 01 22 20

THE COBBLED ROAD

Departure: from the roundabout in the centre of Lavelanet (yellow, then red and white signs).
Time: 5 hours round trip (not counting the climb to the Château de Montségur).
The road between Lavelanet and Montségur has only existed for the past 130 years. Before that, everyone used the cobbled road. Peasants carried cords of wood on their backs which they took to be sold in the village. The cobbled road fell into disuse, but has now been reopened and it makes an enjoyable outing. To get the real feel of the peasant life, try walking it in clogs!

Pays de Pamiers
between foothills and mountains

Pamiers is the most industrialised town in the département, and its population is even larger than that of Foix, the capital of Ariège. It suffered very badly during the Wars of Religion, which can be seen from the cathedral and its surroundings which bear many traces of the city's eventful past. The composer Gabriel Fauré was born here and the rhythm of his second quartet could have been inspired by the obsessive cadence of the local forges.

Pamiers

The cathedral

Place du Mercadal

Open daily, 8am-6pm.

All that remains of the original structure is its magnificent four-storey brick belltower, constructed in pure Toulouse style. The nave was destroyed during the Wars of Religion and was rebuilt in the 17th C. It has a lovely 18th-C. organ. The choir is decorated with 19th-C. frescoes and paintings. Outside, follow the Promenade du Castella, created on the site of the former castle, which overlooks the town.

Vals

7½ miles (12 km) E of Pamiers via the D119, then the D40

A church in the rocks

This little village, halfway between Pamiers and Mirepoix, harbours a very strange church. This mysterious little chapel is carved out of a huge boulder and is covered with magnificent frescoes of Catalan origin. A staircase of 23 steps leads down into the depths to a lovely crypt dating from the time of Charlemagne.

Mazères

12½ miles (20 km) N of Pamiers via the N20, then the D624

Visit to a *bastide*

This *bastide* is in Ariège at the gateway to Lauragais. It was built in the 13th C., mostly from the local brick. The Counts of Foix once chose it as their residence. It is built on a grid plan around a central square and has retained some of the arcades, as well as a 17th-C. market hall with a wide roof. The château of the counts has since disappeared.

The forges of the Ariège

Fortech,
75 Boulevard de la Libération, Pamiers.
☎ 05 61 68 09 17.
Guided tour (2 hours) all year round except in summer, by appointment.
Free admission.
Gabriel Fauré was inspired by the rhythm of the forge in his musical compositions. This factory is one of the most modern in Europe, but you can still discern the melody of the metalworking skills which have been endemic to the region for more than 200 years. Aluminium alloy, titanium and superalloy parts are made here, destined for a number of clients and businesses, including the aeronautics industry, the French army and a number of power stations.

Montaut

6¼ miles (10 km) N of Pamiers via the N20, then the D29

Hand-made soap

La Boutique de l'Écureuil,
Lieu-dit Porteteny.
☎ 05 61 68 32 98.
From Montaut, take the Route de Gaudiès, then turn right towards the hamlet of Crieu.
Open all year round, 10am-noon and 3-7pm, except Sun. and public holidays.
Free admission.
This hand-made soapworks has created a most unusual product – hazelnut soap (15 F). You are not allowed to eat it, but are advised to combine it with other cosmetics which are also created here. Note that this soap is made from hazelnut oil, while most cosmetics are made from hazelnut 'milk'. Philippe Huertas, a master soap-maker, will answer your questions about the processes involved in creating hand-made soap.

Spotcheck

D4

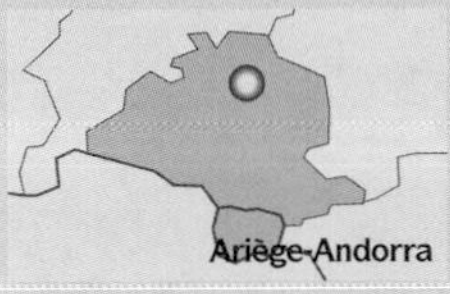

Things to do

- The forges of the Ariège
- Visit a hand-made soapworks

Within easy reach

Mirepoix, p. 212
Foix, p. 208
Le Mas-d'Azil, p. 210

Tourist Office

Pamiers et Pays de Pamiers:
☎ **05 61 67 52 52**

The Mazères church

Saint-Lizier and Saint-Girons

neighbouring towns

Saint-Lizier is the historical capital of Couserans, clinging to its rocky outcrop, and right next to it is Saint-Girons, the administrative and trading capital of the district. In the course of time, the two towns have merged and now offer a complete panorama of regional history from the Gallo-Roman period to the contemporary manufacture of cigarette papers and of course, the gold rush.

Saint-Lizier

The cathedral

Open daily, 9am-noon and 2-6pm.
Free admission.
The cathedral was built between the 11th and the 15th C., but is off-centre (the choir is not on the same axis as the nave). There are **frescoes** and valuable **gold plate**. The cloister, with its 32 arches and marble capitals, is attached to the church and is a masterpiece of simplicity.

The bishop's palace

☎ 05 61 04 81 86.
Museum open daily, July-Aug., 10.30am-12.30pm and 2-6.30pm; out of season, 2-5.30pm (Nov.-March, groups only).
Admission charge.
This 17th-C. bishop's palace overlooks the medieval city and is now used as a museum which houses local exhibits. **The ethnographic museum** contains some curiosities, such as the *bretch*, a cradle once carried on the head, and the *escoutaous*, a collar which dogs used to wear to protect them against attack from wild animals. In the summer, there are **exhibitions by contemporary artists** in a lovely ground-floor room. Thanks to its dominant position, the view from the palace is superb.

Looking for animal tracks

L'Œil aux Aguets, Rue Neuve
☎ 05 61 66 47 98.
Walks reserved for those under 15 years old: 136 F/day. From 8 to 15 years old, observations in the mountains: 159 F/day.
Jean-Louis Orengo arranges these excursions to help children under 15 learn about the wildlife of the Pyrenees. In one or more days the children will learn to recognise and follow the tracks of local animals. They come back (after staying overnight in a shelter) with casts of their own tracks!

Saint-Girons

Unforgettable *croustades*

Martine Crespo, 38 Rue Pierre-Mazaud ☎ 05 34 14 30 20.

The *croustades* of Saint-Girons consist of layers of delicious flaky pastry stuffed with prunes, pears, apples, etc. The latest creation is a *croustade* flavoured with Pyrenean mountain cheese. They seem simple to make, but it takes a lot of skill. At any event, they can be eaten without too much difficulty! (53 to 68 F for 6 pers. depending on garnish.)

Moulis

3 miles (5 km) SW of Saint-Girons via the D618

The santons of the Pyrenees

Jean-Marie Mathon, Aubert-Le-Moulin ☎ 05 61 04 61 88.
Open daily, 9am-noon and 2-7pm.

The ***pyrenousts*** are to the Ariège what *santons* are to Provence. In his workshop, Jean-Marie Mathon, a craftsman, sculptor and the last santon-maker in the region, will show you how these delightful figurines are created. They usually depict old occupations, mythical characters, animals, old traditions and even the architecture of the Pyrenean valleys. Each decorative, hand-made figure is unique (from 60 to 500 F.) and they make an unusual souvenir of your visit.

Prat-Bonrepaux

8¾ miles (14 km) NW of Saint-Lizier via the D117

Panning for gold

Jean-Luc Billard, La Gare ☎ 05 61 96 61 63.

The rivers of the Ariège are apparently 'hiding-places for nuggets'. To get the feeling of what it is like to be part of the gold rush, follow the greatest of the prospectors, Jean-Luc Billard. In summer

he will take you to dig around in the mud and gravel and you will find a few 'spangles' (you get to keep the gold). In July and August, courses run from one to three days, 250 F to 700 F).

Spotcheck
C4

Things to do
- Discover the Pyrenean santons
- The Festival of Saint-Lizier

With children
- Learn to recognise animal tracks
- Pan for gold

Within easy reach
Foix, p. 208
Saint-Gaudens, p. 202
Le Mas-d'Azil, p. 210

Tourist Office
Saint-Girons:
☎ 05 61 96 26 60

THE FESTIVAL OF SAINT-LIZIER
Mid-July to mid-Aug.
Association Austriart (☎ 05 61 96 07 89). Each summer the cathedral welcomes singers from all around the world (such as Jessie Norman, Pierre Amoyal and Bernard Soustrot), as well as young soloists who have competed in international piano, cello and harp competitions. There are rehearsals and working sessions for the musicians, followed by a concert. The festival is just as much an attraction for professionals as it is for music lovers.

Tarascon-sur-Ariège and the valleys of Vicdessos and Saurat

Tarascon probably existed as a settlement in prehistoric times, to judge by the number of inhabited caves in the area. Niaux, Bedeilhac and Lombrives have all retained primitive works by their earliest inhabitants. In the nearby valleys of Saurat, Vicdessos and the Ariège, sandstone and talc are still quarried and worked, heirs to a prehistoric tradition.

Tarascon-sur-Ariège

The Pyrenean Park of Prehistoric Art

Lieu-dit Lacombe, Route de Banat
☎ 05 61 05 10 10.
Open daily except Mon., Apr.-Oct., 10am-6pm (from 8.30am in July-Aug.; the ticket office closes at 5pm).
Admission charge.

Visit this open-air museum, covering 37 acres (15 ha), and become immersed in Ariège's prehistoric past. Enter the darkness of the cave of Niaux, decorated in authentic colours

and atmospheric lighting, and see what it looked like in the days of the Magdalenian cave-dwellers. Further on, experience the sounds of 13,000 years ago or learn to make fire or hunt as our ancestors did. Ideal for children.

Péchiney Aluminium

Usine de Sabart

☎ 05 61 02 40 00.
Guided tour Mon.-Fri. by appointment (for groups). Closed Aug. *Free admission.*

This tour will teach you all you need to know about tin cans. In the factory, the liquid aluminium reaches temperatures of 1742°F (950°C). You can watch it flow into the large moulds to be turned into ingots and then into containers for garden peas, or weapons, cars and ships. Nearby, anodes, which are used as terminals on electric batteries, are made. The giant electrolysis session will remind you of science lessons at school!

Hypocras

Maison Séguélas,
Rue de la Croix-de-Quié

☎ 05 61 05 60 38.

Try this ancient local aperitif and promise to drink it faithfully (as did Hippocrates, who invented it 2,300 years ago). The mixture of wine, spices and local herbs was popular in the Middle Ages. Hypocras has been revived by Élyane and Michel Séguélas, who use an original recipe. The effects are said to be agreeably prolonged. It should always be served cold, but not iced (75 F for 1¼ pt (75 cl) 60 F for 18 fl oz (50 cl)).

The hot baths of Ax

6 Avenue Delcassé, Ax-les-Thermes

☎ 05 61 64 24 83. Guided tour Tues.-Fri., by appointment. *Free admission.*

The spa waters of Ax are the hottest in the Pyrenees (172.4°F (78°C)) and have been delivering their therapeutic virtues for the past 700 years. They are rich in sulphur and sodium, and are perfect cures for rheumatism and respiratory infections. Take your cue from the 9,000 people who take the cure every year and jump into the water, for prevention as well as cure. There are daily exercise sessions (Mon.-Sat., 4-8.30pm; Sun., 9am-noon. Swimming pool, sauna, Turkish baths, etc., for only 50 F).

Spotcheck
D4-D5

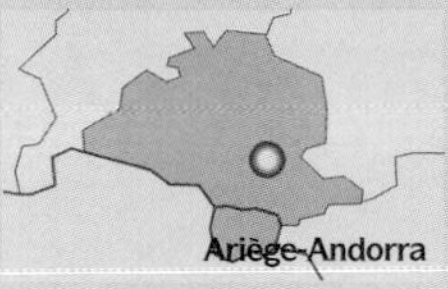

Things to do
- The many Prehistoric caves
- The Péchiney factory
- The talc quarries of Luzenac
- The stonecutter of Saurat
- Orlu Power Station

Within easy reach
Foix, p. 208

Tourist Office
Tarascon-sur-Ariège:
☎ 05 61 05 94 94

Ussat-les-Bains

2½ miles (4 km) SE of Tarascon via the N20

Grotte de Lombrives

☎ 05 61 05 98 40.
July-Aug., guided tour every 30 min., 10am-7pm; June and Sept., guided tours at 10.30am, 2pm, 3.30pm and 5pm; out of season, guided tours at weekends, public holidays and school holidays only (Easter-May and Oct.-11 Nov., same opening hours; 11 Nov.-Easter, 2pm and 3.30pm). *Admission charge.*

This is the largest cave in Europe that is open to the public. You travel into the cave on a **little train** that follows a twisting route through breathtaking fairy grottos with their stalactites and stalagmites and amazing rock formations. According to local legend, it is here that Pyrène, daughter of Bébryx, king of the mountains of the Ariège, lies buried.

Luzenac

11¼ miles (18 km) SE of Tarascon via the N20

The talc quarry

☎ 05 61 64 60 60
☎ 05 61 64 68 00
Guided tour Mon.-Fri., at 4pm by appointment only. Closed 15 Oct.-15 May.
Admission charge.

The quarry is at an altitude of 5,670 ft (1,700 m) and 295,275 tons (300,000 tonnes) of talc are extracted every year, using high explosives. Learn about this surprising local rock, whose brilliance and softness are graded into 13 different qualities, all of them having different uses from cosmetics to heavy industry.

Saurat

5 miles (8 km) NW of Tarascon by D 618

L'or gris de Saurat

39, Ch. des Planèzes
☎ 05 61 05 92 54.

Sylvain Cuminetti is the last stonecutter in France who makes **sharpening stones** from natural materials. The

stones lie next to his workshop, in the only working sandstone mine in existance. He works the stone with a scythe or a saw and employs the same methods his ancestors used 200 years ago. There is a choice of stones for sharpening fishhooks, secateurs and even nail files (from 14 F).

Aynat

4 miles (7 km) NW of Tarascon via the D618

Grotte de Bedeilhac

☎ 05 61 05 95 06.
Open daily, July-Aug., 10am-5.30pm; out of season, 2.15-5pm. School holidays and Sun., 2.30-4.30pm.
Guided tour every 30 min. (time: 1 hour 30 min.).
Admission charge.

The cave was used during World War II for storing equipment because it has a huge entrance, 120 ft (36 m) wide! Enter this dark world which extends back for nearly ½ mile (1 km). In the vast caverns, with their accretions, you will see many wall paintings of animals and strange clay shapes at ground level which are very rare.

Niaux

2½ miles (4 km) SW of Tarascon via the D808

Grotte de Niaux

☎ 05 61 05 88 37.
Open daily, June-Aug., 9.15-11.30am and 1-5.30pm; Sept., 10-11.30am and 1-5.30pm.

Drawing of a gazelle on the walls of the Cave of Niaux

Guided tour every 45 min. (time: 1 hour 30 min.); out of season, guided tours at 11am, 2.30pm and 4pm. Guided tours in English at 9.15am and 1pm. Admission charge.

There are 1¼ miles (2 km) of galleries and cathedral-like vaulted ceilings, which lead you to the **black room** at the back of this extraordinary cave. This is where the cave-dwellers, who lived 13,000 years ago, hid the best of their art. There are paintings of bisons, horses, roebuck and deer, and a host of enigmatic drawings. Wear sensible footwear and be sure to take some warm clothes as the temperature is a constant 54°F (12°C).

Jean-Jacques' textiles

Next to the church
☎ 05 61 01 43 43.
Guided tour Tues.-Sat. by appointment. Closed Feb.

From raw wool to a knitted sweater. The wool of Pyrenean sheep, who are shorn in the spring, is first sorted by natural colour, then rinsed and worked as you watch. You can then see it being carded – when the fibres are all made to lie the same way – before it is spun. On the way out, you can choose knitting wool, tapestry wool, socks, sweaters (from 485 F), blankets (from 650 F), quilts (from 1,000 F), foot-warmers, and much more.

THE MADWOMAN OF THE PYRENEES

The whole district still talks about this strange figure. Less than two centuries ago, just above the village of Vicdessos, hunters found a wild, naked woman wandering around in the mountains. When captured, she explained to the priest, before escaping, that the bears were her friends and kept her warm. She was recaptured and imprisoned in the Château de Foix, but died a few weeks later, and truth thus died with her.

Alliat

2½ miles (4 km) SW of Tarascon

Grotte de la Vache

☎ 05 61 05 95 06.
Open daily, July-Aug., 10am-5.30pm; out of season, guided tour at 3pm and 4.30pm.
Admission charge.

This is the most moving of the Ariège caves. It is next to the Cave of Niaux, and the drawings here reflect the everyday life of prehistoric man. There are hunting weapons, fishing tackle, tools and art objects. You can marvel at the results of 20 years of excavation of an average Magdalenian household more than 4,500 years ago.

Orlu

22 miles (35 km) SE of Tarascon

The hydraulic power station

☎ 05 61 64 20 05.
Guided tour Mon.-Fri., by appointment.
Free admission.

This power station is operated from elsewhere by remote control. In a wonderful mountain setting, energy is created in total isolation, as the power station is fed with water from Lac de Naguilles 615 ft (985 m) higher up. The water turns the turbine which activates the alternator, all (almost) without assistance. Electricity has never seemed so magical.

Faun engraved on a bone found in the Grotte de la Vache at Alliat

Andorra
a trip to the Principality

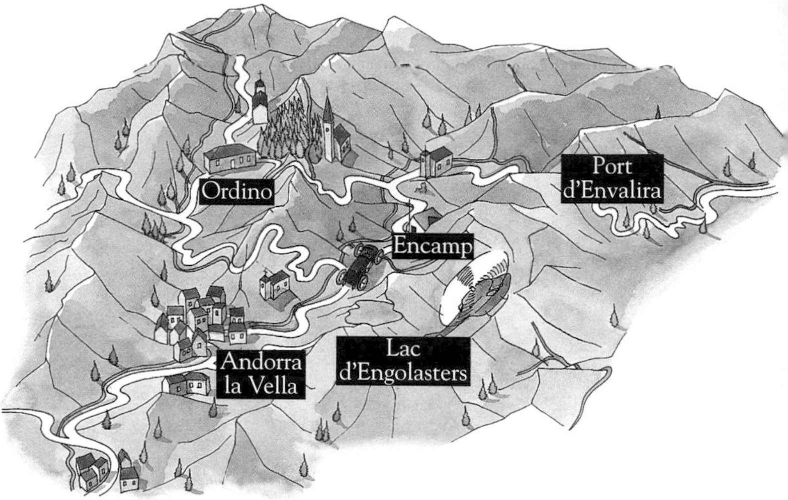

This tiny little principality (180 sq. miles (468 km^2)) perched on a rocky spur, is the highest country in Europe. It has 50,000 inhabitants, of whom 27,000 are Spaniards, 8,500 Andorrans and 4,000 French, and the national language has been Catalan ever since the reign of Charlemagne. Andorra has a very strange status, it is ruled jointly by two powers who are responsible for its fate – the Spanish Bishop of Urgell and the President of the French Republic. The land is a mixture of history, beautiful landscapes and a very healthy economy.

Spotcheck
C5-D5

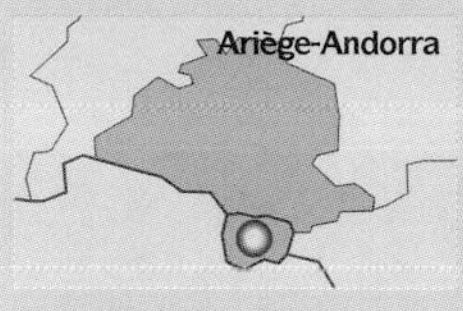

Things to do
- The National Car Museum
- Flying over the principality in a helicopter
- Lac d'Engolasters
- Water sports on the Valira del Nor

Andorra la Vella

Barri Sant Esteve

The **old quarter** of the Andorran capital is perched on a round hill at an altitude of 3,380 ft (1,013 m), and has retained its narrow streets lined with old houses. Inthe Church of **Sant Esteve** there is a beautiful Romanesque Virgin. In the north-east and south-west, the **new town** contains the banks, travel agencies and department stores which have become the main attractions of the city.

ANDORRAN CUISINE

The traditional cuisine of Andorra is simple, made with local ingredients. This is due to the transport and communication difficulties posed by the remote and mountainous geography of the country. Many of the dishes are hearty peasant fare based on pork, such as *botifarra* (sausage), *bulls embolcats i de carnetes* (chitterlings) and *bringuera* (chitterling sausage), as well as ham which is used in an unusual dish called *rostes amb mel* (fried ham with honey), a local favourite. Another dish worth trying is *trinxat* (potato and cabbage hash).

La Casa de la Vall

Rue Carrer de la Vall
☎ (00 376) 829 129.
Open daily, 9.30am-1pm and 3-7pm (Sun., 10am-2pm). Booking essential.
The Valley House is a massive 16th-C. **gothic structure**

which serves as a parliament building for the ruling body of the principality, the General Council of the Valleys, which used to sit in the Church of Sant Esteve. As you wander from room to room, you will discover the history of the Andorran people. On the first floor there are 16th-C. frescoes in the very beautiful reception room, and 12th-13th-C. frescoes in the old chapel (now the office of the trustee), which has an altar screen dating from the 16th C. In the session chamber, is the 'closet with seven keys', which was only opened when all of the parishes were represented, each with its own key.

Ordino

4 miles (7 km) N of Andorra la Vella

La Casa d'Areny de Plandolit

☎ (00 376) 836 908.

Pens and inks in the Casa d'Areny library at Ordino

Open daily except Sun. afternoon and Mon., 9.30am-1.30pm and 3-6.30pm. Guided tour only, in many languages.
Admission charge.
This is the traditional home of an Andorran master blacksmith. From the entrance hall with its domed ceiling, visit the kitchen, the bakery, the dining room and the bedrooms. The wine-cellar is full of casks, and the cellar and workshops still have their tools in place. There's a chapel and a library with 5,000 volumes. From cellar to loft, everything is here to show you how Andorrans once lived. Traces of the owner can be still found in the wrought-iron work and the anvils in the pretty garden.

A vintage Bugatti in the National Car Museum

Views of the village of Ordino

The silent valley

Access from Ordino.
In Ordino, at 4,330 ft (1,298 m), breathe in the atmosphere of the ancient streets of the village and the main square, then visit **Sornas** half a mile (1 km) to the north. The church contains a 17th-C. altar screen. Cross the stream to get the upper part of the village. Here you'll find a footpath which leads through the forest to the **Pic de Casamanya** (9,140 ft (2,742 m)), the second highest peak in Andorra. The views are magnificent.

Encamp

3¾ miles (6 km) NE of Andorra la Vella

The National Car Museum

☎ (00 376) 832 266.
Open daily except Mon., 9.30am-1.30pm and 3-6pm (Sun., 10am-2pm).
Admission charge.
The little village of Encamp boasts an extraordinary collection of vintage cars. Their uniqueness suits the principality very well.
About a hundred motor cars manufactured between 1898 and 1950, more than fifty motorbikes and numerous bicycles are meticulously maintained.

PERFORMANCES IN THE PRINCIPALITY

The geographical isolation of Andorra has forged traditions which are expressed in the most amazing theatrical performances. Two examples are the masquerade of the Legend of the Lake at Engolasters and the famous *Pessebre vivent* (living crèche) at Escaldes-Engordany. In summer, don't miss the International Music Festival of the Valley of Ordino or the International Jazz Festival at Escaldes-Engordany. A more unusual tradition is The Marratxa, a folk dance which is performed only once a year in the Placa de Sant Julia de Loria (4½ miles (7 km) south of Andorra la Vella), on the last Sunday in July.

La Massana

2½ miles (4 km) N of Andorra la Vella

Bird's-eye view from a helicopter

Heliand,
Edifice Comabella,
Avenue Sant Antoni
☎ (00 376) 835 563, 837 929 or 835 461.
Reservations required.

To get a different perspective on Andorra, take a helicopter to get to an even higher altitude and reach really inaccessible places. You can take a quick ride (5,500 ptas or 220 F per person for 10 min.) or visit the lakes and high mountain refuges (10,000 ptas or 400 F per person for 20 min.). You can also hire a mountain guide (20,000 ptas or 800 F) for a maximum of five people.

Meritxell, Canillo and Sant Joan de Caselles

After Encamp (3¾ miles (6 km) NE of Andorra la Vella), turn off on the right of the main road.

The church route

In 1873, at the sanctuary of **Meritxell** (2 miles (3 km) from Encamp), the General Council of the Valleys declared the local Virgin to be the 'patron saint of the valleys of Andorra'. Visit her modern chapel, then stop at two more churches. The church at **Canillo**, at an altitude of 5,100 ft (1,530 m), has the tallest belltower in the country. That of **Sant Joan de Castelles** (12th C.), just next to it, is one of the finest local examples of the Romanesque Lombard style. There is a wonderful representation of Christ in majesty. The interior is wonderful throughout.

The church of Sant Joan de Castelles (12th C.)

The Port of Envalira

16¼ miles (26 km) NW of Andorra la Vella

Ascending to the summit

At an altitude of 8,023 ft (2,407 m), this is the highest peak of the Pyrenees that has a road running through it. Take advantage of this easy climb to the summit, as the view over all the mountains of the principality is spectacular. If you look westwards, you will see the highest point of this tiny country, which is slightly separate from the surrounding peaks. The Pic de Coma Pedrosa is at an altitude of 9,820 ft (2,946 m)), and on the other side, there is

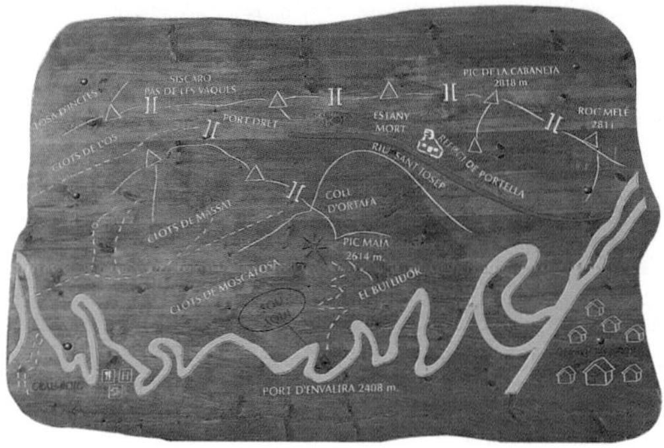

a roller-coaster ride down to the Pas de la Casa and the border with France. On the way, there are some lovely lakes and the geological formation called the Cirque de Font-Nègre.

Engolasters

E of Andorra la Vella

The mountain church

From Escaldes-Engordany via the N2.

The Andorran trio – pure water, an ancient church and a divine view. Leave Escaldes on the road to Encamp, following the river. Then continue until you come to a turning on the right, leading to Engolasters. The view is heavenly. The 12th-C. **church of Sant Miquel**, perched on a summit, is in pure Romanesque Lombard style and is decorated with murals, though they are reproductions. Even higher up, at 5,500 ft (1,650 m), **Lac d'Engolasters** offers unforgettable walks or mountain biking.

Bring your fishing rod!

From April to September, come and tease the Andorran trout in the rivers and valleys and from mid-June to mid-September, in the numerous mountain lakes and ponds. The Tourist Offices will issue you with a fishing licence and give you advice about the best fishing spots. (An ordinary licence costs 2,500 ptas or 100 F. A permit for a whole season costs 5,000 ptas or 200 F; an eight-day permit costs 1,500 ptas or 60 F.)

Valira del Nor

N of Andorra la Vella

Hydrospeed and kayaking

Federacio Andorrana de Canoa-Caiac
☎ (00 376) 868 757.

If you enjoy excitement and exhilaration, practise whitewater sports in the spring. This is when the rivers of Andorra are in full torrent, thanks to the melting snow. For something less hair-raising, try going down the Valira del Nor in a kayak in summer. This delightful stream runs through a peaceful valley. If you want to learn how to use a kayak or how to hydrospeed, the Stade Communal d'Andorra la Vella, on the banks of the Gran Valira, is open daily.

Duty-free Andorra

Cigarettes at bargain prices

Cigarettes are about three times cheaper here than in France! There are variations between one shop and another, which can reduce the price by another ten francs or 60 (per carton). But you won't get away with taking home three or four suitcases! You are allowed to

cross the border with a maximum of *either* 300 cigarettes *or* 150 cigarillos and 75 cigars *or* 14 oz (400 g) rolling tobacco or pipe tobacco.

Alcoholic drinks: be careful at the border!

The price of spirits in Andorra is half what it is in France. But you are only allowed to take a very limited amount out with you. You are not allowed to leave the border with more than 9 pt (5 l) of *vin ordinaire* and 2½ pt (1.5 l) of 22% spirits or 5 pt (3 l) of less than 22% spirit. No restrictions apply in how much you drink on the spot!

A blitz on the supermarket

Even for the sort of thing you will find in the everyday shopping basket, Andorran prices will be an average of 20 to 30% less expensive than elsewhere in Europe. But again, your amount of take-home goods is limited. You cannot leave with more than 1,200 F worth of goods per person aged over 15, or 600 F for every person under 15.

Limits that cannot be exceeded

Food is about 20% cheaper than in France, but the purchase of certain essential items is strictly limited. This is most certainly another legacy of the difficult terrain of the country. For example, you cannot 'export' more than 5½ lb (2.5 kg) of powdered milk, 6½ lb (3 kg) of condensed milk, 13 lb (6 kg) of fresh milk, 2¼ lb (1 kg) of butter, 9 lb (4 kg) of cheese, 11 lb (5 kg) of sugar and confectionery, and 11 lb (5 kg) of meat. Don't exceed the limit, as customs take such offences very seriously.

Bargains in cameras, jewellery and luxury goods

Audio and camera equipment, as well as jewellery, are 20 to 30% cheaper than in France. If you are buying a hi-fi system or music centre, a camera or videocamera, or an item of jewellery, make sure the value does not exceed the limit (3,600 F if you are over 15 years of age and 1,800 F if you are younger). Otherwise, you will be required to pay customs duty on the balance. Keep hold of your receipt.

It's good to know

Be aware that the maximum value of purchases permitted, as quoted above, cannot be divided between several people! For instance, if you are buying a piece of jewellery worth 7,200 F, you cannot split the value between two people (3,600 F + 3,600 F). Any items which cost more than the authorised amount are liable for duty and tax which must be paid individually for the whole value.

NO ADMITTANCE!

Importing certain items into Andorra is strictly forbidden. These include any animal and vegetable products. Pets also cannot be imported, so no cats or dogs can be taken over the frontier. Any species of flora or fauna threatened with extinction can neither be brought in or out, nor can anything manufactured from these species. The same stringent rule applies to medicinal items, unless they are for the exclusively personal use of the traveller.

Index

A

B

C

D

E

F

G

H

I

L

M

N

O

P

R

S

T

U

V

W

PHOTO CREDITS

All the photographs in this book were produced by **Hémisphères Images** (rights reserved: p. 21 t.r.; p. 37 t.; p. 41 b.c.; p. 106 c.; p. 124 t.; p. 200 t.), with the exception of the following:

Jean Clottes (rights reserved): p. 222 (b.).
Jacques Debru: p.4 (c.); p. 6 (c.d.); p. 53 (t.); p. 58 (c., b.); p. 60 (t.); p. 139 (c.d.); p. 152 (t.r.); p. 166 (c.); p. 167 (t.r., b.l.); p. 173 (t.); p. 175 (t.); p. 177 (t.); p. 181 (b.r.); p. 208 (b.); p. 209 (c.); p. 229 (c.).
Delinière: p. 117 (t.).
Pierre Journou: p. 207 (b.l.).
Nicole Pailhaugue (rights reserved): p. 223 (b.).
Gwenaëlle Plet: p. 23 (b.); p. 193 (c.r.).
J. Thirant: p. 193 (b.).
Dominique Viet: (rights reserved): p. 70 (c.);
Office de tourisme d'Auzat: p. 86 (b.).
Photothèque Hachette: (rights reserved): p. 21 (b. r.); p. 34 (t.); p. 60 (b.); © Éd. Rossignol p. 72 (b.); p. 73 (b.l.); p. 74 (c.g.); p. 75 (c.); p. 78 (t.); p. 102 (b.); p. 103 (t.d.); p. 107 (b.); p. 118 (t.); p. 164 (t.).

This guide was created by PASCAL DE CUGNAC and YASNA MAZNIK, with the assistance of ÉLISABETH BOYER, ANNE LEPRINCE, FRÉDÉRIC OLIVIER and AUDE SARRAZIN.

Illustrations: RENAUD MARCA (except page 79, PASCAL GINDRE)

Illustrated maps: RENAUD MARCA

Cartography: © IDÉ INFOGRAPHIE (THOMAS GROLLIER)

Translation and adaptation: CHANTERELLE TRANSLATIONS, LONDON (JOSEPHINE BACON)

Additional design and editorial assistance: SUZANNE JUBY, MARY SANDYS, JEREMY SMITH and CHRISTINE BELL

Project manager: LIZ COGHILL

We have done our best to ensure the accuracy of the information contained in this guide. However, addresses, telephone numbers, opening times etc. inevitably do change from time to time, so if you find a discrepancy please do let us know. You can contact us at: hachetteuk@orionbooks.co.uk or write to us at Hachette UK, address below.

Hachette UK guides provide independent advice. The authors and compilers do not accept any remuneration for the inclusion of any addresses in these guides.

Please note that we cannot accept any responsibility for any loss, injury or inconvenience sustained by anyone as a result of any information or advice contained in this guide.

First published in the United Kingdom in 2000 by Hachette UK

Distributed in the United States of America by Sterling Publishing Co., Inc. 387 Park Avenue South, New York, NY 10016-8810

A CIP catalogue for this book is available from the British Library

ISBN 1 84202 015 3

Hachette UK, Cassell & Co., The Orion Publishing Group, Wellington House, 125 Strand, London WC2R 0BB

Printed in Spain by Graficas Estella

Voucher section

/herever you see this symbol ❀ in the guide, you will find a voucher in this section which will entitle you to a discount or special offer. See the appropriate page in the guide for details of the attractions.

On presentation of this Vacances guide

La Ferme au Cerfs et Sangliers

(deer and wildlife park)

p.117

Offers a free digestif, plus a visit to the Park or visitors to the Ferme-Auberge and child entry to visitors to the Park

Offre le digestif et la visite des Parcs aux clients de la Ferme-Auberge et l'entrée des enfants pour les clients des Parcs

La Ferme au cerfs et sangliers
Henri Saint-Lannes, 32460 LE HOUGA

On presentation of this Vacances guide

Gascogne Navigation

(river cruises)

p.123

A discovery cruise on the D'Artagnan for 40F, plus a 10% discount on motor boat hire

Propose la croisière découverte sur le D'Artagnan à 40F et offre 10% de réduction sur la location de bateaux à moteur

Gascogne Navigation
Quai de la Bouquerie, 32100 CONDOM
☎ 05 62 28 46 46

On presentation of this Vacances guide

La Maison Ryst-Dupeyron

(Armagnac distillery)

p.123

10% discount on all items bought, following a tour of the distillery

Offre 10% de réduction sur les produits achetés lors de la visite des chais

Ryst Dupeyron
Château Cugnac
1 Rue Daunou B.P. 58
32100 CONDOM
☎ 05 62 28 08 08

On presentation of this Vacances guide

La Cité des Machines du Moyen-Age

(display of machinery from the Middle Ages)

p.123

Reduced price entry tickets

Propose l'entrée au tarif réduit

Cité des Machines du Moyen-Age
Village
32100 LARRESSINGLE
☎ 05 62 68 33 88

On presentation of this Vacances guide

La Villa Gallo-Romaine de Séviac

(Roman villa)

p.124

Reduced price entry tickets

Propose l'entrée au tarif réduit

Villa Gallo-romaine de Séviac

Montréal du Gers
32250 MONTRÉAL-DU-GERS
☎ 05 62 29 48 57

On presentation of this Vacances guide

Le Château de Cassaigne

(Armagnac distillery)

p.124

5% discount

Offre 5% de réduction

EURL Roques Exploitation

Château de Cassaigne
32100 CASSAIGNE
☎ 05 62 28 04 02

On presentation of this Vacances guide

Le Domaine des Cassagnoles

(vineyard)

p.125

A free engraved glass

Offre un verre gravé

Domaine des Cassagnoles
32330 GONDRIN
☎ 05 62 28 40 57

On presentation of this Vacances guide

Le Centre de Photographie

(photography centre)

p.126

40% discount on the 'Eté Photographique de Lectoure' and 10% discount on books published by the Centre

Offre 40% de réduction sur le forfait Eté Photographique de Lectoure et 10% de réduction sur les ouvrages édités par le Centre

Centre de Photographie de Lectoure
5 Rue Sainte-Claire
32700 LECTOURE